THE MACHIAVELLIAN'S GUIDE
TO WOMANIZING

D1205008

The Machiavellian's Guide to Womanizing

Nick Casanova

Carroll & Graf Publishers, Inc.
New York

Library of Congress Cataloging-in-Publication Data is available.

ISBN 0-7867-0203-6

Manufactured in the United States of America

10   9   8   7   6   5   4   3   2   1

To G.H., whose sterling character and many war stories provided the moral framework for this scholarly tome.

Acknowledgments

This book would not have been possible without the inspiration of all the women who ever rejected me and sent me off on these flights of fancy.

Contents

Introduction

In the sixteenth century, Niccolò Machiavelli wrote a book, *The Prince*, about how to gain and keep political power through devious means. He has since received more than his fair share of vilification. In the popular mind, Machiavelli's name has become synonymous with duplicity and evil. Whether this is justified is debatable. What is beyond debate is that those who have followed his teachings in the intervening centuries have met with great success.

Had Machiavelli focused his energies on womanizing, this is the book he would have written.

Women who talk about a man who knows "every trick in the book" are referring to this book. Herein are successful strategies in the war between the sexes. This book is not so much an outlining of the rules of the game as an underlining that there are not rules. (In seduction, it's not how you play the game, it's whether you win or lose).

There's not need for guilt. Women are Machiavellian, too. The only difference is that with them it's called "using their feminine wiles." This book will help you develop your masculine wiles.

People say that all's fair in love and war, the point of which is that everything in love is unfair. If you'd prefer the unfairness at your enemy's expense, this book is for you.

THE MACHIAVELLIAN'S GUIDE
TO WOMANIZING

The List

The wish to acquire is admittedly a very natural and common thing; and when men succeed in this they are always praised rather than condemned.

—Niccolò Machiavelli

Popular wisdom has it that the career womanizer is only in love with himself. Actually, he is in love with his list.

Most guys keep a list, tucked safely away in a bottom drawer, of the women they've scored with. (Many women keep similar tallies.) How many on your list?

0–10   This book is worth its weight in gold to you.
11–20   You can obviously use our help.
21–30   This book will help perfect your style.
31–50   Many chapters will have a familiar ring to you.
50+   Your help is needed with the second edition.

The most important thing about your list is never, ever to let a woman know you keep it. If she finds out, she will do everything in her power to keep herself off it. If a woman ever asks you how many women you've slept with, maintain you've only slept with four. Round the number down rather than up, the way you do when one of the guys ask.

The message you must convey is that you care more about

1

quality than quantity, even though the opposite is true. If you must mention your list, make sure it's only after she's on it.

One thing all lists have in common no matter how many names they boast is that there's always room for more.

Are You a Hound?

Is this book for you? To find out, take this simple test: Would you rather spend ten nights making love to the same beautiful woman, or a night each with ten different beautiful women?

If you would rather spend all ten nights with one woman, read no further.

But if you're like most guys, you chose ten different women. This means, whether you realize it or not, that at heart you are a hound. Don't struggle against it—four million years of human evolution have molded you to be this way. In fact, the only real perversity would be to rebel against these instincts.

When you get tired of a woman after a couple of weekends, it is because thousands of generations of your ancestors are in effect urging you to spread your sperm (i.e., your genes) more widely. Don't disappoint them. Let variety be the spice of your sex life.

Women have been selected over millions of years of evolution to have different mating instincts, most of which boil down to selecting a mate who has good genes, who will stay with them, and who will be a good provider. Thus, from the dawn of history, they have fallen for a certain type of guy—the type this book will help you pretend to be.

Politics and fashions change from year to year but basic human instincts would take hundreds of generations to change. So whatever the current status of feminism and sexual politics, rest assured that this book is quite timely.

Part I
Tactics

The Big Lie

Princes who have achieved great things have been those who have given their word lightly, who have known how to trick men with their cunning, and who, in the end, have overcome those abiding by honest principles.

—Niccolò Machiavelli

Most women prefer to think that seduction is a matter of two people who have a lot in common being overwhelmed by the passion of the moment rather than a well-orchestrated attack. And every woman instantly raises her guard against a guy on the make. (For some reason women are unable to accept being just another notch on your bedpost.)

So play along with the Big Lie. Pretend sex is the furthest thing from your mind. Offhand comments such as: "People pay so much attention to sex. It's just not that big a deal" show that friendship is the only thing on your mind. (It also makes you sound more experienced.) "I used to be into one-night stands, but I've outgrown those" also shows that your heart's in the right place.

Don't ever say, "I just want to have a good time." Most women know that translates directly as "To me, you're only a lay." And no woman is susceptible to "Come on—I'm in the middle of a hot streak, so don't ruin it."

Voice your distasteful reaction to singles bars ("They're just *meat* markets!") and recite the Sensitive Person's Pledge of Allegiance ("I could *never* go to bed with someone I didn't care about.").

The hard part is looking sincere while you utter these insincerities."

Sixteen Comments That Show
You're a Sensitive Guy

It is not necessary for a prince to have the above-mentioned qualities, but it is very necessary to seem to have them.
—Niccolò Machiavelli

If your prospective target likes warmth, caring, and sensitivity on the part of a lover, and you have her fooled so far, these lines will confirm that you're Mr. Right:

- I'm not ashamed to admit it. I've cried plenty of times.
- Boxing should be abolished.
- You know, it's funny, but I usually get along better with women than I do with men.
- Did you see the sunset yesterday evening? Wow!
- I can't stand big apartment buildings. I want to live in a house with a garden.
- I have a lot of gay friends.
- I *love* children. And the amazing thing is—there's so much you can learn from them.
- That's such a beautiful dog/cat/painting/whatever she has in her apartment.
- I bake my own bread.
- I'm a charter member of ASPCA/Greenpeace/The Sierra Club.

- I really don't care what a woman looks like, as long as her inner beauty shines through.
- If I seem a little reluctant to become involved too quickly, it's because once, a long time ago, someone hurt me very deeply.
- You really don't appreciate your parents until you leave home.
- Zoos are so inhuman. Animals weren't meant to be cooped up.
- I may look tough on the outside, but on the inside I'm just a frightened Mama's boy.
- I spent a year working with retarded people. It really helped me grow.

These comments are more effective when used in context; but if you can't, just drop them anywhere.

If your prospect likes her men macho, simply reverse the above statements ("They oughta just take all the retards out and shoot them").

How to Sound Sincere

Telling a woman what she wants to hear generally means telling her how much you like her. There are many ways of expressing affection. Some are hokey ("I would give the sun, the moon, and the stars for you, were they but mine to give"); some are weak ("I don't *dislike* you"); some don't make any sense ("I worship the very ground you walk on"); and some are obviously untrue ("I'm happy if you're happy").

9

The following lines, in order of ascending affection, are to be uttered at increasingly familiar stages of the relationship. They sound spontaneous and therefore sincere.

- You know something? You're really good company. I mean *really* good.
- That was the first really enjoyable date I've been on in a long time.
- You know, I like you more than I've ever liked any girl after just two dates.
- I hope we're friends for a long, long time.
- I've noticed something funny recently ... I'm always happy when I'm with you.
- I'm so glad I met you. It scares me to think, if I hadn't happened to need directions on that street corner that day ...
- This sounds trite, but I feel so close to you. It's as if I've known you for a lot longer than just three weeks.
- You're one of the nicest girls I've ever met ... the kind I'd want to ... well ... (At this point look away as if you said something you hadn't intended to let slip.).
- I can't imagine ever changing the way I feel about you.
- I can't think of anyone else I'd rather spend the rest of my life with. (This comes perilously close to proposing.)

You can always resort to "I love you," but this has become a bit of a cliché.

Propose Marriage

A prince ... must learn how not to be virtuous, and to make use of this or not according to need.
—Niccolò Machiavelli

"Never tell a woman you love her, even if you do" is the conventional wisdom. However, implying it strongly can sometimes help you storm the citadel. The best way to do this? Propose marriage. Very few women don't let their defenses down when proposed to. (If the woman actually accepts, it can be sticky extricating yourself.) If your target has you pegged as a womanizer, proposing will defuse her suspicion. And if she is seriously weighing your offer, she'll have the incentive to take a test drive.

If you think she'll doubt your sincerity, don't propose on your first date. A dozen red roses should prove your intent; while they will run upward of fifty dollars, the satisfaction is, if not guaranteed, certainly much more likely. A fake diamond engagement ring, available in any five-and-dime store, is another useful prop.

You probably don't propose every day, so a few rehearsals are helpful. Erupting into laughter while asking for her hand will diminish your matrimonial credibility. If you can't bring yourself to propose, at least hint strongly that you're interested in getting married. This will get her antennae up.

11

Then, when describing the qualities you're looking for in a wife, list hers.

Don't actually get married. The idea may seem vaguely appealing, especially if you haven't worshiped at her altar yet, but remember, eternal vigilance is the price of liberty.

Flattery

Women love flattery—and the less they deserve it, the more grateful they are. Just don't make it too unbelievable or they'll think you're mocking them. Flattery, like humor, works best when it contains a grain of truth.

But don't go to the other extreme. Unvarnished honesty will only backfire, such as: "You must look great when you're wearing makeup"; "Sometimes, when you're quiet, I almost like you"; or "If you just lost twenty-five pounds, you'd be gorgeous."

Ask permission to take her picture. Women either love or hate to have their picture taken: either way, they're flattered to be asked. If she's got a sense of humor, ask, "May I take your picture? I need something to jerk off over."

Ask, "You're not related to (a certain movie star), are you?" If you see the slightest resemblance, be it ever so faint, rest assured she will have already seen it. People always think they resemble a better-looking version of themselves, and your target will undoubtedly be pleased that somebody else spotted the resemblance.

One effective way to flatter her is to praise her to her best friend. This friend will undoubtedly repeat your compliments to your target. Your target should be delighted to hear this. (The sincerity of a compliment delivered to one's face is always suspect, but compliments behind one's back are generally considered to be meant.)

Go ahead and whisper those sweet nothings into her ear, even if that's all they are.

Nine Ways to Tell a Woman She's Beautiful

"Gee, you're looking beautiful" is not unpleasant for any woman to hear, but it sounds like a compliment a father might give. Here are some lines to make her swoon.

—It's really unfair that most women are sort of ordinary-looking and a few get to look like you.
—All four of your grandparents must have been very good-looking to produce someone as drop-dead gorgeous as you.
—I'll bet you've broken a lot of hearts with that face of yours.
—No one could have a face that perfect without plastic surgery. (You're risking that she's had it.)
—Every now and then Mother Nature just takes it upon herself to create a masterpiece.
—You're one of the three best-looking women I've ever seen. (Be prepared to name the other two.)

—I never thought I'd see a girl with a perfect face *and* a perfect body. Occasionally you see one or the other, but never both.

—Helen of Troy must have looked something like you.

—The amazing thing about your face is it doesn't have a single flaw! (If she points one out, say, "No! That just makes you more beautiful.")

These lines work best with a woman whose looks rate a natural six or seven on a scale of ten and through dieting and makeup has made herself a seven or eight. If the woman is a nine or a ten, she'll have heard similar flattery before and will remain unaffected. If she's below a six, she'll think you're mocking her.

Be a Good Listener

One of the oldest jokes around is that so-and-so's best quality is that he's a "good listener." However, since most people's favorite subject *is* by far themselves, to give a woman a truly enjoyable date, be prepared to let her discuss her favorite subject all evening long. (The emphasis is on long.)

Most people—and men are equally guilty of this—define "getting to know you" as telling you all about themselves. The difference between men and women is that women consider this a prerequisite for sex. So act as if she has your undivided attention while she spews out banal details about her friends, her family, her job, her co-workers, her favorite movie stars, et cetera. Profess admiration, approval, astonishment, and sympathy when each is called for.

Should you find your attention wandering, remember that all that is really required to keep up appearances is a few nods of the head and an occasional repeating of her last few words with a questioning tone.

At some point, she may begin to feel self-conscious about having blabbed on, and will ask you about yourself. You need only say, "Oh, my life isn't nearly as interesting as yours. I just work in a boring office every day." Then ask her to elaborate on some aspect of her life, sit back, and try not to look bored.

Listen to her talk long enough, and you may get to hear her moan later on.

Show You're a Nice Guy

Above all else, a woman who's checking you out cares about whether you're a nice guy. There are easier ways to do this than act like a saint all the time. The easiest way is to talk about your volunteer work. (And be sure to pooh-pooh it afterward.)

"Saturday afternoons I work for the ASPCA uptown." After she remarks on how nice you are for doing it, say, "I'm not doing it because I'm nice, I do it 'cause it makes me feel good."

"I think everybody should give a tenth of their income to charity. I do." (Be prepared to list your charities.)

"Once, when I was working at a gym, I saw this old wino outside, so I asked him to come in and take a shower. That poor guy hadn't showered in ages." (The implication is if you treat a bum that well, you'll treat her at least as well.)

"I worked for the Peace Corps in Ethiopia for a year after college. It was frustrating not being able to help those people any more than I could. One year was all I could take."

This technique is most effective when demonstrated first-hand. When you and your date walk by an indigent person, hand him a five (it'll be worth it) and tell him, trying to sound as concerned as you can, "Don't spend it on booze. Buy yourself a sandwich or something." Try not to look pleased with yourself (the kiss of death for any would-be saint).

She may be touched enough by your kindness and generosity to let you touch her later on.

Act Dazzled By Her Looks

If a woman is not secure about her attractiveness, (i.e., if she is a woman), you can often ingratiate yourself with an indirect form of flattery.

You meet a woman, start a conversation, and find she is

interested in, say, meditation. You express a desire to try it, though you haven't the least interest, and get her phone number. A few days later you call and say, "Hi, this is Nick. I'm the fellow who was asking you about meditation the other day." After your target says hello, admit, "I have to confess, I'm masquerading under false pretenses. I told you I'm interested in meditation, and I am, vaguely, but the truth is, mostly I just wanted to stare at you. How about I just buy you a drink instead."

You'll get a positive response for three reasons. First, she will have suspected that your interest in meditation was only a ploy to begin with, and your admission makes you seem honest. Second, your confession makes you out to be the type who can admit fault, always a good sign. Third, of course, is the sheer flattery value of your statement.

When you meet her, carry on a casual conversation, and don't refer to her looks directly. Then, the first time you make a verbal blunder, shake your head and say, "Being around a woman who looks like you has always turned me into a blithering idiot."

Indirect flattery comes across as more sincere because it seems less calculated. After all, you didn't intend to stumble over your words. That the excuse flatters her seems almost accidental.

At some point offer, "I'm *trying* to judge you on the merits of your conversation. I have to keep reminding myself, beauty is only skin deep."

Flattery can be most effective when it approaches your target from an oblique angle.

The Pass

Few things are more embarrassing than an awkward pass. It doesn't help that the woman usually seems able to sense them coming.

One way to avoid this embarrassment is to be humorous: "If you don't get up from this couch by the time I count to three, I'm going to kiss you." Before she can move, quickly count to three. If she rebuffs your advances, it will be more as if you made a joke than a pass, and you won't have to feel foolish.

Or say, "I have a secret to tell you." This is your excuse to lean in close. Then whisper in her ear, "I find you very attractive." It's much easier to kiss her from this position than it is to lunge in her direction and aggressively thrust your face at hers.

But the best way to make contact is not to appear to be making a pass at all. Calmly ask, "Will you do me a big favor?"

"What's that?"

"Give me a hug."

This sounds as if all you want is a little affection, and it's hard for her flatly to say no. Once she's in your arms, it's much easier to progress to a kiss, partly because it's harder for her to break away, but also because she will be touched by this evidence of your warmth. And the mere fact that she's returned your hug will help disperse her own inhibitions. In

18

fact, when you draw away slightly after you hug, while your face is still close to hers, the natural inclination for both of you will be to kiss. If you resist the impulse, chances are *she* will go ahead and kiss *you*—so in a sense *she* will be the one making the pass. If you're feeling playful, pull your head back and say, "Did I give you permission to kiss me?"

One secret to making a pass is to be perfectly still, just like a statue, beforehand. For some inexplicable reason, this seems to have a hypnotic effect on women. Try it. You'll be surprised.

These instructions, followed explicitly, will enable you to hit pay dirt with much greater regularity.

The Massage

Most women love massages; more importantly, they're more acquiescent after receiving one. The only problem is convincing them beforehand that your intentions stop there.

Never ask, "Can I give you a massage?" This places the burden of acceptance on her. Just say, "Lie down on your stomach, I know how to relax you." If she demurs, answer firmly, "Don't be silly. I'm just going to rub your back."

One line of attack is, "If you don't trust me, you don't have to accept one, but my back is really killing me, so could you give me one?" If you're on superficially good terms, she can hardly turn you down. Extend the massage as long as you can, and grunt appreciatively at frequent intervals. At some point murmur, "I swear, I like massages better than sex." This will remind her how nice a massage is, and also make you seem less of a sex fiend. If she doesn't want to be paid back for fairness' sake, she'll probably need a massage after all the time she's spent bent over you.

If this fails, tell her that you are a licensed masseur. Most women have always wanted to receive a professional massage but haven't either because of the illicit implications or because it seems extravagant to pay twenty dollars for a half-hour massage. (A massage table in your apartment can be an invaluable prop.).

Once your hands have started to work their hypnotic magic, it is a simple matter to remove her clothing piece by piece. It helps to reassure her (e.g., "I'm just untucking your blouse so I can do your lower back better"; "I'm just unhooking this clasp because it's in the way"). By this point, she should be enjoying the massage so much that she won't object.

Still, it's important not to show unseemly haste in getting at those hard-to-get-to places.

Telltale Signs

Unfortunately, no one has yet invented the machine that, when held up to a woman in the manner of a Geiger counter, will tell you whether she is willing to go to bed with you. So until someone invents the pussy meter, you will have to rely on the many clues that women drop, knowingly and unknowingly.

Good Signs	*Bad Signs*
Patting her hair or adjusting her nylons upon seeing you.	Taking out her compact and freshening her makeup in front of you.
Looking at you frequently.	Frequently consulting her watch.
Acting flirtatious with you.	Acting flirtatious with other men.
Leaning back and stretching (showing her breasts to best effect).	Crossing her arms and legs.
Laughing at all your jokes.	Pretending not to hear your jokes.
Comparing you favorably with her ex-boyfriend.	Comparing you unfavorably with her ex-boyfriend.
Beating out a drumroll on her thighs, or hips.	Drumming her fingernails on the tabletop.
Telling you she's got a great little apartment.	Telling you her apartment is a mess.
"Give me a call."	"I'll call you."

Too many bad signs means it's time to cut your losses. Walking out in the middle of dinner is bit abrupt—but at least you won't waste any more time that way.

How to Translate Her Words

While you must devote much attention to how women will interpret your words, you ought not to ignore the fact that females are also quite capable of double-talk (at times it seems that's the only talk they're capable of).

When She Says	*She Means*
I'm not ready for a heavy relationship right now.	I'm just not ready for a heavy relationship with you right now.
Oh, God, I'm so tired this evening.	You better not be expecting sex tonight.
I'm underpaid at my job.	I hope you're picking up the tab.
I don't understand how some people can have sex with someone they barely know.	If you want *this* pussy, you better settle in for a *long* siege.
Describe your ideal woman.	Describe me.
We're going to have *lots of time* to see each other.	We'll be seeing each other *lots of times* before I let you fuck me.
Oh, I'm so unattractive.	Tell me I'm beautiful.

| My last boyfriend was incredibly cheap. | You're going to have to spend two hundred bucks up front, *minimum*, before you get in *here*. |
| I love you. | Tell me you love me. |

Going on a date is often like taking an intensive Berlitz lesson in female double-talk. (Some women are so patently transparent that no translation lessons are necessary.)

How to Tell if She's Interested

There are many standard clues that women drop, knowingly and unknowingly.

Does she looks at you a lot? If you catch her staring at you more than three times, she wants you. (Naturally, this assumes you're not engaged in any outrageous behavior that merits gawking.) Think about it. Do you stare at women you want? Yes. Do you stare at women you don't want? No. Women are less visual, but they are not blind.

If she asks about your family, she's interested. (She wouldn't bother if she didn't care.) Of course, if she keeps asking about your older brother, she's probably more interested in him.

If she asks about your likes and dislikes, she's prospecting for future activities for the two of you.

If she says you're "interesting," she's interested.

If she laughs at all your jokes, even the lame ones, you've got her hooked.

If she asks if you have a girlfriend, it can mean that she's interested. (You must judge from the context—she might just be casually curious about your sexuality.)

If you're not receiving the desired feedback, take the initiative: "There's something that's been bothering me recently, and I have to know." When she asks what's wrong, look very concerned and say, "Do you find me attractive?" She may blurt out something revealing as she laughs.

If it's a woman you've just met, there's one way to judge her interest with no loss of face. Simply say, "You're attractive. If I weren't married, I'd ask you out." If she doesn't respond positively, let the subject drop. She may respond, "Oh, well, if you weren't married, I'd go out with you, too." Reply, "Guess what? I'm not married. What are you doing Friday night?"

She can't turn you down without making a liar of herself.

Banter

Teasing a woman about her appearance is a good way to play on her insecurities, compelling her to prove her attractiveness in ways she might not otherwise—like trying to lure you into bed.

If she has so much as one white hair, ask, "Is that a white hair?" Inquire how old she is, then reply, "Really? Normally when I meet a gray-haired lady, I assume she's much older."

If she protests, chuckle and comment, "you look like you've seen your share of tequila sunrises."

Peer at her closely, then express pleasant surprise: "Oh, you're growing a mustache!" (Every woman is self-conscious about the peach fuzz on her upper lip.)

Suggest, "You should do something about that jawline." Add helpfully, "I know the name of a good doctor."

Try, "Have you put on some weight?" When she denies it, express surprise.

If she makes a joke you've heard before (most jokes fall into this category), reply, "I applaud not only the humor but the originality of your joke." Or just nod politely. She may actually attempt to relate a long joke with a beginning, middle, and end (most women are constitutionally incapable of doing so). After she delivers the punch line, ask, "What happened then?"

If she asks what you think of her new dress, reply, "How much did it cost?" When she tells you, wince.

If she stumbles over her words, immediately retort, "Well put."

If she expresses her opinion on anything, you can reply, "Always have to be the center of attention, don't you."

If she shows any tomboyish tendencies whatsoever, furrow your brow and ask, "Have you ever had a boyfriend?"

Just because you don't end up in bed with a woman doesn't mean you can't have fun at her expense.

Off-Color Banter

Taking flirtation a step further brings you into the realm of sexual insult. Keep in mind that this line of talk will go over only with a certain type of woman—one who is extremely forward and flirtatious herself.

Saying either "I bet you're a real nymphomaniac" or "You seem like the type who'd have a real hard time reaching orgasm" will elicit a strong response from your target.

Ogle other women as they walk by. Remarks such as, "Nice ass, that" or "Whatta set of lungs" set just the right tone for your conversation.

If she lights up a cigarette, comment, "They say women who smoke just love giving blow jobs. Is that true?" If she has an attractive mouth, enthuse, "Those lips were just made for blow jobs."

Gesture at her loin area and say, "Bet there're a few miles on that odometer." If she gets mad, reply, "Hit a sore point, did I?"

If she has a bruise on her leg, comment, "If you have to get it cut off, keep in mind I have a penchant for amputees."

If she's wearing tight pants, marvel. "Those pants are pulled up so tight you must have to have one labia pulled over on one side and the other on the other side."

Muse, "You strike me as the type of woman who spends a lot of her spare time masturbating."

If she expresses dismay at any of your comments, reply,

"What are you getting so hoity-toity about? You're not exactly a vestal virgin."

As long as you're playing the role of bad boy, you might as well play it to the hilt.

Playing Hard to Get

This book is mostly about demonstrating counterfeit affection; but there are times when it is better to do the opposite. If you make yourself too available, you can lose your appeal.

You must judge your quarry correctly: Some women need lots of attention, other prefer a little challenge. (It's a fatal mistake to smother the latter.)

Pretending indifference is easy (and often fun). At the early stages of courtship it can be accomplished simply by forgetting her name or not looking at her very much. (Constantly staring is a dead giveaway that you desire her.)

After you call her by the wrong name, immediately apologize and correct yourself. The desired impression will be left. This mistake becomes increasingly insulting the longer you know her. (For utmost effect, moan the wrong name during sex.)

Ask, "Were you the one who used to ride horses?" This is even more effective than calling her by the wrong name (a mere slip of the tongue), because it means you have her genuinely confused with someone else.

If your relationship has not reached the physical stage yet, share a soft drink with her. Each time before you take a swig, thoroughly wipe off the neck of the bottle where her lips have touched it. (Women being women, she will then want proof you're not put off by close physical contact.)

Standing her up on a date (even if you want to go) can convey the correct attitude. Afterward, don't claim an emergency; tell her you simply forgot about the date (but be profusely apologetic).

Don't act like a doormat and you won't get treated like one.

Show You're Attractive to Other Women

If your date is susceptible to mob psychology, all you need do to brainwash her into falling for you is show how desirable you are to other women. Arrange to have a buddy phone your apartment several times during the course of an evening. Each time you answer the phone, your date should hear something like the following. (Talk secretively, as if you don't want her to hear, but loudly enough for her to get the gist of the conversations.)

"Hi, Sue-Ann . . . Fine, thanks . . . I'd like to but I promised George I'd help him move. . . . No, there's no one else here. . . . I'll give you a call. . . . Yeah, soon, bye."

"Hi, Yasmine, you caught me just as I was going out the door. . . . I've got to get to my tailor. He closes in five minutes. . . . Okay, tomorrow evening. See you."

*   *   *

"Hi! How's California? Fine. . . . Listen, you caught me at a bad time . . . Mike's over and we're watching the game. . . . Okay, see you at the airport then. . . . Me, too. . . . Love you, bye-bye."

If your date asks who phoned, reply, "Oh, no one." After the third call, unplug the phone and say, "People I haven't heard from in months are coming out of the woodwork tonight." This obvious lie should convince her you're a hot item.

If your date suggests you're quite a ladies' man, deny it repeatedly; this is tantamount to admitting it. By this point she should be keenly aware of what a prize you are and want you herself.

Making Her Jealous

If a woman is taking you for granted, nothing will revitalize her flagging attention like a healthy dose of jealousy.

There are many ways to make a woman jealous. Some are subtle, some not so subtle. When you pass by another nubile young thing in the street, turn around and check out her backside. Then sigh deeply. If you make eye contact with the passerby, smile at her (this is an outright declaration of war).

Anytime you're near a newsstand, pick up a girlie magazine and flip through it. (This can have an off-putting effect on

29

a first date.) Better yet, leave a few skin magazines around your place. Idly pick one up during the course of a conversation and absentmindedly leaf through it.

Ask your girlfriend, "Do you think Susan is pretty?" She'll respond sharply, "No. Why? Do you?" Reply, "Just curious, that's all."

Tell her, "If I wasn't going out with you, I'd go after Becky." She will interpret this to mean that you'd like to go after Becky, which, of course, is what it does mean.

If a well-dressed nymphet sashays by, examine her closely, then comment, "Nice dress." (Heterosexual males never pay attention to a woman's clothes.)

Ask, "Have you ever had an open relationship?" She'll say something like "No. I think that's disgusting. Why? Do you want one?" Reply, "No, of course not, I was just asking, that's all."

If she should have occasion to ask what you were doing on a certain night, quickly answer, "Nothing . . . nothing." (No one ever does absolutely nothing.)

If she decides to counterattack by ogling a few guys, laugh as if you think she's cute. (Nothing makes a woman more insecure than total lack of jealousy on your part.)

Tell her you got a call from an old girlfriend the day before. When your target asks what she wanted, reply, "She wanted to have a drink sometime, that's all. You know, just as friends."

Too much of this behavior can lead to a fight and even a breakup, but in the right dosages it can tie your target into knots of insecurity, which is just how you want her.

If She Asks You Your Sign

As everybody with an IQ in excess of 93 knows, astrology is a preoccupation of the addlebrained. However, if a pretty woman asks your sign, *don't* demonstrate your wisdom by saying "Jeeeesus *Christ*! You don't believe in *that* shit, do you?"

The best reply is simply "Guess," which identifies you as a fellow believer. If she has asked you your sign, there's interest on her part; this means she hopes you're compatible, and therefore she'll pick a compatible sign for you. So when she makes her guess, reply, "That's right! How did you know?" At this point she'll gladly give a long-winded explanation. Feign interest.

Once she's started out believing you're compatible, chances are you *will* be compatible, partly because her attitude will create a self-fulfilling prophecy, and partly because her attitude will create a self-fulfilling prophecy, and partly because avid astrologers constantly look for facts bearing out their predictions. And after all, how many intelligent men (you've already proved *you're* intelligent by reading this book) will listen spellbound while she expounds on how the gravitational pull of the stars when you're born exerts such a profound influence on your later life?

Now, the stars exert less gravitational influence on you during birth than a cigarette lighter in the operating room, and there's as much real science in astrology as there is in

31

the distribution of Chinese fortune cookies at dinner, but if you play along with her game, chances are greater she'll play along with yours.

If You Excel at a Sport

All men are showoffs at heart, and you are no exception. And with good reason. For the last four million years, women have been evolutionarily selected for mating with men who would be good providers. For most of that time, providing entailed running fast and throwing spears accurately. These days one's ability as a provider has precious little to do with one's spear-throwing prowess, but women still succumb to such atavistic charms. However, if you want to demonstrate your athletic skills, there is a way to do it and a way not to do it.

Don't boast about your prowess, then insist she watch you. She'll be less impressed because of her raised expectations. She'll think you a conceited boor. And she'll feel obliged to praise you afterward, an awkward position for anyone.

Let's say you're a good butterflier. Your approach should be something like this: "I'm due for a time trial Saturday. It will be boring for you, but I'd be grateful if you came: Your presence would undoubtedly inspire me to a better performance."

Portray yourself as mediocre befor hand ("I just hope I can finish the four laps"). And rest assured few women know the difference between a good and a bad athletic performance anyway. (Any guy who lifts knows that bench pressing two hundred pounds is commonplace, but few women know that.)

Afterward, your instinct will be to insist what she just witnessed was a subpar performance. It's better to tell her the opposite ("Knowing you were watching took two seconds off my time").

At the same time, profess embarrassment that you participate in your sport ("Pretty mindless way to spend an afternoon, eh?"; "Pathetic, isn't it, trying to recapture lost athletic glory at my age"; "I can't help it, I'm thirty-two going on fifteen").

Then apologize for having taken up her time ("That must have been very tedious for you").

If it's embarrassingly apparent that you were showing off, say in mock solemnity, "I sincerely hope you don't think I was trying to show off." After she snorts, add, "I admit, I'm shameless."

Among the lower orders, such showing off is called courtship display. The peacock spreads his feathers, rams butt heads, and flies follow elaborate mating dances. It works for them. It can work for you.

Hypnosis

Most women, ever eager to be the center of attention, will willingly offer themselves as subjects for hypnosis if you can convince them you're an expert.

Don't expect actually to hypnotize her. Despite tales of people jumping off buildings or committing murder while hypnotized, any realistic study of the field will show that few subjects can be persuaded to place their hands in fire or do anything they wouldn't do normally. Hypnosis is merely the power of suggestion, and people will generally do only what they want. Herein lies the trick.

If the girl wants sex (this includes most of them) but feels that she ought not to have it with you at this particular moment (this also includes most of them), "hypnosis" can provide her with just the excuse she needs.

Thus you must convince your subject not that she is hypnotized but that she can convince you (or herself) that she is hypnotized. To effect this charade, it is not necessary to have her stand on her head while speaking in tongues. Less drama is called for.

Start by repeating over and over in a rhythmic monotone that she feels very relaxed. Instruct her to hold her arms straight out. Then tell her they feel increasingly heavy. (This requires no great leap of imagination.) Next, tell her she feels drowsy. Continue to tell her how relaxed she feels. Suggest that she feels warm, and would be more comfortable with fewer clothes. Tell her that the massage you're giving her is relaxing her even further. With her "free will" supposedly taken away, she'll feel free to do (and let you do) as she pleases.

She may jokingly blame you afterward for having "hypnotized" her into having sex, anxious to deny complicity in the act.

However, the essential judgment to make beforehand is not how hypnotizable she is but rather how much of a liar.

Pretend You're Married

People often complain that in this era of free sex, the forbidden fruit appeal of sex has disappeared. Well, married men are one of the few taboos left. So why not make yourself seem unattainable? It's easy to do. Just pretend you're married. (In these plague-ridden times, it's also an excellent way of advertising you're disease-free.)

The traditional line used by the average husband is that his wife is a shrew, and he'd like to leave her and marry the target instead. This tactic sometimes meets with success, which is why, of course, it has become a tradition.

However, the opposite (and less clichéd) approach will yield more bountiful results. Wax eloquent about how wonderful your wife and marriage are. This will put your target off her guard: No guy on the make talks about how wonderful his wife is. And it poses a subconscious challenge few women can resist. (If she can distract such a happily married man, she must be quite attractive indeed.)

If your target needs a little encouragement, test the waters by commenting, "If I wasn't married, you're the first one I'd ask out." If she responds favorably, you're home free.

If you commit a *faux pas*, you've got a built-in excuse: "God, it's been so long since I've actually tried to seduce anybody, this kind of stuff just feels awkward to me now."

The hard-core homebreakers will take it as a challenge to see how long they can keep you from home. Nothing works better than, "Gee, my wife must be getting worried." Once you're at the homebreaker's apartment, make the following bogus call (dial eight digits): "Hello, honey? I'm at the office, I have to work late on the new project . . . a couple of hours . . . love you, bye-bye." She'll do anything to keep you from getting home on time.

Every night, armies of married men slip off their wedding bands, trying to conceal their attached state. They should be flaunting it. And so should you, whether or not you're married.

So invest in a wedding ring. It will never occur to your prospect that you're single. Even better, it will never occur to her to try to wrangle some kind of commitment from you.

If You're Divorced

If your target knows you're divorced, her natural tendency is to be swayed by a latent sense of sisterhood and disbelieve your version of events. To counteract these instincts, you must tread very delicately. You must put the subject in such a light as to enlist her sympathy. There are certain things you can say, and certain things you cannot.

You can't say, "She was always arguing with me," a statement that gives off faint reverberations of, "The bitch didn't know how to take orders."

Don't complain bitterly of your ex's spending habits, or your complaint will echo, "Cheap ... cheap ... cheap."

You mustn't criticize your ex's poor housekeeping, or your target will assume you didn't do any yourself. It also brings to mind the image of domestic slavery—which will not evoke feelings of romance.

Do not say that your ex cheated on you. While this will elicit sympathy, it will also make you look like a pathetic cuckold, and your target will wonder why your ex felt the need to cheat—didn't you satisfy her?

Likewise, don't admit that you were caught cheating—a clear indication that you will also cheat on your target.

You cannot even remotely imply, "She got old and I got tired of her."

If your ex has a restraining order on you, don't breathe a word of that.

Here is what you can say:

If you have children, note that she ignored them and didn't take care of them. This implies no fault on your part and makes your ex look quite coldhearted.

Or say your ex was chemically dependent. Don't explode in righteous anger at the recollection. Just shake your head sadly and calmly say, "There was a problem with alcohol there," or "When we got married, I didn't fully appreciate that . . . that she used drugs." This shows tremendous forbearance.

Mournfully mumble, "No matter how many times I tried to get professional help for her, she'd always backslide. I just couldn't bear to watch her do that to herself." Only a saint could put up with an addict for an extended time, and if you fall short of sainthood, well, that's forgivable.

The nerviest approach of all, if you can get away with it, is to claim that you've been married and divorced five times. Everyone has heard of people like this, but very few people have actually met one. While your target won't regard you as a good prospect for a long-term marriage, she'll be fascinated the way a bird is mesmerized by a snake.

Play your cards right and you may just be dealing with the future ex Mrs. you.

Be a Widower

If you are thirty-five and still unmarried, the only conclusion a girl can draw is that you're not interested in marriage—and this will diminish her interest in you. If you are divorced, your target will wonder why your marriage failed. (Are you a philanderer? A wife-beater? Or just plain selfish?)

The solution is to pose as a widower. Evidence of your Dear Departed needn't be overwhelming, just a framed picture or two on the bedstand. (Your prospect would prefer less rather than more evidence of the deceased.)

Your wife died of leukemia almost two years ago (an exact date lends credibility). Anything longer than two years and you might have turned into a hound again; anything less and she'd wonder why you don't seem sad. Leukemia conjures up the image of you faithfully standing vigil at her bedside during those last agonizing months. (Being able to summon tears at will is a tremendous advantage.)

If she blurts out, "That must have been terrible when she died," simply reply, "Any words to describe it would sound trite. Reminisce ("We used to walk here all the time") but stop short of "I'll never love another the way I loved her." It enhances your marriageability to muse, "Right before she got sick, we had just decided to have kids." Always conclude,

"Well—I guess I can't spend the rest of my life mourning her."

It won't occur to your prospect that you are lying unless you get carried away and contradict yourself. As always, the minimalist school of lying works best.

Sympathy Booty

All women harbor the maternal instinct. Although usually suppressed, it's not buried deeply; the slightest provocation can bring it to the surface. How do you focus it on yourself?

Simply relate a story that makes you look tragic but not pathetic, sad but not creepy.

"Last week the doctor told me that I only have half a year to live because of my brain tumor." The Florence Nightingale in any woman will compel her to do anything in her power to ease the pain of your last months. (The only drawback here is you can't continue to enjoy her after the six months are over.)

"When I was ten I was molested by an older man." This makes you look like a sexual victim rather than the victimizer you are.

"Ever since my wife died of cancer last year I haven't been able to feel much of anything for another woman." No woman can resist this challenge. (Tony Curtis used it to good effect with Marilyn Monroe in *Some Like It Hot*.)

Be brave. Always insist, no matter how heartrending your problem, that you don't want sympathy.

Pretend It's Your Birthday

When a woman knows it's your birthday, it seems to strike a generous chord somewhere deep inside. If you let her know subtly, she may even feel slightly guilty she hasn't gotten you a present. It will also give the two of you an excuse to "celebrate" (for most people any excuse will do).

At an opportune moment, ask, "Do I get a birthday kiss?" She will be hard put to say no. After all, it would take a very hard-hearted (or very suspicious) woman to refuse a *birthday* kiss. A birthday kiss sounds chaste, but physically it's the same as any other: upper persuasion for a lower invasion.

If this doesn't lead to immediate results, ask for a massage. Or jokingly suggest that what you'd really like for your birthday is to see her in her birthday suit.

Unless she knows you well, chances are she won't ask you for proof that it's your birthday.

Can You Keep a Secret?

If you know a woman on a flirtatious but not intimate basis, and see her regularly—for instance, in between classes or every morning at a coffee shop—ask if she can keep a secret.

When she says yes, look around to make sure no one else is within earshot, and whisper conspiratorially, "You've got an incredibly beautiful face."

If you get a positive reaction to this, next time you see her, tell her she's got great legs.

Next time, tell her those great legs lead up to a scrumptious rumptious.

Next time, say she's got beautiful breasts.

Each time, start by asking if she can keep a secret. She will, of course, say yes, since nobody admits they can't keep a secret. Then, when you tell her the "secret," she will have tacitly agreed to be part of your little cabal.

Judge from her reaction each time whether she'll be receptive to escalating levels of boldness. If she reacts laughingly, take the next step. If not, simply stop, having offended her only slightly. (How offended can she be by a compliment?)

Next, ask her if she can keep a secret, then tell her you'd like to lay some kisses on her legs. Next, her rump. Next, her breasts. Finally, ask her if there's a time you could plant these kisses on her. Any woman with even a vestigial sense of modesty will feel obliged to say no, so ask if you could just buy her dinner instead. If she has let the flirting get to this stage, she will probably accept.

With a little luck on your part, after the date she'll be hoping you're the one who can keep a secret.

Playing the Ethnic Angle

There are three ways to exploit your target's ethnicity: flattery, teasing, or claiming consanguinity. The choice depends on your target.

Some women (and some ethnic groups) have to be treated with kid gloves. These you should flatter. Flattery generally consists of praising the accomplishments (or sympathizing with the travails) of her group. Another common approach is to claim as your hero a kinsman of hers. Unfortunately, such attempts at flattery are often painfully transparent, and leave both of you feeling awkward.

Tell her she looks like whatever you are. If she's smart, she realizes people often like to claim a good-looking person as one of their own. This is an unintended and therefore more sincere form of flattery.

Another approach is to tease her. When she first tells you what her antecedents are, ask, "Are you ashamed of that?" Later, comment, "You're very well behaved for an Italian."

Or try, "Back in the old country, wasn't there a lot of inbreeding among your people? Don't anthropologists explain your country's history that way?"

Whatever you do, make sure your jibes are gentle ones

that could be aimed at any group (such as Polish jokes). Well-aimed barbs at your own group, however, are acceptable.

If it's at all possible, claim consanguinity. Tell her you're part whatever she is. (Kinship begets trust, and trust begets intimacy.) If you can convince her that you share her ethnicity (to whatever small extent), be sure to mention how much happier her mother would be if she knew that her daughter had a nice Italian boyfriend.

If you can't convince her that you're of the same ethnicity, at least make a joke of it. Say, "You don't think those are my real parents, do you? I was adopted from a Lithuanian adoption agency." Or try, "The [your group] are lost descendants of the [her group]. Recent archaeological finds have confirmed this."

Find out which little town her great-grandparents came from, then say that your great-grandparents came from there, too. And come to think of it, you had Scepettos in your family line. Nothing lends that feeling of immediate closeness like knowing you're cousins three times removed. (It will also lend the extra spice of incest to the relationship.)

Posing as a Foreigner

Ever notice how when you're in a foreign country you can just throw yourself at people's mercy and they're usually very helpful? There's no reason not to do the same thing at home. Just ask a pretty woman in ungrammatical, halting English if she can direct you to a good restaurant. (When she answers, pretend you don't understand, the better to draw out the conversation.)

When she asks what country you're from, be believable (i.e., if you're blond, don't say Tanzania). Whatever you look like don't say France, because everyone who has taken a little high school French will want to try it out on you. (On that score, rest assured no one knows Bulgarian, Cantonese, or Ibo.) If you're not good with accents, just say you're Canadian. After you've managed to get the directions to a good restaurant, ask her if she'll be your guest. Relay—awkwardly—that you'd be very grateful if you could practice your English with her.

As a foreigner you can get away with all sorts of gaucheries that would be unforgivable were you an American. In fact, she'll probably think they're cute. For instance, while you're talking about your country, point at your chest; then, when talking about her country, point at her chest, lightly touching her breast with your finger.

The most satisfying aspect of this encounter comes after you've had sex, seeing her expression when you announce in your normal voice, "Well, honey, that's your lesson in foreign culture for today."

Your Hero

If your target places a premium on virtue, you can leave the impression that you share the same values by talking about someone you admire. That someone cannot be one of your actual heroes—a macho football player, a playboy actor, or an influential billionaire. You must pretend to admire a saint.

Bring up the subject by asking your target who her heroes are, as if you want to know her better. Feign fascination with her reply. Then, if your target fails to ask you the same question, prompt her with, "I always find it interesting who people's heroes are." She should pick up on this cue. If she doesn't, plow ahead anyway: "You know, I've always admired ..."

Candidates for your pantheon include Mother Teresa, Albert Schweitzer, and Father Damien. Shrug resignedly: "I wish I were that good. But I'm afraid I'm a sinner." (Everyone knows sinners are more fun.)

If your candidate has a little bit of the gold-digger to her (most women harbor a latent tendency), add, "I'm too interested in things like money. Well, maybe someday." She'll find it reassuring that you intend to get rich first. No woman minds being with a rich saint.

Another tactic is to rave about what a gentleman a certain friend is. Spin a yarn about how your friend had said his girlfriend broke up with him when in fact he broke up with her and you only discovered the truth accidentally when you talked to her later on. ("I figure most guys are doing well enough by not exaggerating their exploits. I never figured I'd meet a guy who'd lie the other way. What a *great guy!*") The implication is that you might be inspired to behave similarly. (Don't use a buddy she knows or she won't believe you.)

Impress her with your virtuousness and you may get to impress her with your virtuosity later on.

Paying For It

You're at your wits' end. You've tried every trick you know to get your date into bed, but she is behaving like an immovable object, forcing you to the unpleasant conclusion that you're not an irresistible force.

There's one last hope: Her greed may outweigh her pride.

Look her straight in the eye and say, "I'd give anything to make love to you." Pull out your wallet and whisper, "Even two hundred dollars." Lay the bills down—but overact just a touch, to leave open the possibility that you're kidding.

If two hundred dollars doesn't do the trick, and you can afford it, offer more. You can always take the money back right after you finish; there's very little she can do about that. Or just tell her you'll pay her the next day, then don't. It's hardly the type of thing she'd take you to court for.

Don't make the mistake of thinking she's not "that type of woman," because every woman has her price.

If She Likes Her Men Macho

While the book thus far has concentrated on how to show you're sensitive and caring, there are women who want a Stanley Kowalski.

The secret to appearing tough is never to appear to try to seem tough. A good tactic is to talk about how scared you were in some dangerous situation most people would never dream of getting into. ("The first time I went skydiving I almost pissed in my pants. Couldn't wait to get up the second time, though.")

If she asks where you went to school, tell her Bridgewater Prep. When she says she hasn't heard of it, grin and comment, "I don't imagine too many of your friends went to reform school."

A tattoo will further burnish the image. (Just get the kind you stick on and wash off.) The skull and crossed rifles motif lends just the right touch.

Casually mention your stretch in Folsom. ("I was a frightened boy when I went in, I was an animal when I got out.") If she asks what you were in for, answer, "armed robbery" ("I was young and I was foolish").

If the subject turns to sports, yours used to be kick-boxing. ("Not that noncontact bullshit.") No matter how small you are, there's a weight class for you.

Other facts to remember: You grew up poor; you understand cars inside and out but know nothing you'd learn from a book; and your politics are three steps to the right of Attila the Hun.

Always use ethnic slurs. And remember that your testosterone level is suspect if you pay any attention to traffic lights.

This type of woman likes a man who's assertive, so don't act tentative when you move in for the clinch.

Save Her Life

How many adventure movies don't have at least one scene where the hero saves the beauty's life? In how many of those adventures does the woman not fall for the hero? Tells you something, doesn't it?

Even if the woman doesn't fall for you, if you save a woman's life it would be incredibly petty of her not to give up the booty.

If you're not in a position to save your target's life, simply set up such a situation. If you have a buddy she hasn't met before (preferably a threatening-looking fellow), arrange with him to meet up with you and your date in a relatively secluded area. Make sure he has a weapon (a starter's pistol will do, but be sure it's unloaded), and apply your talents as a choreographer. The scene should run roughly as follows:

You and your date are walking down a lonely country road, and your buddy rushes up, pulls out his gun, and says, "Hand over your money and I won't hurt you." You kick the gun out of his hand (tell him beforehand to hold it low), then place your foot on his stomach and send him sprawling. You scramble over to retrieve the gun, and the "mugger" runs away.

Take a deep breath, look as if you're trying to hold back your anger, and say, "One of these days I'm going to meet someone like that and hurt him . . . bad."

Then wink at your target and yell at the retreating figure, "Hey, you forgot your gun!"

She's yours.

The most enjoyable part of this escapade will come after you've tagged her, and after you've grown tired of her, when you introduce her to your buddy.

Relaxing a Nervous Woman

If a woman is nervous, it's not just her problem. It's also *your* problem, because a nervous woman doesn't feel sexy.

The solution is to make her feel she's not alone in her nervousness. Nothing makes a nervous Nellie less nervous than the knowledge that you, too, are nervous. So even if you're so relaxed you're on the verge of falling asleep, tell her that you were racked with anxiety before asking her out, you were a nervous wreck before meeting her, and you're a basket case right now.

Or just say, "You intimidate me." If she expresses surprise, mention that you're not used to being around someone so accomplished. Then list her accomplishments (there's got to be *something* she's good at). Knowing that you're intimidated will relax her, and also give her that warm glow that comes from being appreciated.

Sometimes during a first date the tension builds until the

pass is made, because both parties know it is coming; use that as an excuse to kiss her early. Just say, "Forgive me, but I think this will make both of us a little less nervous," and kiss her. Then say, "Now you don't have to worry about me making a pass at you anymore."

You can also take some of the pressure off her by saying, "Listen, I'm not ready to sleep with you tonight, so let's just talk. Okay?" She may resent the implicit assumption that *she's* ready to sleep with *you*, but in a subtle way it will make her feel a little less like the meat in the lion's cage.

Tease Her About Her Age

As the sociologists constantly remind us, ours is a culture that worships youth. If you are chasing a woman several years your senior, she will undoubtedly be painfully aware of that difference. Teasing her about it will bring an awkward subject out into the open and make her more relaxed about it.

So if she's six years older than you, tell her she's old enough to be your mother.

Or tell her she looks like an older version of so-and-so.

Tell her she reminds you of a woman whose only public image is that of an older woman, such as Golda Meir, Margaret Thatcher, or Indira Gandhi. If she tells you about some altruistic act of hers, tell her she's just like Mother Teresa. When she protests that she is not nearly that good, say that oh, no, you meant the way she looks.

Ask to see a picture of her when she was young.

Ask if she's embarrassed to be robbing the cradle.

Ask her impression of the decade she was born in, as if she would have been old enough to have formed a distinct impression of the era's popular culture when in fact she was only a toddler. (If she was born in the midsixties, ask if she went to Woodstock, and so on.)

Benjamin Franklin once said that older women are superior because they are grateful for the attention they receive. This may be true, but they are generally not grateful when that attention is directed at their age, unless it is done in a lighthearted, teasing sort of way calculated to put them at ease about what they might otherwise consider a deep, dark secret.

Wistfulness

For many women, sentiment is an unavoidable stepping-stone to horniness. Here are a few standard clichés designed to put things in the right perspective for them.

If your target is approaching thirty, touch on the subject indirectly. "They say youth is wasted on the young. It's so true." Or, "So many people don't take advantage of their youth and beauty, then regret it later on."

The brevity-of-life theme strikes a responsive chord in most women. "When you think in terms of evolutionary time, we're not even here for the blink of an eyelash. Life is so ephemeral, it's a shame not just to reach out and enjoy every day as much as you possibly can."

If your target is holding out on you, continue in this vein. "When you're seventy years old and your life is behind you, do you think you'll be happy you were virtuous and chaste, or do you think you just might regret your missed opportunities?" Or say, "Look around. See all these people? In ninety years every one of them, including you and me, will be long dead and buried. Then it will be too late."

Put it in historical perspective. "Catherine of Russia used to enjoy a different man every night. The Empress Wu of China had a bed constructed so she could enjoy thirty-three men at the same time. All I'm asking you to do is enjoy one man, the same man, for a long time." If the discussion drags on, ask, "Would you rather live your life or just talk about it?"

Tell her, "I used to be like you. I always used to live for tomorrow. One day I woke up and realized I had to live for today."

If you can stomach all these clichés, they should put your target in a more pliant frame of mind. If you're with a woman you find barely attractive, these lines are a good way to convince yourself to go for it.

Paying Lip Service to Friendship

One of the great myths is that a man and a woman can be just friends, with no sex involved. This myth, popular among women, implies that men enjoy their company, prize their conversation, and value their friendship. In reality, almost no heterosexual men hang out with heterosexual women on a regular basis with absolutely no sex (or attempts at sex) involved.

However, to pass the Nice Guy Litmus Test, you must prove you're capable of being a "friend" in a low-key, no-strings-attached sort of way. This allows your target to feel that the two of you have a solid basis for a long-term relationship, and also allows her to feel less pressured for sex.

Mention early on in the courtship process, "Oh, I have lots of friends who are women. You know, just friends." This will show you to be the sincere, warmhearted individual you aren't.

The irony is that once you are involved in a sexual relationship (often only after having arduously proven capable of a nonsexual one), friendships with other women are not countenanced. Just try telling your new steady girlfriend that you're going out to have a drink with another woman—you know, just as friends.

Female logic has never been known for its logic.

Pretend to Be Someone Else

You've just phoned your target and arranged a date, but the conversation was flat and stilted. If you want to inject some levity into your budding relationship, phone her back and pretend to be your own parole officer. (Make sure she knows you well enough to know you're kidding.)

Say that you've put a tracer on Nick's line and just wanted to check up and make sure that Nick was behaving himself. Ask if she thinks Nick should be put back in jail, and if Nick has been causing any trouble. Your target, if she has a sense of humor, will seize this opportunity to make all sorts of outrageous charges against you. Play along.

When she asks what Nick was in jail for, say sex crimes. When she asks what sort of sex crimes, tell her that several women lodged charges that Nick was too good in bed, that he ruined them for other men. When your target says that she didn't know that was a crime, answer that in your county it is. Say that Nick has learned his lesson, and he has agreed never to be that good in bed again.

Or you can pretend to be Nick's psychiatrist. When she asks why Nick's seeing a psychiatrist, reply that Nick had a nervous breakdown because of a woman he was dating who insulted him. List the warning signs of an impending break-down (things you've already done), and stress that she should be extremely nice to Nick and accede to all Nick's demands. She'll probably say that she's not sure she can do that, as

Nick has been making quite a few demands. Stress that any resistance on her part would be a traumatic enough blow to cause a relapse. The next time you see her, pretend ignorance of the conversation and play off it.

This kind of repartee will not necessarily land your target in bed, but at least it will put the two of you on a joking, relaxed footing—a better vantage point from which to get her there.

If you do end up in bed, and after a few weeks it gets a bit boring, close your eyes and pretend that *she's* someone else.

A Solitary Sport

Unlike real wolves, the human kind does better not to hunt in packs. Despite the occasional situation where a buddy comes in handy, as a rule you'll enjoy more success if you search for prey alone.

Guys in groups tend to approach girls only to show off to each other (this is especially true during high school). In fact, most guys who make ostensible pickup attempts in front of their gang would have no idea how to respond if a woman actually reacted favorably to their advances. (Women sense this, and this is part of the reason why comments from such groups tend to make them angry.)

No woman can do other than ignore a group of guys making lewd comments. Even if the guys were friendly in a polite way, she would feel vaguely that she was inviting a gang bang by being friendly. (And if she didn't feel this way, she still might be confused about which guy she was supposed to respond to.)

And even if she wasn't confused, it would still be hard to let one of them pick her up in front of all the others; after all, it's harder to do anything with an audience. (Think of it as the difference between having sex in private and onstage.)

So see the guys when you want to see the guys, not when you want to meet women. Besides, as with other carnivores who hunt in packs, there is always the conflict in the end about who gets the meat.

Part II
Props

Score with Your Football

When a woman sees you tossing a football, she immediately perceives you as nonthreatening. If you're over twenty-five years old, yelling "And Namath is fading back! Namath is fading back!" as you throw the ball will make you appear particularly innocent. After all, can you imagine Charlie Manson playing football? Neither can she.

Women normally don't frequent football fields (if they do, you needn't bother with props), so you'll want to take your football into town. Have your buddy pass you the ball near a pretty woman, then when it goes bouncing in some crazy direction (preferably hers), apologize for bothering her. If you're lucky, the football will hit her, allowing you to tender heartfelt apologies and perhaps start a conversation.

But this also can backfire. It's more productive simply to ask the woman if she'd like to join your game. If she claims she doesn't know how to play, reply, "You're probably better than Joey over there." (Boyish banter will augment your air of innocence.) If she says she's not dressed properly, look puzzled and reply, "This is touch, not tackle." If she still declines, which she undoubtedly will, say, "Catch!" and gently toss her the ball. Her instinct will be to hold out her arms, and, before she knows it, she's involved. If she says she has to go somewhere—for instance the opera—reply, "Come on, what's more fun, the opera or a football game? Get serious!"

The best thing about the football pass is that you leave no tracks. If you try to hit on every prospect at a party, eventually no self-respecting woman there will have anything to do with you. If you fail to score with your football, just take it around the corner, start your routine anew, and no one's the wiser.

The Business Card

If you have a respectable job at a respectable company, use your business card to advantage.

You're on the train to work. You've been staring at the woman across the way and even made eye contact a couple of times, but haven't thought of an appropriate opening line. Just before your stop, dart over with an apologetic look on your face. "Listen, it's awfully forward of me to say this to a complete stranger, but I couldn't help but notice how beautiful you are. I know it's obnoxious to hand out a business card, but here," you say, handing her your card. "Give me a call tomorrow, please."

You mustn't seem as if this is a habit. And you can't seem pleased with yourself (or your job) as you do it, otherwise she'll be turned off by your conceit. You must come across flustered when you do this, as if you were goaded into this act of desperation by her beauty.

When a woman calls, don't ask, "Which one were you?" Just say, "Oh, I was hoping you would call" and see if you can tell from the conversation which one she was.

If you have a fancy job, you may attract gold-diggers with this approach. If you do, so what? You're not looking to marry them.

It pays to keep some monkey business cards on hand.

Your Bodyguard

If you have a buddy who's large or tough-looking, preferably both, you can impress the impressionable by pretending he's your bodyguard. This game works best with gold-diggers and starfuckers, but even normal women will be bamboozled by the aura of a fellow who needs a bodyguard.

Your buddy should dress in a suit and tie (only lowlifes have bodyguards who don't dress formally) and double as your chauffeur. Rent a limousine for the evening (it's cheaper than you think without the driver).

Your buddy drives, you sit in the back, and you stop whenever you see a pretty woman. He gets out, walks up to the woman, takes off his chauffeur's cap, and politely says, "Excuse me, miss, but Mr. Casanova saw you and would like to meet you." He then gestures toward the rear of the car. Press the button to roll the window down and when the woman leans over to see who's in the backseat, simply say, "You're a very pretty woman. Can I offer you a ride?"

If she accepts, act blasé, as if you are merely accepting your due. You must be very low key and not appear eager. Whatever you do, don't smirk or give yourself away with any stifled laughs.

Be sure to refer to your buddy as your bodyguard, so she gets the message. If your target asks why you need a bodyguard, just reply vaguely, "Lot of bad people out there." When you get out of the car, he should follow you at a discreet distance.

When she asks what you do for a living, pick a role that suits you (e.g., if you're nerdy-looking, don't claim to be a rock star). If you're barely out of college, you probably should just invent a role for your father.

To make it worthwhile for your buddy, just switch roles occasionally. (It's almost as much fun to play the tough bodyguard anyway.)

You're not going to start any long-term relationships this way, but who wants one when numerous short-term relationships are available?

Pull it off, and you may well need a bodyguard just to protect you from all the angry women you've lied to.

A Little Pooch Can Lead to a Little Chooch

The dog is truly man's best friend.

The only thing that makes a woman glow more than praising her dog is praising her child, and the advantage of the former is that chances are it's not her offspring.

So if you see an attractive woman walking her dog, stroll right up and pet it. Don't worry about scaring her. A guy who likes dogs seems sexless and nonthreatening. Face it: A guy who lets his dog eat off his plate simply couldn't be a womanizer. And she'll be pleased that somebody finally appreciates how lovable her dog is.

So pat its head, scratch behind its ears, talk baby talk to it, and let it sniff your crotch. Be rough, like a real dog owner. If you can bear it, kneel down and let it lick your face—the ultimate proof you like dogs. Repulsive as this is, you may be setting in motion a chain of events that will culminate in your licking its owner.

Meanwhile, don't even glance at the woman. Tell her how cute her dog is, ask what breed it is, and reminisce about old Fido—who just happened to be the spitting image of her dog—and how you cried when he was killed by a car.

Be subtle as you steer the conversation from her dog to her. ("Isn't it hard keeping a dog around here? Do you live nearby? As a matter of fact, I'm thinking about getting a one-bedroom there myself. I should check one out sometime. Gee, that would be awfully nice of you.")

If the woman rejects your overtures, a good way to work out your anger (it's unhealthy to bottle it up) is to spit on the dog as you walk away.

Your Dog

Having your own dog can be a great conversation starter. Many people have owned dogs at some time, and feel a bond with other owners. Often dogs can bring back pleasant memories of childhood.

Don't buy an intimidating beast. Many men feel the need

for a dog that enhances their sense of masculinity. But Dobermans, Rottweilers, and pit bulls are not cuddly and do not attract friendly female attention.

On the other hand, you don't want a neurotic little poodle or Chihuahua, which send the opposite message. Labs and golden retrievers strike a nice balance.

A woman who would never dream of approaching you if you were alone will think nothing of coming up to ask about your dog. And unloading her maternal instincts on your pet puts her in a relaxed, receptive frame of mind.

Train your dog to go to women, wag its tail and sniff, but not to bark ferociously. This will give you the opportunity to say, "Sorry to bother you. He seems to like you," and start a conversation.

It is a truism that a man who treats his dog well will treat his wife well. Even if a woman hasn't heard this, she will instinctively sense it. So no matter what kind of husband you intend to be, while courting, lavish affection on your pet.

Having a dog is almost a public declaration that you have affection to spare: not a bad subterfuge for a fellow with lust to spare.

If you don't want the hassle of actually owning a dog, offer to walk a friend's. Just be sure to get acquainted with the animal beforehand. It wouldn't do to have the animal attack you just as you're trying to ingratiate yourself with some dog-loving woman.

Your Lair

Whether you live in a dormitory, a rented apartment, or your own house, certain universal rules of decorating apply.

First, be clean. You may not mind accumulating a leaning tower of pizza boxes, and you may think taking out the garbage a waste of time, but assume your target feels differently. She won't want to lie down amid the trash (no matter how well you feel she'd blend in).

If you have roommates, make sure they're out of eyeshot and earshot.

Decoration designed to augment your masculinity will make you seem either very young or very insecure. Off-color signs ("Lie down. I'm a psychiatrist" or "Trespassers will be violated") will make you appear particularly juvenile.

Pictures of past girlfriends or anything remotely resembling a trophy collection are to be kept out of sight. (A pair of panties nailed to the wall guarantees you won't get hers off.)

A bedroom with a large water bed and a mirror on the ceiling will make her uneasy. And sexual paraphernalia are most definitely to be kept out of sight.

Absolutely do not post centerfolds from girlie magazines. No woman will disrobe in their presence. She won't want the comparison. (Not to mention that you'll come across the type who spends more time masturbating than making love.) Put yourself in her shoes. Imagine she had three photographs of erect penises on her wall, labeled "9"," "10"," and "11"." Would you find this conducive to a romantic evening?

Mood Music

Ever noticed how the background music plays such a large part in setting the mood for a movie? Horror scenes are more terrifying, action scenes more exciting, and romantic scenes more moving. And most of the time, you don't even notice the music; it merely works insidiously on your subconscious.

Well, music works its magic on women, too. You can take advantage of this if she's at your place.

Euphoria-inducing dance music, especially of the Motown variety, is a good way to start the evening on an upbeat note. Then, as attack time draws near, sentimental music will put her in the mood. Serenade her with Tchaikovsky (his three ballets), "Moon River," or any show tune (from a show with a sappy ending).

Don't play your music too loudly. The trick is to alter her mood subtly, not blast her out of her senses. Background music must remain there.

Match your music to your target. If she considers herself a feminist, don't play Elvis. If she considers herself sophisticated, don't play country and western.

No matter what she considers herself, don't play John Philip Sousa or Gregorian chants. Just play soft music with an insistent beat.

Music is the food of love. Make sure she eats hearty.

Home Movies

One underrated technique for putting a woman in the mood is a pornographic film. This does not mean taking your date to the local X-rated theater, an experience as sordid as it is potentially embarrassing. Instead, keep a porn film near your VCR. The choice of hard- or soft-core should depend on your audience.

Don't display the tape front and center stage, but do put it where she won't fail to notice it. Have only one porn video in view: a single tape suggests open-mindedness, a library, perversion.

Don't propose a viewing yourself; let her suggest it, as her curiosity should get the better of her. If she just points at it and laughs smarmily, which is probably what she'll do, ask if she'd like to see it. If she makes a derogatory comment, tell her she should watch it before passing judgment.

Any shame she feels about wanting to see the film should be overcome by your greater implicit shame for having actually purchased it. (Tell her you got it before you had some buddies over one evening.) During the movie, express boredom so she doesn't feel threatened by the presence of a sexually aroused, dangerous male.

Don't assume she'll become overtly aroused by the film (although this may happen). She may even feel disgust. But the viewing should plant a seed in her mind that won't disappear until it has sprouted and grown ripe for the plucking.

Part III
Situations

The Challenge

As January 1 approaches, people think of New Year's resolutions: getting to the gym three times a week, forgoing desserts, and visiting Aunt Mary more often. It's time for you to challenge a buddy to a scoring contest: Get out the old tote board and see who can print with the most women in the following calendar year.

Choose a buddy who will tell the truth, the whole truth, and nothing but the truth about his exploits; otherwise it becomes a lying contest. He should be roughly as prolific as you. Otherwise the competition will be a humiliation for one and a bore for the other.

It is remarkable what a boosting effect such a contest can have on your numbers. When you're neck and neck in an exciting race, your every sense will keenly attune to the hunt. Your mind will focus, your wits sharpen, and your carnivorous instincts erupt in all their glory. You should have your best year ever.

If you find yourself lowering your standards to an embarrassing extent in the scramble for points, you can always tell yourself, "Ah, I just did that one because of the contest."

This book is devoted to changing your target's mind-set. Changing your own can have an even more salutory effect on your dance card.

At the Gym

Twenty years ago, most women thought if they so much as touched a barbell, they would wake up the next morning looking like Mr. Universe. Today the average woman goes to her gym five times as often as she goes to her hairdresser.

In recent years, health clubs have acquired a reputation as the new singles bars. In fact, they're better. The healthy, athletic atmosphere is more conducive to other physical activities (and leotards hide few secrets from an undecided suitor).

One way to meet a prospective target is to see what kind of gym bag she has, get the same kind, take hers, "find out" whose bag you took "by accident," and offer to buy her a drink by way of apology. But there are easier ways.

If you don't mind appearing a novice, ask, "How do you use this machine?" Likewise, asking a woman for help with negatives (continuing past the point where you can lift the weight entirely by yourself) is a good icebreaker.

If you're looking to start a conversation with a woman on the treadmill next to yours, ask, "Do you ever feel, as I do, that this machine is a metaphor for your life?"

Try flattery. "You must have very low body fat" is acceptable in this milieu; or, "You must work on your quadriceps a lot." (Most women don't even know what quadriceps are and will ask.) "Nice pecs" might get a rise (the pectoral muscles are those of the chest).

"Are you a dancer?" is effective because no woman minds being mistaken for a dancer. (Don't ask if she's a shot-putter. And "Are you on steroids?," while flattering to a guy, will not have the same effect on a woman.)

Ask, "Why is it women never sweat?" If she is only lifting a tiny amount of weight, ask, "How did you get so strong?" (Be sure your humor is obviously good-natured.)

Bet her an ice cream cone that you can lift twice as much weight at a certain station. Whoever wins, you've got a date. (If you're riding the stationary bike next to hers, challenge her to a race.)

If you don't score, at least you won't have to gnash your teeth over a wasted evening (there are times a good workout is more satisfying anyway).

At the Beach

You're at the beach, the hot summer sun giving your libido a boost. Young women lie around in various states of undress, some with the upper parts of their bikinis tantalizingly undone. And the only thing you can do about it is jump into the cold water.

How do you approach a bikini without being overly intrusive?

Bring a six-pack in a Styrofoam container. Walk up to a woman with a towel draped over your arm like a waiter and ask, "Would you care for a cocktail before dinner?" If she plays along and asks for a martini, reply, "I'm sorry but we're out of those. We *do* have beer, however."

Ask her to watch your belongings while you take a dip. After your swim, ask her to put suntan lotion on your back. If you're with friends, ask a group of women if they'd like to participate in your "Beach Olympics." Run a race (you in knee-deep versus them in ankle-deep water); play football with a beach ball; have a swimming race to the buoy and back. Have chicken fights (you and your buddy each carry a woman on your shoulders in chest-deep water and they try to topple one another). Something about wrapping her legs around your neck makes a woman feel intimate with you.

The nice thing about meeting a woman at the beach is that what you see is what you get. No dim light and fancy clothes to disguise the fact that she's twice the woman you thought.

The Wedding

Weddings are festive affairs, with flowers, decorations, ceremony, fancy clothes, new hairdos, and solemn vows of everlasting devotion—all things that women love and men hate. But as long as you're not the one getting married, they are a great trawling spot.

Weddings lend a sort of legitimacy to all the attendees. When you saunter up to a woman on the street, a fear lurks in the back of her mind that you might be a rapist or a serial killer. If you approach a woman at a wedding, this fear does not enter the equation.

Being at a wedding is almost like being set up on a blind

date—you have not only been vouched for as an upstanding member of society, you also have the recommendation of having been liked enough to be invited. So going to a wedding is like being set up on twenty blind dates, but with the blindness eliminated: You get to see which ones are pretty.

You have a natural topic of conversation with any woman there ("How long have you known the bride/groom?, "Isn't it wonderful that they're getting married?")

Single women think of weddings as good hunting grounds themselves, although what many of them are hunting for is a ring. They assume that a single guy who knows a groom is probably looking for a wife himself. Do nothing to disabuse them of that notion.

When a woman gets all gussied up for a ceremony where a man and a woman swear eternal devotion and then she drinks a lot of champagne, it's hard for her not to get into a romantic mood. Take advantage of this vulnerability.

Weddings are great as long as you're not the one being sacrificed on the altar.

Let's Have a Drink

The idea here is not to get drunk unless she does. For while plenty of drunken guys have scored with drunken women, and sober guys with sober women, and sober guys with drunken women, very few drunken guys have scored with sober women.

Restrain yourself to a maximum of two drinks to her one.

77

If you're not a drinker, do no more than keep pace with her, or rather, get her to keep pace with you.

Propose a toast to her career. If she's not enthusiastic about her work, propose a toast to her early retirement. Or to her favorite hobby. Or to her favorite movie star. Keep proposing personalized toasts, and she will keep drinking. She may even feel obligated to propose some to you after a while. If she does, warn her that you can't be responsible for your actions if she keeps you drinking.

If she's health-conscious, refer to the pseudobeneficial aspects of drinking. ("Studies have shown that people who have a drink a day live longer than teetotalers. Here's to a long life!") Remind her of the B vitamins and brewer's yeast in beer. Refer to the calcium in a Kahlúa and milk. Mention the vitamin C in a vodka and orange juice. If she scoffs at this routine, give up graciously. ("You're right. Oh, well. Kill a few brain cells?")

If she's the type to rise to a dare, challenge her: "I haven't met the woman yet who could chug one of these things." (Make her feminism work in your favor.)

Or say, "Here's a drink that will put some hair on your chest." She'll probably reply she doesn't want any, thank you. You can either reply that you don't believe she doesn't have any, or that she would look good with some. After a few drinks this line of talk will seem amusing.

Try, "One of these and all your troubles will go away," an offer that if true would be hard to resist.

Should the liquor cause you to behave awkwardly, note, "I find that when I've had enough to drink I become incredibly charming. I do all sorts of clever things . . . like throw up."

"Let's have a drink" is the socially acceptable way of saying, "Let's have sex." If a woman accepts the former invitation it is no guarantee that she will accept the latter, but it certainly increases the odds.

At the Supermarket

Some women go to bars, some go to the beach, and some go to the nightclubs. But all women go to buy food. So whatever kind of woman you're in the mood for, you can do all your shopping at the supermarket.

Your opening gambit should depend on what she has in her cart (or on the checkout counter). Ask, "How do you cook that?" or "What do you use those for?" Most women are only too pleased to show their expertise as cooks and potential homemakers.

Or try being playful. If she has two soft drinks and a package of corn chips, try, "That looks like a nutritious meal" or "Health food nut, eh?"

If her shopping cart is absolutely loaded, try, "Like to eat, eh?" or "Need some help eating all of that?" If she's thin, say, "You must have the metabolism of a hummingbird." Flattery never hurts.

If she has a lot of one item, express mock dismay: "Didn't anyone ever teach you about a balanced diet?"

If ice cream is among her purchases, ask, "Whatsamatter . . . no willpower?"

If she has only a couple items, comment, "On a diet, eh?" (Don't try this with a plump woman.)

If she has some particularly vile-looking food, say, "Gee, that looks appetizing" or "You know, you are what you eat."

There are usually an array of sensational tabloids at the

checkout counter. Point out a headline and warn her, "Better watch out: A three-thousand-pound space monster is headed for Earth!" If the headline is gossipy, use that: "Wow! (Such-and-such-a movie star) is two-timing his wife! Can you believe it?"

As you pay for your groceries, ask if you can help carry her bags. If she declines, retort, "You don't understand. I don't charge anything." It's then easier for her to agree because it's as if she's just playing along with a joke.

The way to a woman's heart (and loins) is through your stomach.

Hot Pickup Spots

There are certain places, not normally thought of as pickup joints, where it is easy to catch a woman with her guard down.

If a woman is pondering her tape selection in a video store, she's probably available. (If she were seeing the movie with a boyfriend, he'd be there to help select it.) And if she's looking for entertainment, it means she has spare time on her hands. One natural gambit is, "Don't get that movie unless you want to be bored out of your mind." If a discussion of movies ensues, ask her over to your place to watch a movie.

If you see a woman browsing in a bookstore, point out, "That's a great book." This can lead easily into a conversation about its author, genre, et cetera. Your target will probably feel safe talking to you in this milieu: There's something innocent about a book-lover. (Rapists and murderers generally won't settle for the quiet thrill of a well-constructed paragraph.)

Evening classes tend to attract bored, single women. By their nature these courses encourage chattiness. A little persistence can turn social intercourse into the sexual kind.

The airline terminal is another fertile location. Traveling always gives one a heightened sense of adventure and romance. A woman in this state is always more receptive to male advances. If she's traveling by herself, she is all the more vulnerable. So pack a bag, concoct a plausible story about a trip, head for the nearest airport, and check out the incoming gates. It may be a bit out of the way, but you could just end up as some lucky woman's vacation adventure.

The wise fisherman never goes to the same pond where the other fishermen congregate. He goes to his own private spot where he can land as many fish as he desires.

If You Live in a Small Town

If there's a beauty you know only by sight, and you're probably going to run into her again, you can take a leisurely, two-step approach to picking her up. First, walk up to her and say, "Excuse me, I'm not trying to pick you up or anything, but I just wanted to tell you you're one of the most beautiful women I've ever seen."

She'll undoubtedly wonder who you are and why you're denying it when you're obviously making a play for her.

At this point, hold up your hands in protest and repeat, "I swear, I'm not trying to pick you up. I just wanted to tell you that." Then walk away.

When she recovers her wits, it will occur to her how nice you are to bestow such a compliment and not even be trying to pick her up. As she basks in the warm glow of your flattery, she'll wonder if she will run into you again.

The next time you see her, she will surely greet you enthusiastically, secure in the knowledge that you are all innocence and good intentions. She may even try to find out who you are and if you have any mutual acquaintances. (This will give your compliment more validity in her mind.)

Now that you've established you're not the type who tries to pick up women, you can do exactly that. If she's flirtatious, you might even venture, "Remember what I said about not trying to pick you up? I changed my mind."

When a woman is approached by a stranger, her usual instincts are to shy away. With this approach, she doesn't even get the chance to back off—and she has a while to fantasize about you before she does.

The only hitch to this stratagem is that it is contingent upon running into your prospect again. In New York City, you can use this approach for months on end and never run into the same woman twice.

The Street Approach

Most women seem to have had the "Don't talk to strangers" syndrome instilled at an early age by their mothers. Thus many women who would be friendly at a party will barely be civil if approached on the street. Luckily, there are ways to overcome this barrier.

The problem with "Do you have change for a quarter?" or "Do you have the time?" is that they don't lead naturally into a conversation. That's why, "Haven't I seen you somewhere before?" was actually a clever line—it called for the two of you to compare all the places you'd ever been. Unfortunately, through overuse, the line has become self-parody, and even a variation sounds like a bald pickup attempt.

One alternative is utter sincerity: "Excuse me, this is terribly forward, but I'd be kicking myself for the rest of the day if I let you walk away without at least trying to meet you. Take a chance and have a drink with me. If I offend you, just walk out." If she agrees, half the battle is won. Unfortunately, this type of honesty is rarely appreciated.

The other approach is less dramatic but more effective. Stand on a street corner with an open map. When a pretty woman strolls by, ask her directions for a destination that lies in her path—but is at least five blocks away. There's a good chance she'll say, "Oh, I'm going in that direction," in which case you have a chance to walk—and talk—with her for five blocks. Even if she merely tells you where it is, this is an opportunity to walk alongside and strike up a conversation.

A skillful pickup leaves the woman thinking, "What a lucky coincidence I met that nice man."

Be a Photographer

One of the easiest ways of meeting, flattering, and getting to know a woman is to ask to take her picture. You needn't pose as a foreign tourist, just as a fellow American seeing his own country.

If you carry a camera, you are immediately perceived as nonthreatening. Shutterbugs do not rob, stab, or molest. They're harmless innocents who like to keep photographic memories. (Only nice people keep scrapbooks.)

When you spot a pretty woman, pretend to take a picture of a nearby building or landscape. As she strolls by, ask apologetically if she'd mind if you took her picture. ("Gee, it would certainly add to the picture if you were in it.") Ask her to take your picture, too.

If you have a fancy camera, tell your target you're a professional photographer. This will bring out the aspiring model in every good-looking woman.

If the two of you click, offer to send her the photos. She'll have to give you her address. Her desire for the pictures may even compel her to chat with you. (By acting friendly she may even convince herself that she likes you.)

The photographic approach is also convenient if you like to keep snapshots of your conquests.

Film can be expensive, however, so if you don't want to waste the money, just run through your routine with an empty camera.

Picking Up Women from Your Car

When you're driving, you constantly seem to see good-looking women. Unfortunately, meeting them from your car is an awkward proposition at best.

The problem is, you can't unobtrusively pull over to the side of the road to start a conversation with a woman. An automobile means freedom, power, and adventure, but it also means a traffic jam if you stop in the wrong place.

If you do try it, play off the inherent awkwardness: "Hi. My name's Joe. I was just driving home but—God forgive me—when I saw how beautiful you were, I just had to pull over and try to meet you."

Or ask for directions. If there are two women, it's quite natural for them to say, "Oh, we're going that way. We'll show you." You can offer them a ride if they are going in your direction. (This is one of the few instances where being with a buddy is actually better.)

Once they're in your car, don't try to impress them by speeding. They'll be ill at ease already; you will only scare them further by flooring it.

If you see a beauty at a stoplight, gun your engine to get

her attention and joke, "Race you to the next stoplight." Let her win, then at the next light say, "Okay, okay, I owe you a beer. Where do you want it?"

If you've got a fancy car, your chances improve. It's harder to turn down a ride in a Mercedes (no one is totally immune to status), and an expensive car lends an air of respectability.

Some cars are by their very nature threatening. A pickup truck is intimidating in its overt masculinity, a car with darkened windows automatically connotes sin, and no woman in her right mind is going to climb into a van with a picture of a naked woman on the side.

Unfortunately, most women don't hitchhike anymore. (Ted Bundy ruined it for the rest of us.) Females who do hitchhike are likely to be teenage runaways, a group not noted for personal hygiene. And if you live in a big city, beware of women who favor heavy makeup and seem to respond almost too well to your overtures. They're probably prostitutes.

When an Apology Is in Order

We've all had the experience of seeing a beautiful stranger across a crowded room. You're supposed to be concentrating on a lecture or presentation but all you can do is gaze at and wonder about the beautiful stranger. She probably realizes you've been staring. This gives you the perfect excuse to start a conversation.

Go up to her and say, in the most heartfelt tones you can muster, "Excuse me, but I owe you an apology."

She, bewildered, will ask, "What for?"

Answer, "For staring at you. I was trying to concentrate on the lecture but I found myself just gazing at you the whole time." Shrug helplessly and say, "I'm sorry, but my eyes just seemed to have a will of their own."

Ask if there's any way you can make up for your rudeness; if she says that's okay and looks away quickly, she's not fertile ground. If she laughs and looks at you measuringly, plow ahead.

To some people, love means never having to say you're sorry. To others, saying you're sorry is one way to get love.

Getting Her up to Your Apartment

Beg, coax, wheedle, and cajole, but the best way to get her up to your apartment is a straightforward lie: "Come on up to my apartment. I *promise* I won't make a pass at you." After you make a pass, when she calls you on your promise, just shrug and admit you lied.

Or try, "Come up to my apartment. I *know* you won't go to bed with me. I just want to be *with* you a little while longer." This will ease her worries about being attacked. Second, she'll be relieved to know that you don't perceive her as "that" type of woman, which seems to be every woman's worst fear. (Once she's reassured you don't think of her that way, she'll be more willing to *be* that way.)

Tell her your roommates are having a party tonight, and ask her to stop by for a while. When she wonders where everybody else is, shrug and say, "I guess the party's just you and me."

Or sweeten the bait. Tell her you have an original Picasso. This approach is like that of the fellow who would tell women he had a nine-inch member: By the time they found out how gross his exaggerations were, he'd already gotten what he wanted.

Getting Her out of Your Apartment

Q: What's the definition of a Cinderella 10?
A: A woman who sucks and screws until midnight and then turns into a pizza and beer.

—Anonymous

Before sex a woman is the most desirable thing in the world. After sex she can seem like the most undesirable. How do you kick her out of your pad without seeming to do so?

Say, "I have to pick up my pit bull at the vet's in an hour. Wanna come?"

Ask if she'd like to shoot some heroin. (If she says yes, you're the one in trouble.)

Close all the windows and pull the shades, saying there's somebody who wants to kill you and you're afraid he may try to shoot you through the window. (Whether she believes you or not, she'll want to get away.)

Admit you're bisexual.

Say, "Oh, Christ, my wife is due back in half an hour!" (Substitute "girlfriend" for "wife" if you're under twenty-two.)

Mention that you were just released from a mental institution. ("I'm okay now. My violence is in the past.")

Repeatedly break wind loudly and laugh hysterically every time.

Blow your nose on your shirt.

When you're sated with sex and the ball game on TV beckons, there's no need to put up with pesky annoyances.

Getting into Her Apartment

You've taken your target out on an expensive date, and you're escorting her home. You don't want to settle for "Thanks for a wonderful evening" and a peck on the cheek at her front door. To avoid this humiliation, you must plot your campaign with great care beforehand.

Bring along a heavy book when you pick her up for the date. Naturally, you'll want to leave it at her place rather than have to lug it around on the date. Afterward, you'll have an excuse to go up to her room.

If you don't have a bulky book handy, or if you didn't pick her up at her place, there's another method. When you're walking her back to her place (there are so many muggers around these days), mention that you have to take a leak. Jokingly ask if she'd mind if you did it there on the street. She'll probably express dismay at your lack of manners. So be a gentleman and wait. That way, when you get to her door and ask if you can use her bathroom, she can hardly refuse.

Getting into her apartment is, of course, no guarantee of scoring. But being kept out is a sure guarantee that you won't.

Keep from Getting Kicked Out of Her Apartment

To penetrate the inner sanctum, one must first keep from getting thrown out of the fortress. This can require both tenacity and cunning.

When one has been particularly insistent in one's attempts at seduction, women have a disturbingly uniform tendency to say, "You'd better leave now." You must keep the referee (she holds that position) from ejecting you from the game.

Say you've misplaced the key to your apartment and must wait for your roommate to return before you can go home. Sporadically make bogus phone calls home and express exasperation at your roommate's tardiness.

Or make a bogus call for a taxi and wait for it to arrive. (Taxis never arrive on time.) Women may let their guard down about sex play if they think they will be saved by the bell before the act can be consummated.

If your car is at her place, pretend it won't start, then make a bogus call to a towing service.

If you are near a body of water, be it a pool, a lake, or even a fountain, "accidentally" fall in before you get to her place. When you get to her place, you'll have to take your clothes off and dry them out before you leave (she can hardly insist you go home in sopping clothes). This leads to a sexually charged scenario at her apartment (with you having to pad around in a towel or her bathrobe). And you'll have a couple hours' grace before you can be booted.

There's no ignominy in having to leave her apartment. The ignominy is in getting kicked out before you've scored.

Sneaking into Her Roommate's Room After Your Girlfriend Has Fallen Asleep

It's 1:00 A.M. You've just thrown a fuck into your steady girlfriend. She's snoring next to you, the saliva dribbling from her mouth. The idea of putting it to her again is not appealing.

Suddenly it occurs to you that Kathy, her luscious roommate you've always had a yearning for, is in the next room, and she's alone tonight. Making as little noise as possible, you gently ease yourself off the bed and tiptoe to the door. You step into the hallway and close the door behind you.

Then the doubts set in. Will Kathy, out of some misplaced sense of loyalty, deny you the booty? Have no fear. There are ways to overcome her nobler instincts. And if Kathy's attitude remains frosty, you can always pretend you couldn't sleep and just wanted to talk.

If you can find a red ribbon, tie it around your throat. Then, if Kathy is awake when you open the door, hold out your arms and say, "Sally sent me as a present to you."

If she starts to object, say, "Shh! Sally will hear." This tacitly makes her an accomplice before she realizes what's going on. If she still objects, remind her how hurt Sally would be if she discovered the two of you together.

The roommate-visitor has two traditional enemies: creaky floors and squeaky door hinges. It's best to have tested these beforehand, but if you do inadvertently make some noise, freeze for at least a minute. It may take you half an hour to get to Kathy's room, but it is well worth the time.

If, when you get back, your girlfriend asks where you were, say, "The bathroom." If she asks why you were away for such a long time, tell her you were constipated. She can't very well ask you to prove it.

Postcoitus Manners

What's the definition of an eternity?
The time between your orgasm and when she leaves your apartment.

—Anonymous

Postcoitus manners can be divided into two categories: if you want to see the woman again, and if you don't. If it's the latter, do as you please. You can pull your pants on and walk

92

out without a further word; or you can use her bedside phone to call your buddy and tell him you scored.

If you want to see her again, however, such latitude is not yours. A woman whose sexual appeal is marginal to begin with can look downright repellent in the cold postcoital light. But if she tries to kiss you, you can't just push her away. You must conceal your overwhelming desire to get away from her. You must even pretend that she is still desirable. And you can't offend her by showing too much urgency in washing her essence off afterward.

Most women can sense that this is the time when a man's affections are at low tide; a few hugs and kisses now will reassure her that your regard for her is not entirely testicular. And this will assure a return bout when you're again in the mood.

Once nature has taken its course, many guys will mutter hurried excuses about having to get a good night's sleep since they have to get up early to go to work. A less transparent tactic is to pretend to fall asleep on the spot. This effectively cuts off all contact. Feeling drowsy afterward is perfectly natural and it probably won't occur to her that you're faking. She may take this as her cue to leave (if it's your apartment), or fall asleep (if it's hers), in which case you can just leave and tell her later you hadn't wanted to wake her.

Being Cute in Bed

You've just boffed Miss Bimbo and you're in imminent danger of either boredom or disgust, probably both. How to stave them off? Joke around a little.

Immediately after consummating the act, stand up on the bed, raise your arms above your head, thrust your pelvis forward, and yell, "I'm a stuuuuuuuud!" Then place your foot lightly on her torso, beat your chest, and let forth a Tarzan yell.

Ask her, "What tune am I playing?" and pretend to play the piano on her body. Let your hands stray a bit, then add, "I know all the right keys." Or pretend to tap out a message in Morse code onto her body and ask if she can decipher it.

Pretend to wrestle or box with her.

Put a "No Touching" sign on yourself.

Do an imitation of her having an orgasm. (If you're not sure if she had one, just do an imitation of her lovemaking.)

Indicate two spots on her body and say, "You're beautiful from here to here." (Exclude at least half her body.) This should start an interesting conversation.

If she should stand up naked, sink to your knees in front of her and recite the following while holding your right hand over your heart and gazing up at her crotch: "I pledge allegiance to the flag of [her first name] of [her last name], and to the sweet pubics on which it stands, with libertine juices for all."

Pretend to be a dog, sniffing at her areas of greatest olfactory output. Pant with your tongue hanging out and wag an imaginary tail.

After you've initiated the next bout, when she is about to reach her moment of peak ecstasy, stop whatever you're doing and insist you're not going to continue unless she'll do your next batch of laundry.

Keep a book on a bedside stand and then, when you're supposed to be in the mist of rapture, pick it up and start reading it. Even better, keep a "girlie" magazine handy, and then, while going at it, pull it out and open up the centerfold on her stomach (or back).

Just remember that while in bed, she's supposed to laugh with you, not at you.

Excuses for Impotence

It happens to everyone. There are times when, for whatever psychological or physiological reasons, the old heat-seeking missile just refuses to do its duty.

Nonetheless, it's hard for any man to divorce himself from his male ego, and if and when this happens to you, you will undoubtedly feel embarrassed. However, trying to salvage your masculine self-esteem by announcing, "I guess you weren't enough inspiration" or "How do you expect a guy to get excited about a flabby body like that?" is not the right course. Blaming her, while providing you satisfaction of a sort, will dissuade her from becoming intimate later.

Tell her instead you were nervous since you're so taken with her and wanted so badly to impress her: "I've dreamed about this moment so many times, when it finally came, I just felt paralyzed." This bit of reverse psychology should allow for a return engagement. Or, in a slightly bolder vein, "I've masturbated over you so many times, now that I have the real thing, it's just too much for me to handle."

Jokingly lay the blame on a third party. For example, "I'm sorry. It's just that I'm so worried about the economy/the possibility of nuclear war/the Mideast situation," to name three problems you can count on not to defend themselves *or* to disappear.

Whatever you do, reassure the woman it's not because she's unattractive.

Then, if you can pull it off, act perfectly unaffected. Smile and say, "Oh, well. I guess this isn't your lucky day. Can I fix you a drink?" If the woman has ever been with an impotent guy before, she has undoubtedly had the additional misfortune of watching him fall to pieces and then having to spend half her evening consoling him. If you can retain your cool, her overall impression of you may be even better than had you given her a thorough fucking.

Convincing Lies to Tell Your Buddies

As everyone knows, the boasting afterward is the most satisfying part of the mating ritual. Having nothing to boast about is no reason to deny yourself this exquisite pleasure.

Any skilled liar knows that the most effective lies are not outright lies, but mere implications. When your friends eagerly ask, "Didja score?" don't admit anything; just look pleased. (You'll not only get a reputation as a successful womanizer, you'll also be admired for your discretion.)

But if you don't derive enough enjoyment from such subtlety, here are some morning-after lines that have the ring of accomplishment:

1. Uhh . . . ask her.
2. We did it four times last night. Well, actually it was three times in the evening and then once again in the morning.
3. It wasn't any big thrill. I mean, she was just like every other woman. I think it's time for me to settle down.

4. Man, I don't even want to *look* at another woman for at least a week.
5. I was surprised she gave in as quickly as she did. I was expecting more resistance.
6. You know, it was sort of embarrassing, because at first I couldn't even get it up. I redeemed myself later on, though.
7. I was surprised—she looks better in clothes. She really does.
8. I'm glad she let me in the second time, 'cause I came awful quick the first time.
9. She had her period, so I had to cornhole her.

After you've told a lie for a certain length of time, it sort of develops into a fact anyway.

Be sure to claim a failure occasionally, in order to help your credibility. (Nobody always scores.)

Hiding an Affair from Your Wife

There's an expression in athletics that a tie game is like kissing your sister. Well, after a while, being married seems like the game ending in a tie. How do you conceal the occasional win from your wife?

You must do just the opposite of what your instincts compel you to. Most men rush home, blurt out an excuse for their lateness, take a shower, then guiltily lavish their wives with affection (if not with sex). This behavior will immediately raise a wife's suspicions. A gift of diamond earrings or the like will confirm those suspicions. The correct behavior is to be your usual uncommunicative self.

When she asks where you've been, you needn't go to the extreme of saying, "None of your business." Just reply mildly that you had to stay late at the office. (It helps to have a coworker who'll corroborate your story.) Casually comment that it was a pain. If she expresses doubt, snap at her. Immediately apologize, but at least you'll have her on the defensive.

Or, when she asks where you've been, retort that you were just out screwing a luscious eighteen-year-old. Since no husband who was recently unfaithful would have the nerve to reply in this way, her suspicions will be immediately put to rest.

If it's worth staying married, it's worth hiding your affair from your wife. Discretion is definitely the better part of an indiscretion.

If You're Older Than She Is

The older you get, the more attractive younger women there are—and the greater the age difference between you and them. You must be prepared to make light of this to surmount the age barrier.

Start by telling her, "I know I'm not young and pretty anymore, but"—shrug modestly here—"I make up for that by being old and ugly."

If you are less than thirty-four, tell her, "I feel a midlife crisis coming on. I need an affair with a younger woman." Add: "I think it would be a learning experience for you to have sex with an older man—just so you could see how little you have to look forward to."

Put her at ease by claiming that at the ripe old age of thirty-four, you're not much troubled by a sex drive anymore, therefore you're not a threat to her. (Even if you're twenty-four to her eighteen, you'll seem old to her. And all women have heard that a man reaches his sexual peak at seventeen.)

Say, "Really, it's quite a relief. Having a strong sex drive just makes you act silly. Now, I can relax and be myself. I'm telling you, for me, sex is just a not-so-fond memory." Add: "At my age, I don't need sex more than once a month, and I just had it last week, so I'm . . . harmless."

If you want to play it a little more romantic, say, "I thought I was too old to have crushes anymore, but here I am at the age of fifty-two with this ridiculous schoolboy crush on you." Shake your head disgustedly and say, "I'm pathetic."

Do resist the temptation to say, "I was young once, too, you know." This really will make you sound old.

Remember, you're only as old as she feels you are.

Throw Her a Bachelorette Party

A woman you've taken a fancy to is about to get married. The invitations have been mailed, the wedding gown selected, the photographer and limousine hired. It's too late to stop it. But it's not too late for a final trip to her altar.

You should weave the following into your conversation with the bride-to-be.

"So, is anyone throwing you a bachelorette party?"

"I had a bridal shower. Is that the same thing?"

"No. I mean a bachelorette party, like the bachelor party he's gonna get."

"I don't think so."

"But you *have* to have a bachelorette party. One last drunken blowout and fling before a lifetime of married boredom."

"What do you mean, 'fling'?"

"Well, it's only fair. He's gonna have one at the bachelor party. They always hire some whore to blow the groom. It's a custom."

"What?!"

"Yeah, it's a custom. Guys keep it secret, but it always happens. If the groom didn't go through with it everybody would call him a wimp."

"Oh, no. You're kidding, right?"

"No. I tell you what. If they're not throwing you a party, I'll throw you one."

Tell her the party starts off with some drinks at your apartment, to get in the mood. After a few drinks, ask her if he was her first choice for a husband. Then ask if she thinks she was his first choice. Both questions should put things in perspective, and the second should strike a nice, deep chord of insecurity, the kind that drives people to act rashly.

If you've had enough to drink, and if you feel you can pull it off, put on some music and do a striptease for her, always clowning just a bit to let her know it's all in jest. (You may need more than a few drinks for this.) Emphasize that after her marriage she'll only have one man for the rest of her entire life. She may find this thought as depressing as you would.

With enough persuasion, you'll be able to give her the wedding present of *your* choice and ensure she has reason to be a blushing bride.

The Blind Date

We've all been told about some wonderful woman we just have to meet. But since the matchmaker almost never has her photo, we've no idea what she looks like. As often as not, she turns out to look as if her plastic surgeon put the silicone in the wrong places. But this isn't always true, so don't turn down a blind date on principle.

In fact, arrange a date. Then buy some flowers, call her ten minutes before you're supposed to meet, and say you're really sorry but that an emergency came up (make it plausible) and you won't be able to go out, but you wanted to drop some flowers off by way of apology. Stress that you want to get together another time. She should be as curious to see you as you are to see her, and her anger should be mollified by the flowers, so she'll probably agree to let you stop by. If she turns out to be a bow-wow, give her the flowers, apologize profusely, make vague plans for the future, and exit as planned.

If you find her attractive, have this speech ready: "I have a confession. I've had blind dates in the past with two girls; both were unattractive. I thought you'd probably be the same, so that's why I decided to back out at the last minute. But now that I've seen how beautiful you are, I'd really like to take you out, if that's still an option." She probably won't have made plans in the ten minutes since you've phoned, and since she'll probably be flattered (even if she disapproves of your tactics), she'll probably say yes.

Just remember that when she answers the door, you must make your decision instantaneously. If you hem and haw while trying to decide if you want to go out with her, she'll realize something is amiss.

The Movie Date

A movie is a great place to bring a boring girl, as it will free you from her conversation for two hours. But while effectively shutting off contact may provide welcome relief, there are ways to amuse your date sporadically and maintain the pretense of social intercourse during the screening.

The one way not to do this is, if you've already seen the movie, to tell her what happens next. There's no better way to ruin a movie.

But do talk occasionally. Lean in close and whisper something innocuous. Five seconds later lean in again and whisper, "The only reason I said that was so I could put my face close to yours." (Wait a few seconds before you move away.)

When the hero first appears, whisper, "That's what I want to look like when I grow up."

Whenever the hero kisses the heroine, try to kiss your date. Eventually whenever two people kiss on screen, all you'll have to do is look at her and she'll start giggling.

If it's a scary movie, start repeating to yourself in a low voice, "It's only a movie. . . . It's only a movie. . . ." Or bury your head in her shoulder and whisper, "Tell me when it's over." Afterward, ask her if she was scared; insist you weren't.

If the movie's lousy, look at her and hold your nose. If you know she felt the same way, stand up after it's over and clap loudly, proclaiming, "Wonderful movie."

When you emerge from the theater, you'll both feel dazed and slightly discombobulated, as if you're coming out of a long hibernation. In this state, she is relatively defenseless; this is a good time to suggest something she might not otherwise be amenable to, like a nightcap at your apartment.

Take advantage of all these opportunities, and the movie will more likely have a happy ending for you.

Cheap Thrills

Psychological studies have shown that when people experience a strong physical sensation, they will associate their heightened feeling with whomever they are with at the time. If you are present when your target has that experience, she will imprint on you. And fear makes people want to have sex. It's why more babies are conceived in wartime.

When two people step off a roller coaster ride, they have a number of heady feelings. They are relieved to be back on solid ground, giddy from the ride, and still tingling from the adrenaline jolt. They are proud of their bravery, and drawn closer by their shared experience. What's more, having been on an exciting roller coaster ride together, each will associate that feeling of excitement with the other. They also will feel a compulsion to duplicate those tingles with other physical thrills.

Your mutual adventure needn't necessarily be a roller coaster ride. Take her swimming in fifty-five-degree water and she'll associate that exhilarating, breathtaking, nipple-tightening sensation with you. Take your target skydiving.

If she's athletic, take her running to exhaustion. The endorphins (the body's natural painkillers) will give her a natural high, and her muscles may be sore enough afterward to require a massage.

Take her snow- or water-skiing, depending on the season and your locale. Or just have a snowball fight or a water balloon fight. Hang-glide, wind-surf, do anything that will stimulate her heart rate and get her juices flowing.

Once her heart rate has topped 120, once the adrenal iceman has stuck his fingers into her stomach, she's not going to be in the mood for a quiet evening curled around a book. After some exhilarating chills and spills, what she wants is action, which is what you are there to provide.

It's a cheap trick, but it works.

The Natural History Museum Date

This is a fun place to spend an afternoon, all the more so with a travelogue designed to amuse both yourself and your target.

There is plenty to talk about. If there is a tableau of Native Americans, say, "That was me in another life. But I killed too many enemy warriors and my punishment was to be reincarnated as a luckless fellow who would fall hopelessly in love with a woman who wouldn't sleep with him."

If the women in the exhibits are wearing revealing costumes, comment, "You'd look quite fetching in that outfit."

If one of the scenes depicts life in the Stone Age, nod

judiciously and muse, "Those were the days a man could just club a woman and drag her off to his cave."

When you get to the animal section, show off your knowledge of zoology. At the hippopotamus exhibit, say, "Man, that is one fat rhino!" At the zebra display, exclaim, "Wow! Striped horses!"

If you see an eland, with its penis extending halfway up its belly, wonder out loud, "Can you imagine having one that small?"

If you see an exhibit of an elk being attacked by a pack of snarling wolves, say, "That's what I felt like when I met your family," or, if more appropriate, "That's going to be you when you meet my family."

Show off your knowledge of evolution as you pass the displays. "The jackrabbits grew such big ears because they were always afraid the other jackrabbits were talking about them. . . . The leopard grew spots because they were vain and wanted their furs to be more valuable."

Expound on the mating habits of the various animals. ("If the male lion is horny enough he'll mate with a leopard and if he's really horny he'll even do a wildebeest.") If you actually know something about zoology or evolution, don't be afraid to speak up.

Natural history museums tend to be great places to play touchy-feely with your target. There are lots of dark corners and deserted hallways that are just tailor-made for fooling around. The fact that you obviously can't go all the way there prevents her from getting too defensive, and she may just get hot and bothered enough so that when you eventually get her home, she'll be ready to demonstrate the mating habits of the North American *Hetero sapien*.

Standing Her Up

If you stand your date up, and you want to see her again, you must have a good explanation handy.

Most habitual liars use the impossible-to-disprove excuse; as a result, it is less believable. The traffic jam, for instance, is more than a little dog-eared.

The firm denial works better. ("*I* was there. Where were *you*?") This leaves the resolution of the impossibility up to her. If she contradicts you, which she will at first, insist you were there. Get angry. It's amazing how many women will end up making your excuse for you. ("Oh. You were probably at the other gate.")

Or alter the circumstances of your plans to meet: If you were supposed to meet at six, insist it was seven. Pretend to be as mad as she is. (Method acting is in order.)

Basically, if she likes you, almost any excuse will do (except "I just didn't feel like seeing you").

A Fight Can Be Good Therapy

Love life dull?

Everyone knows that a good fight clears the air, and that after the makeup and mutual self-recriminations, the love-making is better than ever. Here are some good ways to start a fight.

"No offense, but your breath would halt a rhinoceros in full charge."

Look at the floor and say, "What is it, snowing in here?" then look up at her hair and mumble, "Never mind."

"Isn't it about time you had a face-lift?"

To a large-chested woman: "If you don't wear a bra more often, you're going to be playing soccer with those things in a couple of years."

To a small-chested woman: "Did you have a double mastectomy?"

To a dumb woman, after she has proffered evidence of her stupidity: "Have you ever had your IQ tested?"

In general, sarcasm about any sensitive area will suffice. Then, after you've raised her anger to a fever pitch, let her broil for two minutes, turn off the heat, let simmer for ten minutes, then start a tentative apology. She'll accept it as her due. In a few minutes she'll also be contrite—she may have let fly a few nasty insults herself. Then start with the hugs and kisses, and a few minutes later she'll be hot to trot.

108

Different women have different patterns, but once you've established hers, you can set your clock by it.

Get the Better of a Fight

If you subscribe to the theory that whoever's blood pressure rises less wins the argument, there are several easy ways to better a woman.

One way is calmly to munch on some food while she raves at you. (No one who is furious ever eats.) This will double her outrage.

Pretend to fall asleep while she rages at you. Just say, "Am I tired ... I'm going to take a little nap now," and pretend to doze off. The veins in her forehead will throb.

Leaf through a magazine while she is steaming at you. Appear absorbed in it, and when she tells you to stop reading and listen to her, continue to read and reply. "I'm listening." She'll hyperventilate.

Laugh and say, "I can't tell whether you're serious." (The spectacle of an angry woman *can* be quite funny.) When she insists she is serious, say with a moan, "You are the most moronic bimbo I've ever met, and that's saying a lot." This is guaranteed to drive her into a frenzy.

Say, "You're cute when you're angry," then look pleased with yourself. The fact that you've made such a banal, un-original comment, then congratulated yourself for your wit, will exacerbate her anger even further.

After she screams at you, calmly look her up and down and ask "Do you want to have sex now?"

As much fun as it is to goad her to new heights of fury, remember that at some point you'll have to coax her back down.

Defusing Her Anger

Women, like alarm clocks, are constitutionally programmed to go off at regular intervals. The difference is that when an alarm clock makes unpleasant noises you merely have to press a button to turn it off.

Some men, blessed with more heart than brains, deal with an angry woman by becoming abjectly apologetic (no matter what the situation mallifying the hellcat at any expense. Other men react by becoming angry (again, no matter what the situation), thereby putting the woman on the defensive. Both techniques work. But there is an easier way.

The first thing to do when she gets angry is to ask, "On a scale of one to ten, how angry are you?" After she says ten or twenty, ask, "If you had a pistol, would you shoot me?" (Don't pop this question if a gun is handy.) After she says yes, ask, "Would you torture me first?" Saying yes will help her vent her anger.

Next, offer to let her hit you on the arm. She probably won't, but if she does, don't worry: Very few women throw a punch that can do any damage (except to their hands). Your willingness to atone with corporal punishment should calm her further.

If she continues to rage, solemnly intone, "Well, at least you're in touch with your emotions. That's healthy." After she castigates you for saying something so stupid, say, "Don't keep them bottled up ... that's good." After she tells you to shut up, say, "Come on, get madder. You can do better than that!" This will make her tantrum seem absurd and might even make her laugh (which might well make her even angrier). But at least the spell will be broken.

After soothing her, enjoy the peace until it's time for the alarm clock to go clanging off again.

Breaking Up

Every woman knows "I'm not good enough for you" only means "You're not good enough for me." If you want to split, but you're concerned that hell hath no fury, it's much better to get her to break off with you.

One way to get her to do it is to say, "Damn, my herpes is acting up again." Sit back and watch the relationship rapidly disintegrate.

If she has a different background, use every opportunity to heap abuse on her ethnic group. Sprinkle your speech freely with offensive slurs.

Continually borrow money from her. (Don't pay her back until after she's dropped you.)

Constantly pretend to be drunk at the wheel of your car. (This is fun.)

Step in every dog dropping you see. There are two ways

111

to do this. One is as if by accident, in which case she'll think you're simply clumsy and despise you for that. The other is gleefully to jump on it, in the manner of a child crushing a sand castle. After every splat, grin widely. If she objects to your behavior, act as if she's a bore, and continue anyway. (If she decides to join you, breaking up will be all that much easier.)

If you don't want to dirty your shoes, take a stick and prod at every dog dropping you see. Claim you have an interest in veterinary medicine. ("Hmm, that dog has an iron deficiency.") Then use the stick as a conductor's baton, punctuating your conversational points as you walk along.

That old song to the contrary, breaking up is easy to do.

Answers to Common Excuses

When pressed, many women will often voice one of these universal themes as if they are legitimate reasons for withholding the chooch. Here are some verbal counter punches to confuse, bemuse, or simply stun.

But I hardly know you.	I don't know you very well, either. Do I let it bother me?
I'm having my period.	That's great! This is the one time of the month you don't need any protection.

I'm not in the mood.	Let me lick you for two minutes, *then* tell me you're not in the mood.
You're just not my type.	Close your eyes and pretend it's someone else.
But it's our first date.	Don't think of it as our first date. Think of it as our *last* date.
We have such a beautiful friendship, I don't want to ruin it this way.	Are you kidding? This will make it deeper and more meaningful!
But I have a boyfriend.	Don't worry. I wasn't planning on telling him.

   There is almost no insurmountable excuse for withholding the booty.

Love

Should the subject of love ever arise, recite the following speech. "Love means different things to different people. Usually it's just infatuation, or sometimes sexual fixation, sometimes even a mild affection. But overall, 'love' is the most overused word in the English language."
   "I do know that if someone you really love were to die

you would be absolutely inconsolable for a long, long time, and that a little piece of you would die forever." (This, by the way, is good a definition of love as any.)

Add, "I honestly think some people aren't capable of that kind of love," thereby implying that you are.

This makes you sound like a soulful person with a great capacity for love and raises the possibility in the back of your target's mind that she just might one day be one of those people whose death would render you inconsolable.

Then lighten the mood with, "So, so far I can't honestly tell you that I *love* you, but I do seem to get these feelings around you that I can't quite control." When she asks you what those are, reply perplexedly, "I want to take your clothes off. . . . Is that bad?"

Why Don't You Like Me?

If a woman has rebuffed even your gentlest, most subtle overtures, take the comically direct approach.

Ask, "Why are you so unfriendly to me?" She'll probably reply, "I'm not that unfriendly." Counter with, "Oh, yes you are. If you ever enter the Miss America contest, you're not going to win the Miss Congeniality portion. Don't get me wrong, you'd win the bathing suit portion—at least you'd get my vote—but you'd be dead last in congeniality."

If she insists she is not unfriendly, she will feel obliged to prove it by being friendlier whenever she sees you. Use the opportunity to ingratiate yourself. If she actually tells you why she's unfriendly, use whatever criticism she levels as helpful advice.

114

If you want to make it more awkward for her to rebuff you, phrase the question thusly: "Do I repel you? What is is about me you don't like?" It would take an uncommonly brutal girl to catalog your flaws calmly. If she does respond negatively, she's more likely to say something like "You're obnoxious," that catchall female phrase that in this context translates as "You're too pushy and too blatantly sexual in your approach." Reply contritely, "Sorry. I like you and just wanted to be friends, that's all."

If a crowd is present, and if you can pull it off, ask your target in a tremulous voice brimming with sensitivity, "Evelyn . . . do you like me?" She'll probably be too embarrassed to do anything but laugh in front of the group, so follow up with "*I* like *you*." Let the comment sit for a few seconds.

Another tactic is to say, "I wish you liked me as much as I like you." Admitting you like her makes it very difficult for her not to say she likes you.

By putting your target on the spot you can pressure her either to rethink her attitude, be more friendly, or at least tell you off with a finality that precludes any more wasted time. And time is your most precious resource. Because in the same way that for some people, time is money, for you, time is pussy.

When She Puts an Embargo on the Booty

Withholding of the booty usually happens one to three weeks after it was first surrendered. Men are usually surprised and angered by this tactic. They ought not be.

115

Think of it from the woman's viewpoint.

Before she gave it up, the man did anything for her, spending money left and right, lavishing all manner of praise, and generally tippytoeing about very carefully. But once nature took its course, the relationship took on a different complexion: He treated her with as much respect and consideration as he gave his pillow. She, naturally enough, resents this.

So, she struck back in the most effective way she knew, claiming, "We have to prove we can be friends first," or some such nonsense. Another common plaint is, "When we do this I develop expectations about our relationship." Both translate as, "Is this all you want me for?"

Unfortunately, the only solution is to go back to tippytoeing about the way you did when you first dated her. The embargo will then be lifted, and normal channels of trade reopened.

Spending the Least Money Possible

Many is the fellow who, after a date, totals up the bill only to find he would have been better off opting for the sure return of a whorehouse.

Luckily, there are dates that won't set you back a week's pay. Here are a few.

Have a picnic. Women inexplicably like them, even if they do involve a long drive, ants in your food, and mosquitoes.

Attend a free concert in the park. Since many others will be doing likewise, your thriftiness won't be obvious.

Go get an ice cream cone. Even if it's inexpensive, it does

constitute self-indulgence, which, after all, is what spending money is all about.

Steer the conversation toward music, and rave about a symphony she's not familiar with. Then suggest she come over to your place to listen to it.

If she's a health nut, suggest a workout together. Going for a run is absolutely free.

Rent a movie for your VCR. Or record a movie, then every time you meet a different woman, ask her over to see it, claiming you haven't seen it yet.

If you do go out to dinner, ask if she is a feminist. If she says yes, say, "Great, now we can split the cost of dinner."

If your thriftiness has become embarrassingly apparent, it's time for the grandstand gesture. On a night you know your prospect is busy, tell her you bought some tickets to a play and would like her to accompany you. After she reluctantly declines, ask every other woman you know who is busy that night, and get yourself a reputation as a big spender. In that way you won't seem so cheap the next time you suggest a home-cooked dinner.

If you're so stingy you've been jerking off over the same dog-eared skin magazine for the past three years, rest assured you don't need to pay much more to get the real thing.

How to Boast While Seeming Modest

Everyone admires a winner (most women are groupies at heart), but no one likes a boaster. So when you blow your own horn, make it appear accidental.

The subtle boaster knows that one question leads to another. Always refer to an accomplishment seemingly inadvertently in the context of another subject. ("Yeah, broken bones aren't always that painful. . . . After my accident, I didn't know my leg was broken till four hours later.") Let her inquire as to your accident ("I was ski-jumping"), let her inquire as to your involvement in the sport ("Well, I won Nationals once"), then be sure to downplay it ("Ski-jumping isn't big over here the way it is in Europe").

At home, leave mementos of your glory visible, but not stage front and center. Keep the trophies on your mantel, but leave them face down. Count on her to examine them. Place the certificate on the floor where she'll have to step over it. Bury the newspaper clippings in your photo album, but leave the album where she'll spot it (women are congenitally incapable of leaving a photo album unopened).

Talk about a feat she couldn't dream of replicating, then tell her she could do it. ("Breaking boards with your fists just takes a little practice. You could do it.")

Boasting is as deep-seated a need with men as being told they're loved is with women. But as making their need too obvious can render women unattractive, so it can do the same to us.

I'm Too Handsome

Whether you're a one or a ten, you can score modesty points by complaining about how being too good-looking has been such a burden. If you are handsome, she'll think you're making light of your looks. If you're ugly, she'll know you are.

Mournfully mumble, "My problem has always been that I'm just too handsome. Women are intimidated by me. Not to mention that they're afraid they'll look less pretty next to me.

"And women always assume a gorgeous guy is taken, so they never act friendly. Then, when they do, all the time it's the same old line: 'Why don't you become a model?' As if I haven't heard it a million times before."

Cry out in mock agony, "You don't know what a cross this has been to bear. You don't know how many times I've cried myself to sleep at night. . . . I'm considering plastic surgery to make myself more ugly."

Don't go on too long in this vein or she'll think you really are taken with yourself. Always finish with, "Aah, who am I kidding. I know I look like a toad." Then say brightly, "But if you kiss me, I'll turn into a handsome prince."

If she does, and you don't, explain to her that it's a gradual transformation, so she has to keep trying.

When You've Said the Wrong Thing

Gracefully extracting your foot from your mouth is a useful skill in many situations, not the least of which is a date.

When someone has said the wrong thing, he'll often retreat by saying, "Just kidding." This fools no one. Similarly, the overused "I was just testing you" simply means "I was wrong but I don't want to admit it so now I'm making this lame joke."

If you say something dumb, rather than vainly defending your point, simply poke fun at yourself. Before she can contradict you, add, "Can you believe I just said that?"

If you answer an intellectual question in an embarrassingly stupid manner, shrug and say, "Oh, well, I guess the forty grand my parents spent on Princeton was wasted."

If you've said something overpoweringly conceited and the stench of your egotism fills the room, lean forward and say, "That's what we Princeton men call confidence." This will disperse the lingering odor of your comment.

If you've been overly nosy, say, "Much as I hate to pry, that's what I do best."

If you've said something that comes across as too aggressive or overbearing, say, "I just read *Winning Through Intimidation*." Shrug and add, "I read it twice."

With enough practice, you'll make your *faux pas* look intentional, as if you were just setting yourself up for the graceful recoup.

Special Situations

If one of the following occasions arises, have the appropriate response ready.

When you're talking with the guys, you may categorize yourself as a "tit man" or an "ass man." But if the subject comes up and a woman is present, describe yourself as a "brain man." Women always like this (it's hard to figure out why). If the woman has an exceptionally well-formed posterior, however, it won't do any harm to describe yourself as an "ass man." Whatever you do, don't describe yourself as a generic fan of her worst feature.

Should a woman ask, "Why do you like me?" the correct answer is "I don't know. I just do." Many women have been taught that if you answer that you like them for a specific reason, it means your affection is not genuine.

If your target cries out, "Oh, fuck!" in exasperation, reply, "Fuck? I'll do that . . . you'll be disappointed, but at least I'll have a good time."

If she ever tells you that you look sad, shake your head and say, "Every time I've been with a woman recently, it's been the same old story." When she asks for an explanation, her curiosity piqued, reply in tortured tones, "For me to reach my moment of peak ecstasy, I have to close my eyes and pretend it's you." When she laughs, lean close and murmur, "There's only one solution to my problem."

If you're in a restaurant and see a couple of attractive

women waiting to be seated and the hostess is occupied else-where, walk up, ask. "Table for two?," then seat them at your table.

When it's time to go off daylight saving time in the fall, tell her, "Listen, I know you have qualms about sleeping with me, but we have to turn the clock back tonight anyway, so why don't you just come over to my apartment at mid-night, we'll have some quick fun, then you can go home, we'll turn our clocks back, and it'll be as if it never happened."

Special situations call for special responses.

If Your Reputation Precedes You

If you've been a successful ladies' man in the past, you may acquire a reputation as a womanizer. Since no woman wants to be one in a long line of conquests, that reputation can become self-defeating. So when your latest target flirtatiously says, "I hear you're quite a Romeo," act completely mystified.

Reply, "You know, I've heard that, too, and I have abso-lutely no idea where I got that reputation. I'm not prolific with women at all. Don't get me wrong—I wish I were. But the fact is, I'm not."

Your target may ask, "Come on, you mean to tell me you didn't have a fling with Susan?" Reply, "No, I swear, we were just friends."

If she asks about other women, unless you dated the

woman in question for months and it's absolutely undeniable, deny it. If she asks about a particularly pretty conquest, reply, "I wish. Janet's beautiful. Not like you, but still beautiful."

If your target believes you, she'll be put off guard and possibly even consider you a challenge. If she doesn't believe you, you get credit for not boasting, and she will worry less that her pubic scalp will be held high in victory.

Basically, what you want to tell your target is the opposite of what you tell the guys.

Part IV
The Target

The Bookworm

Contrary to popular belief, bookish women aren't only attracted to bookish men. What's more, they're particularly unimpressed by men who aspire to but fall short of being cultured. So don't attempt to meet her on her own turf. Pander to her fantasies instead.

Intellectual women always wonder if they're not missing out on "life." So act as if you've just stepped out of a beer commercial, in from a long day of work at the fire station and ready to enjoy some of life's lustier pleasures. *Those* guys obviously don't miss out on "life."

Watching beer commercials on TV is probably as close as she's ever gotten to healthy, guilt-free, blue-collar masculinity (it may be as close as anyone's gotten), so don't worry about being transparent. She probably secretly feels that those lumberjacks who daily celebrate "Miller time" are a more appealing breed than the wimpy eggheads she's accustomed to.

If you deliberately appear less educated than you are, she may find you exotic. If she asks if you've read a certain book, always reply, "No, but I saw the movie." Tell her you've never been out of your home state (any member of the intelligentsia will find this fascinating). And even if you only drink sherry and an occasional brandy snifter, when you're with her drink domestic beer (and never light beer).

If you're having trouble extracting the final thrill from her, pander to her fears. She'll undoubtedly have read a lot of psychology at some point, so remind her, "They say it's unhealthy not to have sex—you'll go crazy." (Young intellectuals often worry about that.)

To seduce the bookworm, use your brawn, not your brains.

The Jockette

She's healthy, she's fit, and she's probably got a trim, appealing figure. She's also proud of her ability in her sport; this is the key to how you seduce her.

Let's assume she's a tennis player. The easiest date to get with her in the first place is a tennis date. Even if you are a far superior tennis player, make sure the match is close. A close match will get her competitive juices flowing (which in turn will stimulate the other kind).

If you crush her, she'll be embarrassed and humiliated—hardly the proper frame of mind for romance. And you will only exacerbate the situation by making comments like, "I thought you said you were good" or "Are you sure this was your sport?" (Although one must admit the pleasure derived from making these comments is often commensurate with the pleasure of a love match.)

If you let her crush you, she will lose respect for you. (This also is not conducive to romance.) So if you're outmatched, pick another sport in which to challenge her.

One stratagem, if you are overwhelmingly better in the

game at hand, is to pretend to make the competition close, but do so in such an obvious manner that she cannot but notice the pretense. You'll not only score points for being nice, she'll admire your athletic prowess as well. However, if her athletic ego is on the line (and you'd be surprised how often it is), it's better not to be too obvious.

If you have been having a drawn-out courtship on the court (or elsewhere), when you are ready to go for the kill, let her win the last game. Being aglow with the thrill of victory will put her in the mood for other thills.

The Virgin

An oft-heard truism is that a woman's first experience with sex is usually a great disappointment. This is often simply because her expectations were too high. A woman as yet uninitiated has heard many times that sex is the ultimate thrill. So, when she eventually tries it, reality almost invariably disappoints. (From that point, it will gradually grow into an acquired taste for her.)

The key to having your way with a virgin is to inflate her expectations even further. Promise her that sex is pleasurable beyond her wildest dreams. Promise that she'll feel the earth move. Promise a once-in-a-lifetime experience (at this stage she can hardly argue that point).

At the same time, a virgin will naturally also have misapprehensions about intercourse. One is that the first time will be painful. (It may be.) Another is that she might not be "good in bed." (Every woman is good as long as she's lubricated and willing.) Another fear is that there will be all sorts of blood when she has sex for the first time. (There may or may not be.) Another is pregnancy. (This should be one of your fears as well.) Another is that she will somehow become addicted to sex. (This is ridiculous.) Reassure her about all these fears except the last.

Once she gives in, she may be disappointed. So what? You won't be.

Adding a cherry to your list is a much more glorious achievement than scoring with another mattressback.

The Beauty

Beauties can be divided into two categories: those who know it and those who don't. A surprising number don't know it, especially the younger ones. (As a rule, men tend to think themselves a little better looking than they are, women a little worse.)

If your target is unaware of her beauty, and a bit insecure, tell her how gorgeous she is. It won't be the first time she's heard it, but rest assured she'll lap it up anyway.

If the woman is aware of her attractiveness, you're in for a hard time because she expects the world on a platter (for good reason, as she usually gets it that way). Her Achilles' heel is that she has probably developed a complex about people liking her for her looks and not for herself (again, for good reason). This is the crux of your game with her.

Whatever you do, don't compliment her on her beauty. Pretend you don't find her attractive in the least, and act accordingly: friendly, but not overwhelmingly attentive. She is used to men fawning all over her, and is not only inured to the flattery but may even find it irritating.

At the same time you play down her looks, however, be sure to flatter her wit, intelligence, and other attributes. This will reassure her that you appreciate her for herself, unlike all those other superficial men. She'll undoubtedly find you a refreshing change.

If the subject of her appearance does come up, tell her, "You know, I find it a bit mystifying that everyone else seems to think you're so good-looking. Don't get me wrong—I think you're perfectly nice-looking. But personally, I just don't see you as beautiful."

Pretend you admire her mind, and she'll reward you with her body.

The Aging Beauty

Any compliments on her beauty will work wonders with this creature (except "You must have been really beautiful ten years ago" or "You look really good for your age").

If you can do so subtly, convey that you think she's younger than she is. ("Do you live with your parents?" or "Do you go to school near here?") If you're substantially younger than she is, describe a third party by saying, "He's about our age." If you're her age, flirtatiously ask if she's ever dated an older man before. Act astonished if she tells you her age (*not* by saying, "Is that all?").

If you refer to a historic event of more than a decade ago, preface it by saying, "You're too young to remember, but . . ."

Whatever you do, don't tell her she's young at heart.

These days many females are hypersensitive about being called a "girl" rather than a "woman"; the aging beauty is not. Comparing her favorably with young beauties is also helpful.

After enough flattery, the aging beauty may acquiesce out of sheer gratitude.

Your Best Friend's Girlfriend

This very sensitive situation must be handled with the utmost delicacy and tact.

The best approach with your buddy's girlfriend (who has probably begun to think of you as a friend) is simply to say that you hate to have to tell her, Joe being the good buddy that he is, but you just can't stand to sit by and watch her being made a fool of while Joe cheats on her with every woman in town—a fact that only she seems to be unaware of.

She will not only lose whatever motivation she had to remain faithful to him, she'll also want to take revenge by cheating on Joe with the nearest guy available, and, well, there you are.

After the two of you are finished, tell her that you were

only kidding about Joe, that he has in fact been faithful to her, and that you're surprised she took you seriously. You'll get hysterics, rage, and recriminations, but you can weather the storm securely with the knowledge that this should effectively prevent her from telling Joe what you've done.

Your Girlfriend's Best Friend

If you used to find Susan and Janet equally attractive, after you've scored with Susan, Janet will undoubtedly seem the more desirable of the two.

But Janet, as Susan's good friend, will probably consider you off-limits. So instead of asking her out, tell her you want to see her to talk about Susan.

When you get together, tell Janet you think Susan's being unfaithful. When Janet asks why you're suspicious, say a man has answered Susan's phone twice. (Be prepared for unwelcome news if Janet confirms your "suspicions.") Next tell her you've decided to be faithful to Susan anyway. Let Janet be the one to suggest you're doing yourself an injustice.

Then steer the conversation to their friendship. "At first I thought you two were such good friends. But Susan is such a backstabber."

"What does she say about me?"

"Oh, I shouldn't say."

"Come on, tell me."

"I shouldn't."

"Come on, you can't just say that and then not tell me."

"Well, for one thing she says she thinks you might be a lesbian."

One pleasing aspect of this scenario is that Janet, in her efforts to prove a normal sexuality, should provide a particularly energetic performance.

The Divorced Mother

Every divorced mother thinks her child makes her a less desirable mate in the eyes of a new man. (Usually she's right.) So she is hypersensitive to the way you react to her child.

Soothe her insecurities. Act as if her kid is the most adorable child in the world. *All* women think their child is beautiful, so no matter how ugly the child is, compliment his or her beauty.

Talking to a child is easier than it seems. Just talk about the child's interests—do not fear, he or she will let you know what those are. Play with the child, make him or her laugh, buy the child ice cream. Mommy will glow.

Insist that the child come along on your first date. You'll get off cheaper this way (you can't take a five-year-old to an expensive restaurant). You'll also tire the child out and make the child feel that he or she has had enough attention, so that when the time comes for making a pass at Mommy, the kid will have long since trundled sleepily and willingly off to bed.

You'll also leave Mommy feeling so good about having

indulged Junior that she'll feel like indulging herself later that night.

The Married Woman

We've all read fairy tales that end with the prince and princess marrying and living happily ever after. With apologies to the Brothers Grimm, fairy tales are exactly what these stories are.

Married women are one of the best sources of poontang, if only because there's only one other guy to compete with, and he's usually not that attentive. Most men consider a wedding band off-limits; this sets the stage for you.

Don't try to bed a married woman by questioning her husband's fidelity. Most wives have a pretty good idea whether their husband cheats. If her husband is a philanderer, she knows it already and it will do little good to belabor the point. If he's faithful, bringing up the subject will just make her feel guilty.

Instead, simply say, "If you weren't already married, I'd ask you to marry me." This will make her curious as to what she missed. It will also strike a wistful chord, and for many women, sentiment is a stepping-stone to horniness.

If the married woman expresses dismay at your advances, sing the womanizer's constant refrain: "I thought you *wanted* me to." If this causes further protestation, plead, "You don't know how many times I've insulted women by not trying anything."

The best thing about the married woman is that she doesn't expect a lot of your time, she doesn't expect expensive gifts, and she doesn't expect you to make a commitment—she only expects you to screw her.

The Recent Widow

You'd have to be awfully slimy to attempt this, but if you've read the book this far, you probably qualify, so here's a good tactic for you.

The recently bereaved wife is at her most vulnerable. She is emotionally open. She needs consoling. She feels a universal kinship with her fellow beings, which is kept buried most of the time. And she feels a certain soulfulness that overrides the usual feeling of distrust and suspicion.

When you express your condolences, profess your love for the dear departed, whatever your actual feelings were. Let her know that you share her grief and sense of loss. Be sure to add that her husband would have wanted her to be happy.

It is natural to give her a hug. It is natural to let that hug go on for an extended period. It is natural to hold her hand as a gesture of consolation. Any sort of physical contact will be interpreted as a physical manifestation of your emotional support.

It is also natural for feelings of lust to overcome a man and a woman who are in close physical contact for any length of time, no matter what the circumstances. Let your hug turn into a kiss, then rest your head on her shoulder. Shake your head mournfully and mumble, "I don't know what's wrong with me, this is really horrible, but I want to make love to you. . . . I can't believe I feel this way at a time like this. I'm sorry." With her emotions at a fever pitch, unable to stand her grief, she may just take distraction where she can.

If your conscience starts to bother you, as indeed it should, you can tell yourself as you slither away that at least you made her feel better temporarily.

Stewardesses and Cocktail Waitresses

What do you think of these? Easy sex? So does everyone else. Therein lies the problem. With a reputation like that to live down, these poor women are constantly trying to prove they're not what you think. The biggest mistake you can make is to communicate, consciously or otherwise, that you take their favors for granted.

So don't leer, don't make suggestive comments, and don't talk down to them. The classic wisdom is correct: "Treat a lady like a tramp and a tramp like a lady." (Not that these ladies are tramps, merely that their occupations have that certain aura about them.)

This holds particularly true for the girl your buddy has already had. Saying, "Come on, you let Bernie, why won't you let me?" will only outrage her. (Bernie will be pretty mad, too.)

Do everything short of calling her "Your Highness." Light

her cigarettes, open the door for her, offer her your jacket if it's cold out, and let unctuousness drip from your every word. Roll out the red carpet, and she may just lie down on it.

The Gold-Digger

The gold-digger is the womanizer's mirror image: instead of using money to get sex, she does the opposite. Gold-diggers include just about every good-looking wife or mistress of an unattractive rich man.

However, just because their souls are rotten doesn't mean their bodies aren't heavenly. So play their game. It's not hard to pretend you're rich.

Pretend you're shopping for a country house. Bring your date along as you look at different properties. (Looking at houses may sound boring to you, but it's the type of activity a gold-digger thrives on.) As long as you ask the realtor intelligent questions, he'll think you're seriously in the market. Your date will be convinced you're rich, and you won't have to spend a penny.

Or ask your target to go gallery-hopping. This will leave her with the proper impression. (Only people with money to burn buy art.) Pretend to come close to buying a couple of pieces, but at the last minute find something wrong with each.

"I lost twenty thousand in the market today" will perk up the ears of any gold-digger. She may try to console you in the way she knows best.

If you see her for any length of time, you do eventually have to spend some money. You can fend her off temporarily with, "How come you're always trying to get money out of me? I thought you liked me for *me*." This should shame her into holding off for a little while, but gold-diggers are essentially shameless creatures, and she'll revert to form soon enough.

With the gold-digger, the question you must ask yourself is this: Is the screwing I'm getting worth the screwing I'm getting?

The Social Climber

She goes to parties for the pleasure of turning down all the guys who ask her to dance. (This makes her feel desirable.)

She'll climb all over herself trying to get into the trendiest nightclub, not so she can meet guys, but so she can make the Scene.

It's hard to hold her attention in a conversation because she is constantly distracted by what's happening on the other side of the room.

Her interests are fashion, money, and celebrities. She is first cousin to the gold-digger.

It's easy to be fooled by her because she does love to flirt. In fact, this is her favorite form of sex. She'll talk about guys she'd love to rape but her actions don't speak nearly as loudly as her words.

On a date, she prefers to stay out till all hours of the night rather than going home and getting it.

She would rather be gossiping with her friends than be giving her friends something to gossip about.

Her Achilles' heel is that she's a star-fucker. If you can convince her that you're a star of some kind (sports stars don't count unless they make a lot of money), you have a chance. Otherwise, it's best simply to avoid her. And once you get to know her, there's no doubt about her identity.

The cardinal rule of womanizing is: You can't trust a woman who doesn't like sex.

Dumbbellina

She doesn't know anything about politics, she doesn't know anything about sports, and she doesn't know anything about business. But she always seems to know that you want her only for sex.

Unfortunately, her primary basis for self-respect seems to be that she won't sleep with you immediately. First, you must show that you respect her. Pathetic as this sounds, it's the truth, and it is unwise to ignore her needs.

So every time she opens her mouth, look at her with open admiration and say, "That's really smart." She'll probably believe you. (Whatever you do, don't ever call her stupid.)

Resist the temptation to correct her if she makes errors. And don't try to argue broad philosophical or political issues with her. Steer the conversation toward innocuous topics, such as her favorite foods and places she's been.

She's the perfect candidate for a movie date.

Few things are more obnoxious than the dumb woman who is loudly opinionated, and you'll be encouraging her in this direction with your respect. But if you play your cards right, you can manage a fairly swift screw and an even swifter getaway.

People who don't command respect often demand it, and the less they deserve it, the louder their demands. If the person happens to be a woman whose body you crave, you must pay lip service to her demands before she will pay lip service to you.

Women from the Office

Despite coworkers who caution with such worldly admonitions as "Don't piss where you eat," the office is a great source of poontang. The only dynamic you must battle is that every career woman's biggest fear is that people will regard her primarily as a piece of ass and only secondarily as a professional.

To surmount this obstacle, you must pretend that this is your biggest fear as well. So when you ask Ms. Coworker out for a drink after work, insist she not tell anyone. In this way she'll regard you as a coconspirator, not a potential informant. When the possibility of an affair arises, swear her to secrecy (because you don't want to jeopardize your career). Convince her you have the same vested interest.

If the woman is a professional, or sees herself as one, drop a few lines about how hard it is for women to get ahead in your business. (Whatever field you're in, you can be fairly sure this is the case.)

If, on the first date, she expresses reluctance to have sex on the grounds that it is only your first date, use the following logic: "Normally, when a man and a woman go out on a first date, they have dinner and see a movie, right? That's a total of about two hours of actual talking and getting to know each other. Well, you and I have seen each other at the office every day for the past year. And each day we've talked about ten minutes. That's about two thousand, five hundred minutes of talking, which is more than forty-one hours, which is the equivalent of twenty dates. Now do you mean to tell me that on our twenty-first date you're *still* not going to come across?"

Just because a fellow can't sleep his way to the top of a corporation doesn't mean he can't enjoy a few of its fringe benefits.

Part V
Obstacles

When One Girlfriend Runs into Another

This ticklish situation calls for an immediate, proactive response.

The one thing you cannot do is act visibly embarrassed, which will ruin your chances with both women. You must brazen it out (assuming the women don't know each other). Turn to the woman you bumped into and introduce the woman you're out with this way: "Becky! I was hoping we would run into you. I want to introduce Sheila, my cousin from Massachusetts. She's down for a few days and I'm showing her around." This should allay Becky's suspicions.

As soon as you've parted company with Becky, turn to Sheila, who will undoubtedly be fuming, and say, "Sheila, please don't take this the wrong way. Becky wanted to go out with me but I turned her down. If she sees me out with another woman it would just be rubbing her face in it. Really. I didn't want to hurt her feelings, that's all." This way, you get credit for kindliness as well as faithfulness.

When you get home call Becky to tell her how happy you are that she got to meet your cousin. Should she express doubt regarding your blood ties to Sheila (especially if Sheila shot you a killing look at the time), scoff at her suspicions. "Come on! Do you think I'd ever actually introduce some woman I was on a date with as my cousin? What kind of woman would put up with that kind of slap in the face?

And what kind of guy do you think I am to do that to a woman?"

If she answers this last question spitefully, act hurt. "Becky . . . do you really think I'm like that?" If she answers affirmatively, get angry. ("I'm really insulted. I'm not sure I want to see you anymore.") This should cause her to backpedal.

Don't act mollified. After all, she has a hell of a lot of nerve accusing you of being such a sleazeball.

When She Has a Boyfriend

If a woman hides behind the old excuse "I have a boyfriend," keep pressing the attack.

Immediately reply, "I know *lots* of women who have enough love in their hearts for *two* boyfriends." If she looks hesitant, ask, "Is your boyfriend the jealous type?" She'll probably say "Yes," to which the proper response is, "Is he big?"

Ask where he lives. If he lives far away, say, "That's not a boyfriend. That's a pen pal."

Ask, "What's his address?" When she replies "Why?" tell her you've decided to kill him. (Make sure she knows you're kidding.)

Explain to the woman that she ought to date you just to make the boyfriend jealous. After all, a jealous boyfriend is an attentive boyfriend, and there's nothing that will make him more attentive than being kept in a constant state of insecurity. As, "Is he taking you for granted? You ought to teach that bastard a lesson." Explain that jealousy is just the right stimulant for a flagging relationship.

If she still refuses to see you, accuse her of not caring about her boyfriend.

If She Is Still Recalcitrant

If you continue to pursue an uncooperative subject, it's best to do so in a joking manner that will keep her too amused to be angry.

When she doesn't respond to your suggestions, cry out, "You keep missing your cues! Now let's take that scene again."

If you have any unique qualities, play on them: "This is probably the last chance in your entire life to make it with a guy named Casanova."

Tell her, "You can't reject me. These are my formative years. This could be a traumatic experience for me."

If she complains about anything at all in her life that has gone wrong, nod your head knowingly. "See? That's what happens if you don't go out with me."

If she remains unmoved, ask, "Do you have a heart?" When she says "Yes," ask, "Is it made of stone?"

If she spells out the fact that she doesn't like you at all, in fact can't stand you, reply reprovingly, "You—you won't even let a guy *dream*, will you?"

Eventually your target may surrender through sheer exhaustion.

If you feel you've come on too strong, you can lighten up your final impression with, "Well, I hope you didn't feel too much like Jodie Foster to my John Hinckley."

Turn Rejection into an Opportunity

Many guys, upon being rebuffed, become antagonistic. But burning your bridges is a silly mistake. This is the best time to show that you are good-hearted, sincere, and secure enough to suffer rejection calmly. Also, once a woman has turned you down, she feels she can lower her guard, and you can then make headway.

If she tells you she's unavailable, just say, "Well, I'm sorry to hear that. For whatever it's worth to you, I really do have an *insane* crush on you." Draw out the word "insane."

If she claims to feel bad about hurting your feelings, reply, "You don't have to feel bad—I've had lots of experience being rejected by women." This establishes just the right tone of modesty and humor. Then claim, "You're not missing much anyway: I'm just your average guy—three parts conceit and two parts insecurity." (No average guy would say this.)

If she suggests you should have no problem finding someone else, reply, "It's hard to get excited over a Big Mac once you've seen filet mignon."

Later, ask, "Can you tell just by looking at me that my heart is broken?" She'll probably laugh and deny it. Mournfully mumble, "I'm going to kill myself."

The next time you see her, say, "I read in a book the other day that when you're trying to get over a crush on someone, you're supposed to imagine them in a ridiculous situation. So recently I've taken to imagining you without any clothes on. That doesn't seem to help at *all*!"

It takes time to seduce women who are currently off-limits, but if you work slowly on ten or twelve at a time, you may later be able to pick them off one by one.

If You've Come Across a Bit Too Strong

We have all at times been overly pushy in a doomed attempt at scoring. In situations like these, there's nothing for it but to eat humble pie and lie like hell about your future intentions.

First apologize for acting "way out of line" and reassure her, "You know me, I'm the type of guy who's all talk and no action anyway." Most women will actually give this line some credibility.

Tell her, "From now on, I want you to think of me as you would one of your gay friends. In fact, think of me as your competition for men." Mince around and overplay it a bit. Then say, "I'm sorry, I have a tendency to turn everything into a joke."

Add, "You're not really my type anyway. In all honesty, you could invite me to your apartment, ask me into your bedroom, take off all your clothes, lie down on your bed, spread your legs and ask me to make love to you, and I'd probably just say thanks but no thanks. That's the truth."

If she expresses disbelief, admit, "Okay, okay, maybe that's not true. But I tell you what: I'm going to cure myself. Every

time I have a lustful thought toward you I'll slap myself."
Hold up a finger and pedantically state, "It's called aversion
therapy. Pretty soon, whenever I see you I'll just wince." At
regular intervals, glance down at her body and then slap
yourself (lightly).

If she still expresses dismay at your aggressiveness, reply,
"Okay, okay, you win. But just think of the status involved:
How many people can say they've got their very own per-
sonal stalker?"

Getting Your Last Digs In

When a woman rejects you, and it's plain you'll have no
future chance with her, you'll likely be momentarily non-
plussed, and the opportune moment may pass before you can
gather your wits to deliver the appropriate farewell. Thus
it's best to have the right insult on file.

The best insult is one tailored specifically to her. Obviously this book cannot determine your target's sensitive
points. But if you're not certain what they are, the following
parting shots should have a nicely deflating effect on her ego.

If you haven't scored with her yet, let her know her only
meaning was as a statistic: "Damn! Joe's still winning the
bet."

"What bet?"

"The one on how many girls each of us screw this year.
He's leading, eight to six. And I thought you were a sure
thing, too."

If she rejects you in person, say, "Wait a sec," then phone another woman and ask for a date. If the other woman doesn't pan out, turn back to the first woman and say, "Come on, go out with me just tonight." (The implication is that she was second choice all along.)

If the woman is terminating a relationship, muse, "I guess from now on when I cheat on you I won't really be cheating anymore."

Pointing out a physical flaw works wonders. ("That blubbery ass didn't do a whole lot for me anyway.")

Dredge up a past trauma of hers and imply that she deserved it.

Say, "I've been meaning to tell you, I tested positive for gonorrhea last week. You better get yourself checked out." (She'll not only worry herself silly, she'll also waste the time and expense of a doctor's appointment.)

Hide your own emotional turmoil as you deliver your parting shot. If you are matter-of-fact about it, the insult will have more bite.

How to Cure a Broken Heart

The first rule of womanizing is: Never fall in love. Should you break that rule and be spurned, you may feel inconsolable.

Well-meaning friends will try to comfort you with such clichés such as, "There are many fish in the sea" or "It was her loss." These are the wrong clichés.

The right cliché ordinarily refers to another ailment: "The best medicine is a hair of the dog that bit you." In other words, jump aboard the first girl you can get your hands on. It is physiologically impossible to suffer from a rock-bottom depression if you have just gotten laid.

If you can't find a willing woman, then go out and get rejected by at least three more women. This will put the initial rejection in perspective. It sounds silly, but it works.

Another distraction is physical pain. Run two miles absolutely all out. The burning of your lungs will make the ache of your heart seem faint by comparison.

If you're susceptible to melancholia, you have undoubtedly been so affected before. Examine your history. Was the last heart-breaker still filling your thoughts three months later? This one won't be, either.

Then again, if you're dumb enough to fall in love, you deserve what you get—so pay no attention to this chapter.

If She Sees This Book on Your Bookshelf

If Machiavelli had had a prince for a disciple, the first thing he would have recommended him to do would have been to write a book against Machiavellianism.
—Voltaire (to Frederick the Great of Prussia)

If your target should spot this guide in your apartment, tell her it was a gift and the only reason you haven't thrown it out is you don't want to hurt your friend's feelings: "I guess it was Bill's idea of a sick joke. What gets me is that some borderline perverts out there might actually try stunts like those."

If she says she's read it—and you've already used one of the tactics suggested herein—immediately claim you read only the first few chapters before you stopped in disgust. (If she's read the book and you've used several of the tactics, she won't be in your apartment in the first place.)

If she hasn't read the book and you've used several of the tactics, by all means prevent a casual perusal. If you must, take the book from her and toss it in the toilet, saying, "That's where it belongs." She won't try to retrieve it.

The main thrust of this book is that the less you seem like you'd follow its advice, the greater your chances of success.

Afterword

Normal girls are unable to resist if you exhibit a sense of humor, charm, and a minimal amount of kindness. Even if you're a brazen cad, girls can often be fooled by an act which combines equal parts self-deprecation, wit and flattery. All you really need is the requisite nerve (or perhaps gall) to pull it off. You also want to make her feel very special—as if you don't always chase every girl you fancy. If you read this book you will see exactly how to go about it. Jealousy, gratitude, admiration and other emotions can be manipulated to have just the effect you desire. Novice or expert, you'll undoubtedly chuckle over the most exuberantly risqué tactics you've ever heard. All is fair, as you constantly hear, in love and war. So study up and give yourself an unfair advantage.

About the Author

NICK CASANOVA lives in Manhattan and was single until the age of thirty-one.

Flat...g

Flatlining

Race, Work, and Health Care in the
New Economy

ADIA HARVEY WINGFIELD

UNIVERSITY OF CALIFORNIA PRESS

University of California Press, one of the most distinguished university presses in the United States, enriches
lives around the world by advancing scholarship in the
humanities, social sciences, and natural sciences. Its
activities are supported by the UC Press Foundation and
by philanthropic contributions from individuals and
institutions. For more information, visit www.ucpress.edu.

University of California Press
Oakland, California

Library of Congress Cataloging-in-Publication Data

Names: Wingfield, Adia Harvey, author.
Title: Flatlining : race, work, and health care in the new
   economy / Adia Harvey Wingfield.
Description: Oakland, California : University of
   California Press, [2019] | Includes bibliographical
   references and index. |
Identifiers: LCCN 2018055945 (print) | LCCN 2018058803
   (ebook) | ISBN 9780520971783 (Ebook) | ISBN
   9780520300330 (cloth : alk. paper) | ISBN 9780520300347
   (pbk. : alk. paper)
Subjects: LCSH: African Americans in medicine. | Medical
   care—Social aspects—United States. | Equality—
   United States.
Classification: LCC R695 (ebook) | LCC R695 .W56
   2019 (print) | DDC 610.089/96073—dc23
LC record available at https://lccn.loc.gov/2018055945

Manufactured in the United States of America

27 26 25 24 23 22 21 20 19
10 9 8 7 6 5 4 3 2 1

Contents

Illustrations

FIGURES

TABLES

Acknowledgments

No book is written without the input of many other people, whose efforts lift it above what it would otherwise be. In my case, I am incredibly fortunate to be surrounded by a community of family, close friends, and colleagues who have gone far beyond what I could have fairly expected in their efforts to make this book possible.

This book is dedicated to my daughters, Johari and Jada Wingfield. Mommy loves you girls so, so much! Every single day you make me proud to be your mother. I love our fun family adventures and enjoy every day that I get to spend watching you two grow into curious, smart, strong, brave, wonderful children. I also owe heartfelt thanks to my husband, John, the love of my life, who patiently listened to more data, theories, and information about health care, work, race, and the new economy than I know he ever really wanted to hear. John went through countless iterations of this project with me, was a sounding board for various concepts and analyses, and, maybe best of all, talked me down one Friday afternoon when I decided the entire book was terrible and needed to be rewritten from scratch. Thanks for

telling me to "take the weekend off, clear your mind, and let the game come to you." I could not have done this without you and all your support. You are absolutely the best husband ever.

I thank other members of my family, too, for their constant encouragement. My parents, Brenda and William Harvey, always had my back, provided free child care, and were instrumental in helping me to achieve work-life balance. My sister, Amina, and my brother-in-law, Matt, still owe me on the child care, but they made up for it by always being ready for a Dearmon-Wingfield weekend away. I suppose I also owe Amina thanks for snapping at me, "Get off the computer and quit working! We're on vacation!" Brandon Wingfield continues to grow into an amazing young man and is the only person to watch (and quote) *Black Panther* with me when I need to unwind ("We will not have it!"). I am always aware of how fortunate I am to have such a wonderful, supportive, amazing family. And although we aren't blood related, I also consider Ashley Herndon, Felicia Jackson, and Karmen Davis to be the family that I was lucky enough to get to choose. We are and will always be the best ones!

Professionally, I owe an enormous debt to Christine Williams for the unwavering support, advice, and mentoring that I got from her while writing this book. Christine was a champion of this project from its earliest stages, when it was a vague, half-formed idea that I thought might maybe, possibly, perhaps, make an interesting project. She read drafts, participated in countless email exchanges, talked through ideas with me on the phone, and never stopped challenging me to make this work better. (My favorite example of this happened when I emailed Christine an early, extended abstract summarizing the project, and she wrote back, "Adia. This is boring. You can do better than this.") Christine simply refused to let me coast, pushed me to use my own

voice, and insisted that I make this project live up to the potential that she saw even before I did. The finished product has her stamp and influence on just about every page.

I also thank my collective of sociology friends who provide a friendship that transcends academia and the work that we all do. Thanks to Anna Branch for our conversations about the constant craziness that somehow keeps popping up in both our lives despite our best efforts to eradicate it; Angie Hattery for keeping her sanity so I wouldn't lose mine; Brandon Jackson for understanding about "black actors"; Karyn Lacy for telling me, that same Friday that I contemplated rewriting my entire manuscript, to "take the weekend off, watch *Training Day,* and come back to it on Monday"; Rashawn Ray for hanging out with me and the family in Maryland; and Wendy Simonds for her hospitality and guest room.

Several other colleagues read versions of this book and helped hone and improve my ideas. I appreciate Marianne Cooper, Michele Lamont, Vinnie Roscigno, and Kevin Stainback for taking time from their busy schedules to read and comment on various chapters from this project. I would like to single out Joya Misra for reading an early version of the entire manuscript. I also owe Jake Rosenfeld (Dame Dash!) a special shout-out for not only reading the entire draft but also being willing to give the whole thing a second read when I thought it needed different framing. Additionally, I thank the sociology faculty, students, and staffs at Harvard University, Indiana University, Johns Hopkins University, Lindenwood University, Northeastern University, Southern Illinois University, University of California at Davis, University of Illinois-Chicago, University of Mississippi, University of Oregon, University of Tennessee at Knoxville, and University of Texas at Austin, and I also thank the faculty, staff, and students affiliated with the Clayman Institute for Gender Research at Stanford

University for coordinating my visits there and for their feedback and thoughts on this project.

Finally, I appreciate the institutional and individual support I received from a number of quarters. I began this project while still at Georgia State University, and I thank the faculty, students, and staff in the sociology department for providing a warm, collegial departmental home during the nine years I worked there. I also thank everyone at the (newly reconstituted!) sociology department at Washington University in St. Louis for being such amazing colleagues. I am so proud of what we have built so far and am honored to count you all as coworkers and friends. Special thanks are due to Che Charleston, Lauren Fannin, Justin Hare, and Kate Thorne, who provided valuable research assistance at various stages in this project. I also thank Koji Chavez, my postdoctoral research associate par excellence, who provided incredibly thorough research assistance, statistical analysis, and interview data. Koji went well above and beyond the call of duty to go wherever data collection took him, even if that meant unsavory bars with questionable situations. I also acknowledge the Weidenbaum Center at Washington University in St. Louis for research support that made this project possible, and Betsy Sinclair, Steve Smith, and Patrick Tucker for their assistance with the TAPS data.

Last but not least, I thank all the doctors, nurses, physician assistants, and technicians who participated in this research. I am grateful to everyone who pointed me toward a potential interview respondent for this study, and especially appreciate the three doctors who let me shadow them during their workdays. I learned so much from all the health care professionals who were part of this study, and deeply admire your commitment, dedication, and passion. The work you do does not get nearly the attention or support it deserves, but I hope I have done it justice here.

Introduction

In a society that remains sharply stratified along racial lines, black professional workers today are uniquely situated to offer insights into the current state of racial inequality in America's workplaces. After all, they occupy a complicated position at the center of many contradictory narratives. They are underrepresented in high-status positions, yet perceived to be sought after because of their race. Organizational culture and discourse often lean toward colorblind narratives, even as companies say they want to attract more workers of color. Meanwhile, the professional jobs that blacks have only recently been able to access are increasingly subject to more instability and fewer worker protections. As employees in environments that often are only nominally integrated, black professionals find that their work lives reveal ways that race continues to function as a significant factor in these settings.

As important as this story is, however, it is part of a larger narrative. Racial inequality has always been linked to issues of labor, work, and the broader economy in which these are situated. During slavery, racism powered the nation's economy. After emancipation,

racial segregation enabled many whites to access jobs that moved them into the middle class. Today, blacks remain underrepresented in the professional jobs that offer comfortable incomes, relative job security, decent benefits, and personal autonomy. But now, more organizations and industries acknowledge the need to attract more workers of color who can reflect a rapidly changing customer base. What can black professionals' encounters with workplace racial inequality tell us about how organizations function in the modern economy?

As it turns out, quite a lot. This book focuses on black health care professionals to illuminate how organizations have changed in ways that create new forms of racial inequality. Black professionals' work experiences reveal contemporary forms of institutional and interpersonal racism. But these racial encounters are also linked to the ways organizations can devalue and appropriate black labor in the current neoliberal economy.

Take Randy Goodwin, for example. Randy is an ER doctor whose experiences growing up in an urban environment directly translated to his commitment to work in the public sector, despite the economic sacrifices this requires. Randy grew up not far from the hospital where he now works, and he talks a lot about the ways that his personal and professional lives overlap as a result. In this setting, Randy actually sees his racial status as an advantage. In fact, one of the things that's striking about Randy's life and work is that while he has had some of the standard racial encounters you might expect to find in the life of a black person working in an overwhelmingly white field like medicine, he states that race is much more salient to his life as something that helps him relate to patients. Most of the patients who visit his ER are people of color; and in that context, he sees race as something that helps create a rapport that allows him to do his job effectively.

At the same time, however, he notes the ways race establishes subtle differences between him and his white colleagues. While he may have more common ground with the black patients from his old neighborhood, he is also painfully aware that this connection and the occupational advantages it brings are not always, or even often, recognized or rewarded by the organization in which he works. In a public hospital in an era when privatization runs rampant, everything—including health care—is commodified, and public services are racialized and stigmatized. Randy thus finds himself doing this work without a comparable commitment from his white colleagues (who often denigrate their poor black patients) or his institution, which rarely provides the resources and support that would help him do his job even more effectively. In the public sector, where blacks are much more likely to be patients than doctors, the facility where he works relies on his labor but doesn't appear to value it.

While Randy illustrates one way organizations depend on black workers, Theresa Evans, a family nurse practitioner at a private clinic in Arizona, connects her experiences with workplace racism to ways that the industry needs to improve at both structural and interpersonal levels. Unlike Randy, Theresa refers to herself as having always been the "token black," suggesting that this description best explains most of her time spent working in nursing on elite floors and in elite clinics. Theresa has had to deal with fellow nurses who tell her that she doesn't "deserve" her highly coveted day-shift position; learn quickly that she cannot afford to make mistakes, because they will be exaggerated and scrutinized in ways that her white colleagues' errors are not; figure out how to respond to coworkers who racially stereotype black patients while praising her for being "different"; and swallow her frustration at being assigned the most difficult, demanding patients.

It upsets Theresa that the organization where she works does not do much to address the challenges she faces. But she observes that her issues with nursing are not just personal. They are also a result of the structural processes that keep black nurses in the minority. Theresa asserts that many potential black nurses are excluded from nursing school as a result of a combination of institutional and cultural factors. The emphasis on standardized testing, the high costs of education, and the unspoken beliefs about what a nurse should look like remain embedded, even as the nursing profession acknowledges the need for greater diversity. Given that Theresa has few black colleagues and a perception of organizational inertia, her overt experiences with workplace racism have particularly attuned her to the ways her hospital's policies influence the racial climate at her job.

In a third example, Amber Davis's experiences as a cardiac monitor technician offer an additional contrast to those of Randy and Theresa. Amber's accounts of her work illustrate how much black health care workers' concerns are shaped by occupational status. At the public hospital where she works, Amber no longer frequently encounters patients who treat her more like a personal assistant than a nurse's aide. However, she does have to deal with nurses who are always "full throttle" and appear to assign black technicians work that falls outside the bounds of their job descriptions.

Organizational decisions exacerbate this challenge. Amber readily acknowledges that one of the worst parts of her job are the nurses who seem constantly ready to berate her. But she also observes that nurses themselves are in a tough position that makes her situation even harder. From her perspective, hospitals attempt to cut costs by understaffing and, as a result, encouraging overwork and having one nurse do the job of

two. This can save the organization money, but it also makes nurses' work extremely difficult. And at Amber's facility, when the nurses get frustrated they lash out—often at technicians, who are lower in the occupational hierarchy and thus have few recourses. Unfortunately for Amber, organizational policies that save revenues can make black technicians like her easy targets for hostility.

.   .   .

Randy, Theresa, and Amber hold three very different positions in health care. Consequently, they report dissimilar accounts of their work. But in describing their experiences, these three illustrate some of their commonalities—their determination to effect change for communities of color; their frustration with their workplaces' seeming inability to meet minority patients' needs; and their complicated, at times contradictory, racial encounters with patients and coworkers. To a large degree, these experiences are linked to bigger questions and debates in American society about the changing roles of race, gender, and work—specifically, the disjuncture between the need for a multiracial labor force in a racially stratified society, and the declining amount of resources committed to a public sector that serves a disproportionately black patient base.

For instance, Randy's commitment to working in the public sector has implications for how we staff, structure, and value the institutions that provide services to patient populations who are disproportionately poor and of color. Theresa's account of herself as the "token black" in nursing raises questions about the success of efforts to establish greater racial and gender diversity in predominantly white professions. Finally, Amber's perceptions of the links between herself and the overtaxed nurses at

her hospital offer important insights about the hidden costs for lower-status professional workers.

By showcasing black health care workers' stories, this book meets two objectives. First, it highlights both the multifaceted positions black professionals occupy in contemporary US society and the way their modern racial experiences are fundamentally informed by gender and occupational status. There is no question that many blacks in post–civil rights America have opportunities that were largely unavailable just a few generations ago. However, the US remains as fraught with racial divides and tensions as ever. Thus black progress, particularly the movement into elite, predominantly white, professional employment, engenders backlash, mistrust, and in extreme cases, violent manifestations of white rage (Anderson 2015; Hochschild 2016). Black professionals' accounts of their work lives highlight the divides and fault lines that underscore black progress.

Second, and equally important, this book delineates how aspects of black professionals' work have developed because of, and are intimately connected to, broader systemic changes. Today, organizations assume less responsibility for labor, work is more insecure, and economic inequality continues to worsen. As US society continues to produce a new economy where work, organizations, and occupations are all very different from years past, it is critical to assess what these changes mean for black professionals. This book examines how organizations in their modern form create new mechanisms of racial inequality that have largely gone unexplored.

This focus on black professionals allows me to make several provocative arguments. First, I suggest that as organizations accommodate more people of color in various roles (e.g., as workers, consumers, patients), incremental approaches do not allow

these institutions to meet these workers' needs. Strategies such as professing a commitment to diversity, offering cultural competence training, or even serving primarily disadvantaged populations do not necessarily mean organizations are equipped to handle the racial challenges black professionals in their employ will encounter. Rather, I argue, in order to meet black workers' (and consumers') needs, these institutions require a complete overhaul that recognizes the critical role black professionals play in executing their missions and goals.

Second, in order to achieve this, organizations must forge a stronger social contract with the workers in their employ. In the new economy, many organizations prioritize work arrangements that leave employees stressed out, economically insecure, and uncertain about their long-term financial stability (Chen 2015; Cooper 2013). Researchers and policy makers now suggest that organizations should instead adopt an approach that allows them to offer more social and economic support for workers they hire. This can be done through policies that promote work-life balance, reduce conflicts for working parents, and/or offer better pay and more consistent, regular hours. In addition to this, I argue that organizations should be driven by a race-conscious approach that recognizes the challenges facing workers of color and assumes responsibility for resolving them.

Flatlining is an analysis of race, gender, work, and inequality in contemporary society. As organizations struggle with their attempts to maximize racial diversity while seeking greater profit margins, their actions have consequences for the black professionals they employ. These outcomes include but are not limited to specific forms of additional, racialized labor; ambivalent or distant relationships with white colleagues; and valiant personal efforts to change and undermine institutionalized racism. This

book highlights how both the work black professionals do and the organizational shifts that drive it have far-reaching implications for a society that continues to struggle with reconciling race, work, and opportunity, and it offers ideas for how organizations can resolve some of these issues.

CHAPTER ONE

Health Care, Work, and Racial Outsourcing

Over the course of their careers, black health care workers make many observations, decisions, and choices that have both short- and long-term implications for their work. They choose to specialize in certain areas of health care and decide whether to go into private practice. They take note of the ways that race has an impact on their work, their opportunities for advancement, and the ways they are treated by colleagues and patients. They react to the ways health care has increasingly become more of a business than a service, and assess what that means for their own occupational options. But none of these occur in a vacuum. In this chapter, I examine broad structural changes of the last half century and show how they set the stage for the racial encounters black workers like Randy, Theresa, and Amber experience in professional settings.

ORGANIZATIONS AND WORK IN THE
CHANGING ECONOMY

In many ways, the story of contemporary work is a story of "what is" versus "what used to be." We hear laments over the loss of "what used to be" when politicians and policy makers talk about "growing the economy," the importance of "saving middle-class jobs," and of late, the need to "make America great again." When these parties make these claims, they are referring to a time when, for white men, the unemployment rate was low; labor-force participation rates were very high; work was consistent, stable, and pretty readily available; workplaces were hierarchically organized; and companies paid wages that offered a middle-class standard of living (often on only one income). Workers could easily spend their entire careers with one company that provided decent benefits. While there was a disparity between workers' earnings and that of the head of the company, it was typically not astronomical.

Despite what politicians like to tell us, those days are over. Starting in the 1970s, wages began to flatten and ceased to keep pace with productivity. What this means is that even as workers continue to produce results, wages have not kept pace with their efforts. Simultaneously, gains from workers' labor have increasingly gone to very highly placed managers and CEOs (Bivens and Mishel 2015). The US economy, then, is left with record levels of income inequality and limited social mobility (Piketty, Saez, and Zucman 2016). This disparity not only has left a large segment of the population economically insecure but also has helped lay the groundwork for major crises such as the housing crash of 2008, the recession that followed, and the looming student loan debt bubble.

What drives this growing inequality? A significant factor is the neoliberal ideology that became more dominant in the 1970s and 1980s. Neoliberalism, loosely defined, advocates for the primacy of unfettered markets that are neither subject to nor shaped by government regulations. It prizes individualism over collective action, advocates increasing financialization and privatization, and endorses the maximization of profits and shareholder value. Neoliberal agendas encourage limiting the role of the state and promoting austerity measures in order to push for unlimited free market competition. When policy makers decry government regulations, tout the benefits of tax cuts for the wealthy, attempt to prevent workers from collective bargaining, divert corporate profits to stockholders before (or instead of) workers, and seek to shrink or privatize the public sector, this is neoliberalism in action.

With the rise of neoliberalism, major changes in work, organizations, and industry followed. Collective bargaining has taken a massive hit, with clear consequences for workers. Whereas in the early 1970s, a quarter of all workers were unionized, by 2016 just over one in ten were. This is significant because the decline in unionization has had a marked impact on workers' ability to pressure management for greater compensation (Rosenfeld 2013). One result of this wage stagnation and union decline is increased economic inequality between most workers and those at the very top of the economic scale.

Organizations have also changed in ways that facilitate greater inequality. While they once were strictly hierarchical, they now are flatter and allow workers to be more self-directed. These are organizations that have fewer levels of middle management between executives and staff and, thus, require more independent, unsupervised work—think Google, LinkedIn, and

other companies in Silicon Valley that encourage employees to work in ways that allow them to be their most productive. This means workers can have greater autonomy and more control over their career paths than was true for employees in the past. Organizations now expect workers to be nimbler and more flexible, to change jobs more frequently rather than devoting their entire career to a company, and to take greater responsibility for moving into and out of jobs, organizations, or even the workforce itself.

In tandem with giving workers more autonomy, however, organizations also assume much less responsibility for employees than they have in the past. In postwar America, organizations would shoulder hefty retirement and medical costs associated with labor, but today these are considered "externality costs" that cut into an organization's bottom line (Acker 2006). Companies now shift these costs back to employees, who are increasingly responsible for greater shares of their own retirement and health care costs. This allows corporations to boost profits and is consistent with broader norms that now cast labor as a cost to be cut rather than an important investment.

These organizational changes have dramatically restructured the way work is done. It now is much more insecure and contingent. As a result, employees switch jobs more frequently. In the absence of middle-management layers, teamwork is more prevalent, and routes to upward mobility are rarely as hierarchically organized as they were in the past (Williams, Mueller, and Kilanski 2012). Workers are also more likely to find jobs through networking, which can become essential to the hiring process, particularly for securing professional, high-status work (Rivera 2014). On the face of it, these organizational changes might seem to provide employees with more control over when,

how, and where they work, attributes that are especially valuable in a neoliberal economy, where individualism is prized. But there is a downside to this, particularly for workers of color in contemporary organizations.

HEALTH CARE IN THE NEW ECONOMY

The aforementioned changes certainly apply to the health care industry. Table 1 shows the way health care has changed over the course of the twentieth century. Debates about the role of the public sector, insurance costs and coverage, and the integration of private industry have long shaped the ways health care is organized and how it has changed over time, leading to a current system that is highly stratified and sharply tiered.

The American Medical Association, the main lobbying group and organization representing doctors, launched in the early 1900s. The timing was important, as this move allowed doctors to represent their interests when reformers and forces in government pushed for insurance as a means of addressing health care costs. Though physicians fought health insurance in the early part of that century, they eventually lost this battle in the post-Depression era, when economic collapse brought more attention to and support for insurance and benefits that could protect citizens. However, physicians' opposition to President Harry Truman's proposal for a single-payer health care system in the 1940s helped defeat this initiative. Doctors' collective power, status, and prestige also increased in this period.

Around this time, employers began to assume more of the burden of rising health care costs. Because of wage controls that limited what they could offer in financial compensation,

TABLE I

United States Health Care System, 1900–2018

Year	Timeline of Events
1900s	Beginning of organized medicine. American Medical Association achieves greater influence. Military prohibits men from serving as nurses.
1910s	Progressives push for health insurance. Doctors are opposed.
1920s	Physicians see higher income, more prestige. Costs of medical care begin rising.
1930s	Great Depression occurs. Draws attention to the need for certain benefits (unemployment, health care). Many parts of the country begin experiencing a nursing shortage.
1940s	During World War 2, the federal government establishes wage and price controls. Companies respond by offering workers benefits, including health insurance. President Harry Truman proposes single-payer system. Doctors' groups are opposed. Fails partly because of the prospect of extending benefits to black workers.
1950s	Health care is 4.5 percent of the gross domestic product. Tiered system of health care (private care for wealthy; public, poorly funded care for everyone else) is firmly established. Price of hospital care doubles.
1960s	Nonworking adults find that accessing health insurance is extremely difficult. Federal measures are enacted to address worries about the shortage of doctors. Medicare and Medicaid are established.

1970s	Health care costs continue to rise dramatically.
	Causes of this include high costs of Medicare, growing hospital profits, inflation, and expensive new technological advances.
	Large numbers of (mostly white) women begin to enter the medical profession.
	President Richard Nixon's national health insurance plan fails.
1980s	Health care becomes increasingly privatized.
	Medicare and private insurers move away from "payment by treatment" to "payment by diagnosis" model.
1990s	President Bill Clinton's health care reform fails to pass.
	By decade's end, nearly 20 percent of Americans have no health insurance.
	Many of these are families with young children.
	Health care costs continue to rise, and do so at double the rate of inflation.
2000s	Some politicians and policy makers begin to argue that the current Medicare structure is unsustainable.
	The number of uninsured Americans continues to rise.
2010s	President Barack Obama signs Affordable Care Act into law.
	This is the most comprehensive health care legislation passed since Medicare and Medicaid in the 1960s.
	Opponents argue the law is "socialized medicine," push for repeals that would strip protections for those with preexisting conditions like pregnancy or asthma.
	By 2018, the act reduces the number of the uninsured by 20.5 million.
	California passes law allowing nurse practitioners and physician assistants to perform abortions.

SOURCE: "Healthcare Timeline," from "Health Care Crisis: Who Is at Risk?" Public Broadcasting Service, n.d., www.pbs.org/healthcarecrisis/history.htm.

companies began to offer health benefits to attract workers. This began the trend of linking health care to employment, but it is important to reiterate that these benefits were not widely shared. Organizations began to assume some responsibility for the increasing costs of health care at a time when the workers who could take advantage of this were, owing to employment discrimination, mostly white men. Women of all races, and particularly women of color, faced overt, systemic discrimination that left them underrepresented in jobs that included health care benefits, forcing them to shoulder these costs on their own or rely on a partner's coverage if available (Branch 2011).

Problems with the health care system continued over the latter half of the twentieth century. By the 1950s, health care expenditures had risen to almost 5 percent of the gross national product. Additionally, elderly populations faced increasing difficulty accessing health care. These concerns over cost and access contributed to success in passing Medicare and Medicaid, though they did not lead to the same levels of widespread support for comprehensive, national health insurance. However, worries about a projected practitioner shortage led to federal measures designed to expand training and health education that would widen the pipeline for those interested in health care work. Thus, lawmakers were able to pass legislation intended to expand access to care, address rising costs, and increase the number of providers trained to give care. Unfortunately for many Americans, health care still remained tied to work.

These changes helped but did not provide a panacea. In the 1970s, factors like inflation, high Medicare costs, and the growing use of technology in medicine meant that costs continued to spiral. At the same time, the number of the uninsured also continued to grow. The population of health care practitio-

ners began to change somewhat as the number of (mostly white) women in the profession increased rapidly; but at this point, "American medicine [was] now seen as in crisis."[1]

Through the 1980s and 1990s, an increasing push toward privatization meant that health care became more and more bureaucratized. This limited doctors' interactions with patients and shortened the time they spent actually dispensing care. It also positioned insurance companies between patients and practitioners. Privatization has also reduced available public funding that can subsidize the high costs associated with education and training required for health care careers. Neoliberal principles of free markets, deregulation, and profit maximization pushed health care further and further under the control of private industry, making care itself a commodity rather than a basic right available to all. Government attempts to rein in costs and modify health care during this period were unsuccessful, as evidenced by the failure of then-president Bill Clinton to persuade Congress to pass health care reform in 1993.

Fixing Health Care: Race and the Two-Tiered System

Today, health care has morphed into a sharply tiered system that is profoundly unequal and in which care is highly commodified. For those who are well off and can afford private insurance, there are extensive treatment options, preventative care, and highly sought-after specialists. For those who cannot afford this, care in the poorly funded, under-resourced public sector is often the only option.

1. From "Health Care Crisis: Who Is at Risk?" Public Broadcasting Service, n.d., www.pbs.org/healthcarecrisis/history.htm.

Political attempts to "fix" health care reflect the tug-of-war over this two-tiered system. The Affordable Care Act (ACA), signed into law in 2010, requires everyone to have health insurance and is grounded in the belief that health care is a basic right that should be available to all Americans. Furthermore, it reflects a perspective that all Americans bear some responsibility for each other. By pooling resources, everyone theoretically has access to care that could save lives, thus protecting vulnerable and poorer citizens and ultimately strengthening society. From this standpoint, requiring everyone—even the young and healthy—to purchase insurance means that risks go down for those who are poorer or chronically unwell. In 2015, speaking to the Catholic Health Association in Washington, DC, President Barack Obama himself made this very case: "America is not a place where we simply ignore the poor or turn away from the sick. It's a place sustained by the idea that I am my brother's keeper and I am my sister's keeper. That we have an obligation to put ourselves in our neighbor's shoes, and to see the common humanity in each other."[2] In this telling, the ACA was premised on the assumption that Americans share a common bond of citizenship. That connection was the foundation for a vision in which raising taxes for those in the top income bracket, and mandating that everyone must purchase insurance to create a common pool, was an acceptable trade-off for establishing health care as a right and benefit for all.

This is a sharp contrast to the logic underlying the Republican-sponsored American Health Care Act (AHCA), Better Care

2. "The President's Speech to the Catholic Health Association on Health Care in America," The White House, Office of the Press Secretary, June 9, 2015. https://obamawhitehouse.archives.gov/the-press-office/2015/06/09/presidents-speech-catholic-health-association-health-care-america.

Reconciliation Act, and Graham-Cassidy bills, the former of which passed the House while the latter two died in the Senate. These bills were grounded much more firmly in the ideals of individualism, profits, and commodification. During debate over the AHCA, Congressman John Shimkus (R-IL) questioned why he should be required to pay for health care services, such as maternity care, that he personally would never need to use. Representative Mo Brooks (R-AL) argued that the AHCA would "allow insurance companies to require people who have higher health care costs to contribute more to the insurance pool that helps offset all these costs, thereby reducing the cost to those people who lead good lives. They're healthy; they've done the things to keep their bodies healthy."[3] If the ACA was based on the logic that "we're all in this together," the AHCA, Better Care Reconciliation Act, and Graham-Cassidy were driven by the view that "I shouldn't have to pay for your health care."

Though ostensibly race-neutral, these competing arguments illuminate the racial beliefs embedded in the current stratified health care system. In an increasingly multiracial society, the premise of collective responsibility that underlies the ACA means that wealthy white families will be called upon to show some level of economic, political, and social support for poor black, Asian, and Latino communities. Thus, basing this legislation on the belief that "we're all in this together" means, in practice, that whites must see racial minorities as people with whom they share not just a fundamental connection but also a sense of

3. Sarah Kliff, "GOP Legislator Says Healthy People Lead 'Good Lives,' Should Get Cheaper Health Insurance," Vox, May 2, 2017, www.vox.com/policy-and-politics/2017/5/2/15514006/mo-brooks-preexisting-conditions. This article quotes an argument by Representative Mo Brooks against requiring insurance companies to cover preexisting conditions.

responsibility. Projections that America will become a majority minority nation by 2044 mean that this prospect of mutual connectivity is no longer an abstract hypothetical. Rather, as the US rapidly grows blacker, browner, and more Asian, this collective orientation suggests that these groups are entitled to the benefits of inclusion that they had previously been denied, and that this may call for some sacrifices from white communities.

The racial subtexts of arguments to repeal and replace the ACA are vastly different. Conservative objections to the ACA cast it as a stealth version of reparations, with Obama advancing the legislation as a sneaky way to give undeserved benefits to black Americans. From this standpoint, the ACA was "job-killing Obamacare" that taxed Americans in order to fund health care. By this logic, the ACA hurt "working" Americans by reducing their employment opportunities. Voters with strongly held racial stereotypes, beliefs, and perceptions were less likely to support health-care reform under Obama, indicating that support (or the lack thereof) for health care reform was driven as much by racial attitudes as the actual proposals being put forth (Tesler 2014).

Perhaps no conservative made this case against the ACA and for the AHCA more clearly than former Representative Joe Walsh. In a May 2017 conversation between Walsh and MSNBC commentator Ali Velshi, Velshi pointed out that health care outcomes, as a whole, in the US health care system rank last relative to those of other industrialized nations. Walsh replied, "You can't compare the rest of the world to us. They do not have the big diverse populations that we have. They do not have the inner city populations that we have.... Sweden does not have our inner city population. Norway, these countries do not have—you're talking about countries the size of India with

homogenous populations. You can't compare them to what we have."[4] Contrasting the health care systems of Norway and Sweden, with their predominantly white populations, to the health care system of the US, with its "inner-city populations," Walsh made clear that part of the reason why a more collective orientation to health care would not work is that it would necessarily require whites to be comfortable with their tax dollars paying for a health care system that, in part, supported minority communities. In this framing, then, the ACA involved a black president requiring hardworking white populations to pay for health care for "diverse," "inner-city" populations whose expensive health care outcomes stem from a failure to lead "good lives."

HEALTH CARE IN THE PUBLIC SECTOR

What do these divides mean for work in the public sector, which disproportionately services patients of color? To assess this, it is important to explore just how this arena has changed over the past few decades. It used to be that the public sector provided viable employment options that offered black professionals stable work and economic security. Yet in the post–civil rights era, as black workers gained more access to jobs in this sphere that could provide middle-class status and upward mobility, legislators and policy makers began to decry the public sector, characterizing it as a bloated site of wasteful spending that inhibited free enterprise (Thistle 2004). Public sector workers, by extension, became

4. Matt Shuham, "Walsh: 'Inner City Diverse Populations' Prevent Universal Health Care," Talking Points Memo, May 3, 2017, https://talkingpointsmemo.com/livewire/joe-walsh-large-diverse-inner-city-populations-universal-health-care.

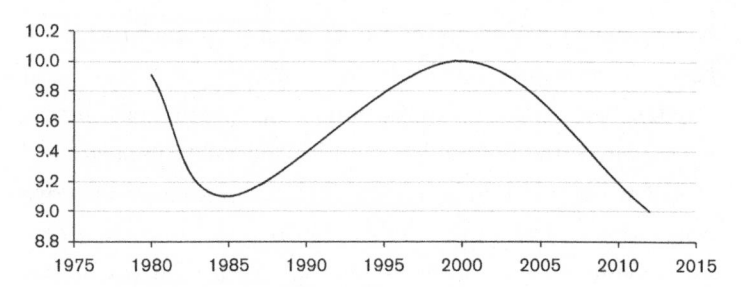

Figure 1. Government employees as a percentage of US population, 1975–2015. Sources: Bureau of Labor Statistics; Greenstone and Looney, 2012.

"entitled," "lazy," and "undeserving"—stereotypes that evoke distinctly racialized imagery and which were used to justify repeated attempts, in a neoliberal economy, to cut spending that supported these workers' jobs.

Privatization followed shortly thereafter. Furthermore, it had the intended effect of shrinking the public sector, where black professionals had been earning comfortable incomes that met or even exceeded the wages their black counterparts earned in the private sector (Pitts 2011). As figure 1 shows, the current ratio of government employees to population now stands at "the lowest level of public sector employment in over 30 years" (Greenstone and Looney 2012). This trend reverses racial and economic progress that had been occurring in the aftermath of the civil rights movement, and creates downward economic mobility for black workers who had previously had access to stable employment and wage parity via public sector work (Greenstone and Looney 2012; Laird 2016; Roscigno, Wilson, and Byron 2012; Wilson and Roscigno 2016; Wilson, Roscigno, and Huffman 2013).

These challenges certainly exist in public health care facilities today. Hospitals like Atlanta's Grady Memorial Hospital and Chicago's Cook County Hospital have a long history of

relying on public funding in order to provide care to uninsured, chronically underserved populations who, in urban areas, are largely black and/or Latinx. As nephrologist Will Ross, the dean for diversity at Washington University in St. Louis, notes, "Local public hospitals have long served as medical providers of the last resort for the uninsured poor, anchoring the safety net that provides access for the disadvantaged, especially in large urban areas." These hospitals "provide 17% of all uncompensated care nationally" and serve a patient population that is unlikely to be insured and is generally overlooked by other institutions.[5]

So how are these public hospitals managing in the stratified, highly unequal health care system of today? Atlanta's Grady Memorial Hospital offers one instructive example. Grady was founded in the late 1800s explicitly to care for the poor and offer emergency treatment, and was rare in that it provided services to black and white patients alike (albeit in segregated facilities). Grady grew to provide services to a population where nearly two million residents were uninsured. Even after the passage of Medicare and Medicaid meant the hospital would receive some reimbursement for expenses, it still continued to struggle with insolvency and bankruptcy. This took a toll on health care providers and patients, and in 2007 the hospital nearly lost its accreditation, owed over seventy million dollars to local medical schools whose doctors trained there, and had a sixty-million-dollar budget shortfall. Yet Grady could not close, as it not only provided critical care to poor patients in the immediate region but also provided

5. Will Ross, "Urban Health and the History of Public Hospitals in the US," May 12, 2015, http://digitalcommons.wustl.edu/cgi/viewcontent.cgi?article=1001&context=historyofmedicine_presentations. Dr. Ross gives an overview of how public hospitals have disproportionately provided care to poor, uninsured, and/or minority communities.

trauma, burn, and stroke care that other hospitals in the Atlanta area simply were not equipped to offer. Despite Grady's economic woes, "closing the hospital's doors would not only have hurt thousands of employees and patients, it also would have been catastrophic for hospitals throughout metro Atlanta. No longer would suburban medical facilities be able to send indigent men and women to the massive structure alongside the Downtown Connector's 'Grady Curve.' Victims of car crashes and gunshots normally treated at Grady would flood other hospitals' smaller and less-prepared emergency rooms."[6] The hospital was in an intractable position because it could not close, but it also could not meet its operating costs.

In order to solve this problem, city and community leaders turned to privatization. Oversight moved from the Fulton-DeKalb Hospital Authority to a nonprofit corporation that could manage the hospital's affairs. This paved the way for philanthropic gifts from the city's business elites. Perhaps predictably, however, this change in oversight led to concerns that the hospital would lose sight of its commitment to caring for Atlanta's poor and indigent populations (who, it is worth mentioning, are disproportionately people of color). And while the transition from a public to a privatized model did allow for new upgrades, new facilities, and electronic medical records, the hospital also cut jobs, raised patient fees, and closed community health centers and dialysis clinics—which meant that poor residents continued to visit the hospital only for emergencies and not for preventative care. Under this privatized model, the hospital now

6. Max Blau, "How Grady Memorial Hospital Skirted Death," *Creative Loafing Atlanta*, February 28, 2003, www.clatl.com/news/article/13072642 /how-grady-memorial-hospital-skirted-death. This article charts the economic collapse and resurrection of Grady Hospital.

works to attract wealthier, whiter patients with private insurance. And critically, as of 2012, the hospital was expected to bring in an annual income of about twenty million dollars.

Grady's story offers some insights into how health care facilities in the public sector respond to the diminishing resources allocated to them. One option is to focus on maximizing profit. Indeed, as political pressure turns health care into a commodity, the decision to designate turning a profit as an organizational priority may seem to make the most sense. A trade-off, however, is that this move to a profit-based model may compromise aspects of the commitment to caring for the poor and underserved. Grady thus offers a useful example of how many health care organizations struggle with this challenge of serving communities of color in an era where public sector privatization means resources are scarce, turnover is high, and turning a profit takes on heightened importance.

BLACK HEALTH CARE WORKERS IN THE NEW ECONOMY

The same changes that restructured health care have also had an impact on workers in this industry. Insurance requirements, hospitals' unwillingness to hire administrative staff, and regulations specifying that doctors must complete certain records themselves mean that physicians now spend nearly twice as much time completing paperwork as they do treating patients (Sinsky et al. 2016). Yet fee-for-service payment models mean that many doctors attempt to shorten the amount of time spent with patients in order to complete more appointments and maintain a higher bottom line. While nurses are able to spend the majority of their time on patient care, they, too, see more

patients, particularly as the number of uninsured Americans continues to decline (Cohen, Martinez, and Zammitti 2017; Westbrook, Duffield, Li, and Creswick 2011). As is the case for many organizations in the new economy, it is becoming increasingly common for care facilities to encourage team-based approaches, where doctors, nurses, and technicians enter into more collaborative relationships. And although they are professionals, health care workers may also find themselves doing contingent work, where hospitals employ them on short-term contracts that provide few or no benefits. Health care work parallels work in many other industries in the new economy, then, in that even professionals do more with less institutional support.

Black doctors, nurses, and technicians largely entered the industry at a time when professional work was becoming less secure and health care in particular was increasingly subject to racially charged debates. For a long time, blacks had been largely missing from medicine and nursing. This was not due to a lack of interest but rather a result of racial segregation in the work and educational spheres, which excluded them from training for and employment in health care work. Before the Civil Rights Act, blacks wishing to undergo medical or nursing training typically acquired their education in segregated, underfunded schools. They then served mostly black populations in segregated communities, though they continued to assert the need for more integration and racial inclusion in medicine and nursing (Hoberman 2012).

A few decades after the civil rights movement, however, professional organizations began to heed the call to bring more practitioners of color into the industry. The predominantly white American Medical Association and other organizations now publicly concede, in response to active, consistent pressure from organizations like the predominantly black National Med-

ical Association, that there is a need to attract more practitioners of color (Hoberman 2012). They advocate adopting a *racial
realism* perspective in health care—the view that in some cases,
workers of color bring special skills and talents, making greater
diversity a concrete benefit (Skrentny 2014). Because of a long
history of racism in the medical profession, black doctors and
nurses may be more likely than their white peers to engender
trust and positive relationships with their black patients, as
many patients prefer to see, and respond better to, doctors who
share their racial background (Sewell 2015). As the country
stands to become a majority minority nation, the medical population needs to include more doctors of color to serve this more
diverse patient population effectively. Women have also become
a greater part of the medical profession, though their presence
alone has yet to transform the field in ways that make it more
likely to meet their needs (Boulis and Jacobs 2008).

Although the medical establishment has proclaimed its commitment to bringing in more doctors of color, black doctors are
still, at about 5 percent of the population of practicing physicians,
underrepresented relative to other racial groups in medicine. Black
women comprise 3.4 percent of all doctors, with black men even
more underrepresented at 2.8 percent. (See figure 2.) Black physicians are also more highly represented in some subspecialty areas
than others, with higher numbers in obstetrics/gynecology, com-
bined residency, and preventative medicine. They are least likely
to be represented in otolaryngology (ear, nose, and throat), immu-
nology, and genetics. (See figure 3.) Interestingly, the fields where
black doctors are most likely to be found are also some of the areas
where women of all races have made the most recent inroads, particularly in ob/gyn and preventative medicine, where women now
constitute 43 and 37 percent of physicians, respectively (Boulis and

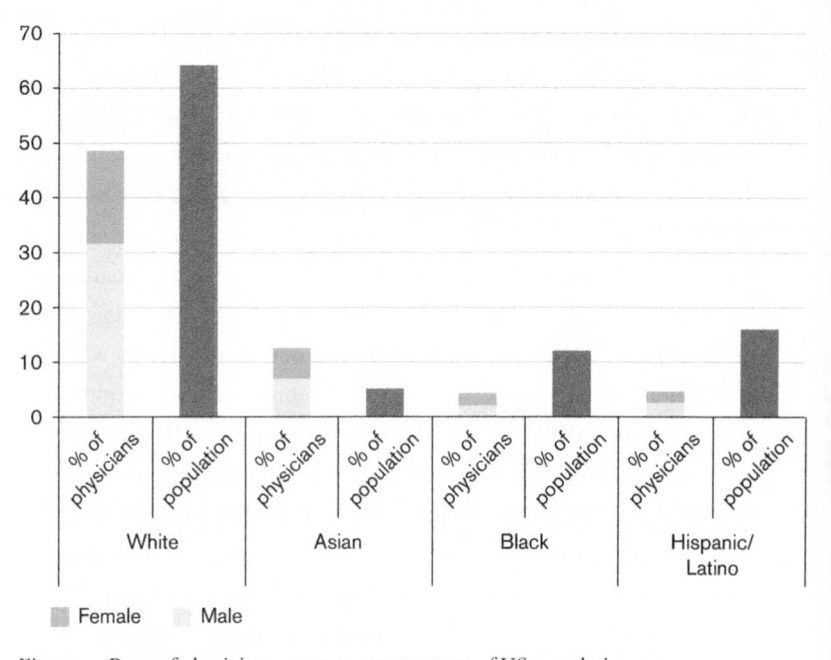

Figure 2. Race of physicians vs. race as percentage of US population, 2014.
Source: Association of American Medical Colleges, "Diversity in the Physician
Workforce: Facts and Figures 2014," www.aamc.org/data/workforce/reports/439214
/workforcediversity.html.

Jacobs 2008). This suggests that while medicine overall remains predominantly white and male, some areas are diversifying faster than others.

Nursing, like medicine, is making an effort to address its largely homogenous workforce. Professional organizations like the American Nursing Association, the Nursing Association of America, and the American Academy of Nursing have all publicly made the case for more diversity in nursing. The rationale is similar to that offered for medicine—more diversity will help better meet patient needs and improve outcomes. Data from the 2013 National Survey of Registered Nurses indicate that while whites constitute only

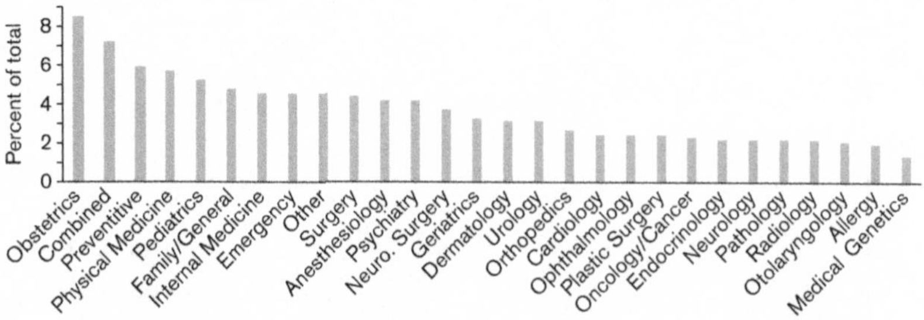

Figure 3. Black doctors by subspecialty area, 2013. Sources: Association of American Medical Colleges Data Warehouse: Minority Physician Database, AMA Masterfile, and other AAMC data sources, as of February 28, 2014.

63 percent of the US population, they make up 83 percent of RNs. Black women comprise only 8.5 percent of nurses, with black men even more underrepresented in this profession, at only 1.2 percent of the field. Because racial minorities constitute a rapidly growing 37 percent of the population, there is a stark demographic mismatch at play. (See figure 4.)

However, there are some important differences between nursing and medicine that affect their efforts to diversify. For one thing, nursing is in the process of pushing for higher minimum educational standards. It used to be that an associate's degree was sufficient training for the profession; but of late, health care organizations have raised the standards so that many nurses need more credentialing. A bachelor's degree or higher is now a common requirement in many areas. However, this creates its own set of problems as many areas, particularly rural ones, are simply not equipped to train nurses. Thus, attempts to professionalize the field further may actually compete with the efforts to attract more workers of color.

As a field where an overwhelming number of practitioners are women, nursing is also a bit different from medicine in that

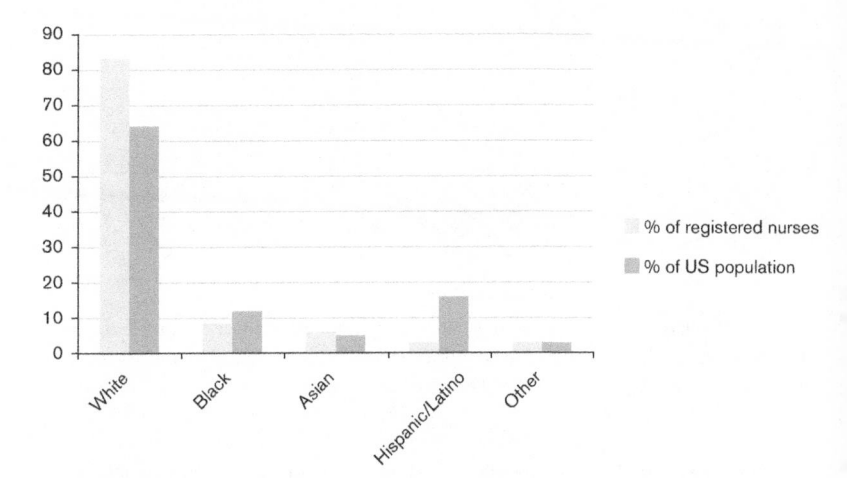

Figure 4. Race of registered nurses vs. race as percentage of US population, 2011.
Sources: National Nursing Workforce Study, 2015; Humes, Jones, and Ramirez, 2011.

it seeks to diversify in part by attracting more men to the field. The preponderance of women in a profession lowers its status and pay; by appealing to men, advocates hope to help raise the field's profile (Reskin and Roos 1990). In one recent marketing initiative, Johnson & Johnson's Discover Nursing/Campaign for Nursing prominently features (white) men in its commercials and web advertising. The American Association of Colleges of Nursing recommends targeting men in marketing materials, emphasizing the more physical, rather than caring (and stereotypically feminized), aspects of the profession and direct outreach to all-male high schools. Unlike in medicine, where bringing in more women means incorporating them into an already high-status occupation, attracting men to nursing requires dealing with the lower status that is too often linked to predominantly female spaces. Ironically, for men of color, these interlocking issues of gender and status may be less problematic,

particularly if they are offset by racial occupational segregation that concentrates black men into lower wage work (Duffy 1997; Wingfield 2009). White men remain a more difficult target, given the feminization attached to nursing and the ways that entering this profession can represent a threat to cultural ideals of white masculinity (Dill, Erickson, and Diefendorff 2016; Sharone 2013; Williams 1995).

Both medicine and nursing profess a commitment to bringing in more workers of color, but doing so is not simple. As evidenced by the fact that the top ranks of many high-status occupations remain overwhelmingly white and male, organizations are notoriously poor at actually achieving the diversity they say they want. Much of this has to do with how organizational approaches have changed in ways that actually obscure attention to, rather than resolve, racial/ethnic and gender disparities (Kelly and Dobbin 1998). In the 1970s, explicit affirmative action guidelines pushed private-sector companies to attract and employ more workers of color. At the professional level, organizations did this in two ways: either by hiring workers for "mainstream" jobs (e.g., corporate counsel, vice president of marketing) or for "racialized" ones (head of community or urban affairs). Racialized jobs offered professional salaries and titles, but few of them provided routes to upward mobility. They limited integration within the corporate culture and carried the expectation that these workers would deal with "minority issues" both within and outside of the company (Collins 1988).

Today, most large private-sector organizations have some sort of diversity program in place. While this might sound promising, in many companies "diversity" is often defined so broadly and vaguely as to be essentially meaningless. Instead of rectifying the structural, cultural, and institutional processes that perpetuate

discrimination and keep men of color and women of all races out of high-status occupations, managers can now claim they embrace diversity by emphasizing the need for "diversity of viewpoints," "diversity of opinion," and "diversity of thought." These objectives allow managers to utilize this language even while they ignore organizational processes that can keep blacks out of the top ranks of organizations or underrepresented in occupations altogether (Berrey 2013 Collins 2011; Moore and Bell 2011). This explains how, at Apple, Denise Young Smith, a senior vice president for diversity (and herself a black woman) could claim that "there can be 12 white, blue-eyed, blond men in a room[,] and they're going to be diverse too because they're going to bring a different life experience and life perspective to the conversation."[7]

In this context, many organizations do not bother utilizing measures that would effectively change the racial or gendered makeup of their workforces. One study of 708 different firms found that many commonplace diversity initiatives—structured mentoring networks, diversity seminars, and the like—had varying degrees of success in fostering change (Kalev, Dobbin, and Kelly 2006). Diversity seminars actually backfired in that they made white men more antagonistic to these sorts of initiatives. Established formal mentoring relationships were modestly successful for black women, but by far the most effective technique for improving diversity involved formally assigning managers the organizational responsibility for creating change. That

---

7. Harriet Alexander, "Apple's Head of Diversity Apologises for Saying a Group of 12 White Men Can Be as Diverse as a Team with Women and Minorities," *The Telegraph*, October 17, 2017, www.telegraph.co.uk/news/2017/10/17/apples-head-diversity-apologises-saying-group-12-white-men-can/. This article describes remarks by Denise Young Smith, who was then Apple's head of diversity, about how groups of blond white men also represent diversity.

is to say, when managers knew there would be adverse consequences for their failure to show that they had measurably
improved diversity, they generated results. Unfortunately, however, many managers do not take note of these evidence-based
studies, and they either persist in pursuing strategies that are
proven to be ineffective or do not devote attention at all to nar-
rowing racial gaps (Embrick 2011). This means that while discussion of diversity is commonplace and even acceptable, the ability, will, and support necessary to achieve it is often missing. In
the most severe instances, organizations establish diversity policies that become a shield against lawsuits rather than equipping
their managers to develop concerted, intentional efforts to create systemic change (Edelman, Fuller, and Mara-Drita 2001).

Yet this point should not be taken to suggest that diversity
policies, broadly speaking, have yielded no gains whatsoever.
Clearly not every organization places so little emphasis on
improving racial and gender diversity. In 2016, in response to
the highly publicized police shootings of the black men Alton
Sterling and Philando Castile, PricewaterhouseCoopers's CEO,
Tim Ryan, initiated ColorBrave, a series of open, informal
workplace discussions about race and racism that address these
issues head-on. In other companies, affinity groups—collectives
organized around common bonds of race, gender, LGBTQIA
status, or other categories—can offer critical social support in
settings where these members are underrepresented (Kulik
and Roberson 2008, but see Williams, Mueller, and Kilanski 2012
for an exception concerning women in science). Additionally,
organizations that offer an "integration and learning" approach
categorize diverse viewpoints as valuable resources. In this context, organizations value greater diversity as something that can
facilitate creative thinking and new ideas, and that can enable

managers not only to diversify their staffs but also to maintain the advantages of this over the long term (Ely and Thomas 2001). In the corporate sector, there is variation in the extent to which organizations address these issues head-on and in the strategies they use to do so.

Efforts to create more racial and gender diversity in health care, then, have some similarities to what has been happening in the corporate sector. For one thing, the two-tiered system of health care means that many organizations that provide care have become increasingly corporatized and adhere to a business model in which profits matter and patients become customers. At the same time, there is a growing recognition that the demographic composition of health care workers has to change. As in the corporate sector, though, health care organizations approach this differently, with varying degrees of success or visible results.

GOALS FOR THIS STUDY

In this book, I argue that when organizations wrestle with determining how best to reach diverse communities while, at the same time, trying to maximize market values and minimize the resources they devote to labor, this leads to a process I term *racial outsourcing.* Racial outsourcing occurs when organizations fail to do the work of transforming their culture, norms, and workforces to reach communities of color and instead rely on black professionals for this labor. As a result, I contend, black professionals do *equity work,* which I define as the various forms of labor associated with making organizations more accessible to minority communities. Equity work is driven by black professionals' experiences with workplace racism and shaped by gender and occupational status, so that black men and black women

workers in various occupations do this work differently. In some cases, equity work is explicitly mandated by organizations; in others, it is a result of the racial solidarity many black professionals bring to their work. But ultimately, both racial outsourcing and equity work represent new mechanisms of racial inequality, where organizations abdicate the responsibility for creating diverse institutions and, instead, rely on black professionals to make the institutions and their services available to an increasingly minority population.

The next three chapters are devoted to three different occupations to highlight how even among workers who could all be considered professionals (e.g., their jobs require credentialing, training, and some postsecondary education), occupational status hierarchies still determine the ways racial outsourcing and equity work manifest. (See table 2.) Chapter 2 examines black doctors' exposure to racial incidents and the connection between these encounters, racial outsourcing, and equity work. As I show, their racial encounters are heavily structured by occupational status and gender; yet organizational policies, which are usually limited to occasional cultural competence training sessions, are ill equipped to deal with these racial realities. As a result, racial outsourcing occurs as black doctors are left to rectify the issues they face without any organizational support. They do so through equity work that includes pursuing structural solutions to the racial issues that plague the medical profession.

Chapter 3 focuses on nurses. In contrast to doctors, nurses argue that racial issues they encounter are widespread and take both structural and interactional forms. Yet because black nurses perceive their organizations as offering only empty sloganeering and rhetoric in relation to diversity, they move to enact measures that help address both institutional and interpersonal racism. In

TABLE 2

Black Professionals, Organizational Policy, and Equity Work

Occupation/ Sector	Types of Racial Encounters	Organizational Policies	Equity Work
Doctors	Mostly structural, few interactional	Cultural competence	Structural change
Nurses	Structural and interactional	Diversity statements	Patient advocacy
Technicians	Interactional	Diversity training for higher-status workers	Opting out or doubling down
Public sector workers	Structural and interactional	Under-resourcing	Staffing, compassionate care

the absence of any institutional intervention designed to improve existing issues, racial outsourcing leaves black nurses to do equity work in which they attempt to protect patients from the racial incidents they experience themselves.

In chapter 4, I show how black technicians' relatively low-level position in the occupational hierarchy informs their experiences with racial outsourcing. Black technicians encounter overt racism from patients' families and from nurses, who are above them on the occupational ladder. Yet black technicians do not have the status to effect broader, institutional changes. For them, racial outsourcing occurs when organizations require equity work in the form of extra labor to help patients of color. Equity work also occurs when they use their cultural capital toward the same end. Lacking the status and independence afforded black nurses and doctors, black technicians reveal that at the bottom of the occupational hierarchy, racial outsourcing

tends to be externally imposed, and equity work is formally embedded in their work responsibilities.

After these chapters focusing on different professions, chapter 5 considers how racial outsourcing is a core aspect of work in the public sector. Currently, less funding and fewer supplies and other resources go to public facilities, even though, as health care becomes increasingly stratified, these organizations serve a growing population of patients of color. In this chapter, I show how public care facilities cope with this disjuncture by relying on racial outsourcing, leaving black doctors, nurses, and technicians to do equity work in the form of offering respectful, professional care while many of their white colleagues instead rely on racial stereotypes. Furthermore, I show here how racial outsourcing and equity work in the public sector leave black professionals feeling distanced from both their white counterparts and the institutions in which they work. I also discuss the gendered consequences of this for black women doctors, which take the form of feelings of frustration and alienation that then require emotional labor to conceal.

I conclude *Flatlining* by reiterating my central argument: in the modern work world, organizations engage in racial outsourcing, leaving black professionals to do the equity work of connecting organizations to communities of color. While this process does not render black professionals as economically disadvantaged as their poor or working-class counterparts, it still has adverse consequences. Namely, it creates disappointment and disillusionment with how organizations treat minority communities; leads to racial isolation from white colleagues; and perhaps most importantly, leaves black professionals shouldering the added responsibility of making organizations more accessible and available to communities of color in an increasingly multiracial society. This

book identifies racial outsourcing and equity work as new mechanisms of racial inequality for blacks in professional settings.

I also use the conclusion to address the implications of this research in three areas. I discuss what these results tell us about the ways health care, as it adjusts to the organizational changes of the modern era, does so through racial, gendered, and classed practices. Following this, I consider what implications my findings may have for black professionals working in other fields. I conclude the book with an assessment of how we can use the results of this research to change workplaces to become better equipped to meet the needs of an increasingly multiracial America.

CHAPTER TWO

"There Was That One Time . . ."

I first met Dr. Lance Sutherland in his sunny, book-filled office overlooking the downtown area of a major city. At the time of our interview, Lance was eighty and had been retired from a storied medical career for quite some time. When I entered, I noted the plaques and photos that lined the walls. The plaques commemorated various accomplishments, notable achievements, and the awards that Lance had earned during his five decades in medicine. I couldn't identify everyone in the photos, but I did take note of a prominently displayed picture of him with a past US president. It was a dignified office that conveyed status, power, and influence.

Given this biography, it is perhaps not a surprise that Lance's reputation preceded him. I was familiar with some (but by no means all) of his accomplishments and wanted to interview him precisely because I assumed that at his age and with his highly distinguished resume, he would have extensive stories to share about the changes that had taken place in medicine and how they had affected him over the course of his career as a black

physician. I expected that a black man whose influence had at one time reached the White House would, at minimum, have very interesting stories to share about the ways race affected his work, whether and how that had changed over time, and what he believed that meant for the future of the health care industry.

As it turns out, I was only half right. My interview with Lance was indeed an engrossing one. He described growing up in a small, segregated southern city and being inspired by the lone black doctor in his town, whom he described as "powerful, magical, very important, and mysterious." This doctor and his expansive knowledge, capability, and healing powers inspired Lance to pursue a medical career of his own. After completing high school in his small town, he attended a historically black college for his undergraduate degree, then went on to earn his MD at a predominantly white university in the northeast. This marked the beginning of Lance's illustrious career in internal medicine. He eventually rose in the profession to become a university president, which led to roles advocating for public policies designed to increase the number of people of color in medicine.

I was wrong, however, in my expectation of how Lance would describe the way race affected his occupational experiences. I assumed that given the time in which he came of age, and given his work in a profession where he regularly was the only black person in elite white spaces, Lance's career would resemble that of Vivien Thomas, a black practitioner affiliated with the Johns Hopkins University in the 1940s and profiled in the 2004 HBO film *Something the Lord Made*. In other words, I was expecting stories of exclusion, isolation, and a constant uphill battle against racial stereotypes. But when I asked Lance about the ways he believed race had affected his work over the course of his career, he replied,

I'd have to say that I really have been fortunate. I have not really felt the sting of discrimination, segregation. Now, I rush to say that I also think it's because of the career path that I've taken. The academic community tends to be much more progressive than the population at large. At the same time, I'm fully aware of bias. I was looking for it as a student and then as faculty. And you could say, "Well, because I was the one black student, and then later, when I joined the faculty, I was the first full-time black faculty, this was the result of equal opportunity at the time." But in my dealings with co-faculty members, there was nothing that I could really say that happened where I was not given a fair chance because I was black. If it happened, I wasn't aware of it.

I found this analysis remarkable given that, as Lance acknowledges, he was a pioneer in many of these spaces. At the time when Lance was advancing through medical school, pursuing his residency, and establishing his reputation in internal medicine, he would have been one of the earliest beneficiaries of desegregation rulings that prohibited legal racial segregation in public and private spaces. As a result, the idea that he was not aware of any racial biases directed his way seemed amazing. But I came to learn that many other black doctors had similar assessments of the ways race affected their work. Importantly, these perceptions revealed how racial encounters are fundamentally informed by gender and occupational status, and that these experiences are critical for shaping how black doctors experience racial outsourcing and the equity work they do as a result.

"THERE WAS THAT ONE TIME, BUT . . .": RACE IN EVERYDAY INTERACTIONS

When black doctors I spoke to described the ways that race affected their work, they would usually acknowledge an interaction where

they had to deal with a patient or colleague's negative racial stereotypes. To be sure, these were annoying and frustrating. However,
respondents also very clearly pointed out that these types of occurrences were rare and not at all representative of their daily
experiences.

Dr. Jayla Flood, a black woman pediatrician in private practice, offered one such account of an isolated incident that made
us both laugh:

> I've had a handful of negative experiences that I felt were attrib-
> uted to the color of my skin. One was blatant. I remember one,
> probably the first year I started practicing. Sometimes the patient
> rooms are open, the door's open, so you can hear the conversation
> in the room before you walk in. And the way that we're set up, I
> have my ledge, where I just sit at my ledge and work between
> patients and document my notes before I go in. And I heard a little
> girl who's probably about three or four talking to her mom about,
> "Where is the doctor, is she coming?" And the mom said, 'Yes, she's
> coming soon,' and you see her little head pop around the corner.
> And then it got silent. And then she goes back in the room and says,
> 'Uh-oh, Mommy. It's a brown lady!' *[Laughs.]* You can just hear the
> mom get all flushed and flabbergasted, and she closes the door and
> says something to her. But I just kind of blew it off and went in.

When Jayla related this story to me, she was not upset, and we
both chuckled at the dramatic tone she adopted when sharing
the little girl's dismay. As she notes, this was one of a small number of incidents in her professional career where she felt her race
led to negative treatment. In fact, immediately after sharing this
account she went on to say, "And I don't know what it is, but I
think the culture has changed. That was in 2006. And now when
I go in, I've had positive reactions where moms of the Caucasian
race will say, 'I intentionally chose you as my doctor because I
want my children to see that people of color can do anything.'"

Jayla's extremely favorable experiences with white patients, coupled with the infrequency with which she encountered racial hostilities, offer a stark contrast to many other accounts of blacks' interactions in predominantly white workplaces (Braboy, Thoits, and Taylor 1995; Evans 2014; Feagin and Sikes 1995; Pierce 2012). In Jayla's experience, racial issues have not disappeared. But they are contextualized by interactions with white patients that are generally favorable and positive.

Edgar, a physician practicing internal medicine, categorizes his racial encounters in a similar fashion. He states,

> There's going to be somebody who's going to be uncomfortable with a big burly black guy, regardless of what their color is. I'm also very straightforward. So someone might be uncomfortable with my directness. But we usually get around that. I don't have any issues with it at all, truthfully. I mean there have been issues, but they've not been *my* issues. They've been the patients' issues. I can think of one time when I was working in the ER and, God bless him, there was a fellow who came in who was piss drunk, having chest pains, had no insurance. I'm the only one manning the ER. He comes in and decides he wasn't gonna let no nigger doctor take care of him. So he fixed me by getting up and walking out. That was beyond my control. That was his cultural bias that basically put his life on the line. It's extremely rare for me. That may have been one of only two experiences that I've had, in thirty-something years, of white patients that were negative.

Edgar's account is similar to Jayla's in that, contrary to what we might expect from research and many firsthand accounts, his interactions with patients are not really characterized by hostility, suspicion, or mistrust. To be sure, he has what I describe as a "that one time" experience: there is "that one time" when he can cite a clear example of racial mistreatment. But he also classifies that experience and a second one as isolated rather than

routine, suggesting that in three decades of treating white patients, the number who have been openly negative to him can be counted on one hand.

Tasha shares another of this sort of example. Her account is particularly significant because she works in an extremely rural, predominantly white part of the country that is actually known as a hotbed for white supremacist organizations and activity. Given these demographics, I went into our interview fully expecting that she would share a litany of stories about racial challenges with patients, their families, and perhaps her coworkers too. However, her accounts of how race shaped her work also fall into the "that one time" pattern: "I had one little girl—here's a fun story. She's seventeen, one of those kind-of-rebellious kids, smoking pot, that sort of thing. And—I love adolescents. She says, 'You know who you remind me of?' I was like, 'Oh, God.' She says I remind her of Tastee from *Orange Is the New Black*. And she says, 'Can I call you Tastee?' And I was like 'No!'" The popular Netflix series *Orange Is the New Black* is about women serving time in a minimum security prison. So when the patient tells Tasha that she resembles this character (who, incidentally, apart from race and body type, bears no similarity to Tasha at all), she is likening a professional black woman in a field where black women are woefully underrepresented to a fictionalized television criminal.

This was among the more egregious cases of racial stereotyping that black doctors in this study shared with me. Yet even for Tasha, living and working in a geographic location with very little racial diversity and even fewer black professional workers, this sort of experience was more of a rarity than a regularity. In many cases, black doctors' interactions involved explicit racial stereotypes only occasionally, typically from patients rather

than colleagues, and they did not consider these to be something that routinely affected their work.

My own field observations yielded additional data supporting respondents' assertions that they were generally accepted in their workplaces without routine racial incidents. As a means of collecting data, I shadowed several doctors employed in different facilities to get a sense of their daily work lives (this is detailed further in the appendix). During a visit to City Hospital, a public hospital located in an urban area, I sat at the front desk of the emergency department during a lull in activity. I was using this time to jot down some field notes when suddenly a white male emergency medical technician rushed over to me. "The patient in exam room six? We need to remove her mask immediately," he said. "It's important to do that so that we can check her in." I looked up, startled. I realized quickly that he was talking to me. Not knowing how serious the situation was, I tried to direct him to Sasha, a young Latina resident sitting a few seats down from me. "You should talk to her," I said quietly. "She would be able to help you."

"No!" He replied adamantly. "It has to be you. We have to get this mask off and it has to happen now." He wasn't quite yelling, but it was definitely clear that my ability to blend in might have gone too far. I motioned to Sasha, who was busy entering notes into the computer.

"I don't think I ... Sasha should be able to help you with this." I looked around for Dr. Goodwin, the doctor I was shadowing, so that he could sort out the situation. Of course he was nowhere to be found. And the EMT only grew more frustrated with me and with my inaction.

"I don't understand. You are the attending, no?" he queried. At this point he really looked perplexed. Finally, Sasha looked

up from her computer and saw that I was in over my head. She took a few steps over and said, "Oh, I'll take care of it. Exam room six?" The EMT looked back and forth between the two of us, completely flummoxed. Finally, Sasha explained with the phrase I had been avoiding: "She's not a real doctor."

This attempt at clarification did not resolve the EMT's confusion. He simply looked back at me and said, "You're *not* a doctor? But you have on the white coat!"

In the moment, I think, we all made the snap decision that it was too complicated to explain the parameters of my research project to the EMT before attending to the patient in exam room six and her troublesome mask. But my experience in that instance lends important credence to the doctors' arguments that overt racial stereotypes and biases are not a constant part of their day-to-day work lives.

For South Asian doctors, wearing the white coat functions as a critical way to signify their authority to others and counter stereotypes that they are dangerous foreigners or threatening "others" (Bhatt 2013; Murti 2012). It is also common for blacks to take extensive steps to legitimize themselves as people who belong in professional settings (Lacy 2007; Wingfield 2012). This is necessary because there are numerous examples of the ways that race functions as a marker that minimizes blacks' credibility, status, and belonging, regardless of what they are wearing, what they are doing, or where they are (Houts Picca and Feagin 2013; Shapiro 2004). Of course, in my example, there were other doctors of color employed at the hospital, so seeing a black woman as the attending would not have been completely out of the ordinary. Even so, the fact that in my case, wearing a white coat was all it took for an EMT to be convinced of my status as

a doctor (despite my visible apprehension and repeated attempts to demur) lends credence to black doctors' assessments of the ways race affects their work.

It may seem surprising to some that black doctors, working in predominantly white settings, characterize their work interactions in this way. Most of the research on blacks in mostly white environments (including but not limited to workplaces) is replete with accounts of overt racial hostility and mistreatment (Cose 1993; Feagin and Sikes 1995; Moore 2007; Pierce 2012). What explains why black doctors' descriptions of their work run counter to the conventional wisdom gained from so many other studies?

I theorize that the social organization of doctors' work likely helps inform this aspect of black doctors' racial outcomes. Health care is a particularly hierarchical industry, and doctors are unequivocally at the top of the status heap. This allows them significant control over their time and schedules to an extent not available to lower-status workers (Clawson and Gerstel 2014). Furthermore, the way their profession is structured means that doctors do not have to spend extensive time engaging in interactions with patients, and those in private practice can enjoy relatively large amounts of autonomy. At a typical doctor's visit, nurses and technicians spend a more significant amount of time with patients while getting vital statistics and entering data into the computer, and doctors may spend relatively brief amounts of time with patients while offering diagnoses. Nurses may even be the ones who offer treatment, in the form of shots, medicine samples, or certain basic procedures. Consequently, doctors' high status, coupled with occupational norms that often allow them to work alone, may free them from some of the more routine forms of racial harassment.

Black doctors may also benefit from patients' self-selection. As health care has become increasingly commodified and treated more like a business, patients have been able to adopt more of a consumer mind-set and exercise choice in determining who will be their physician. This is particularly true for patients with private insurance, who may be able to select from an array of doctors "in their network." In this context, patients may not be surprised to see black physicians and, indeed, may even follow the path Jayla described, where they intentionally select black doctors to treat them. This would explain why these physicians note fewer explicitly racist interactions with patients than, for instance, black pilots with passengers, or black law professors with students—patients can choose black doctors more easily than passengers can choose their pilot or students can choose the professor from whom they take a required course (Evans 2014; Moore 2007). Note that this would likely not be the case for patients who seek emergency care and have to be treated by whatever doctor is available at the time. Not coincidentally, emergency room doctors were the ones in my study most likely to report more frequent, explicitly racist exchanges with patients.

That said, it is important not to misunderstand these findings. The fact that black doctors do not encounter a constant barrage of overt racial hostilities does not mean they feel race has no impact on their work. Owing to the relative rarity of occurrences in which black doctors have to contend with white patients who openly stereotype, mistrust, or second-guess them (and the fact that in some cases, like Jayla's, they have actively positive relationships with white patients), they simply do not view overt racism as something that constrains their daily interactions. But routine interactions are only one way in which race can be a factor that affects work.

CULTURAL AND STRUCTURAL RACISM

For black doctors, race is much more salient as something that affects them through cultural and structural processes. As I have shown, they do not typically encounter routine examples of overt racism in their everyday interactions at work. The absence of explicit forms of racism, however, leaves them more attuned to the ways cultural cues and structural patterns create differences between their experiences and those of their white coworkers. With cultural cues, black doctors note that racial stigmatization creates a climate in which they have to challenge tacit expectations of poor performance. When it comes to structural processes, they contend that broader patterns of racial inequality embedded in educational systems leave black students without training, support, and mentorship necessary for success in the medical field. In the absence of everyday indicators of racial bias, the racial dynamics embedded in the cultural and structural aspects of work become more obvious.

Cultural Barriers: Colleagues' Perceptions of Incompetence

Culture refers to the ways individuals create and attach meaning to shared symbols that help them understand an environment. These practices can inform basic interactions and often take place within organizations or social environments more broadly. Cultural schemas can include the processes that create or stigmatize racial groups, as well as the ways social actors negotiate these processes (Lamont, Beljean, and Clair 2014). For instance, black Americans have long navigated the cultural meanings attached to hair, skin tone, and body type and the ways these

meanings contribute to racialization and stigmatization in relationships, work, schools, and the criminal justice system (Hunter 2015; Monk 2015; Viglione, Hannon, and DeFina 2011). Black doctors note that race affects them as they cope with the consequences of racial stigmatization. Through pervasive stereotypes, tropes, and imagery, blackness is widely stigmatized as connoting inferiority and devalued status. Middle-class black women contend with controlling images of themselves as "mammies" who should be willing to devote themselves to predominantly white institutions, or "educated black bitches" whose ambitions and professional successes render them unrelatable and intimidating (Collins 2004). Meanwhile, middle-class black men wrestle with the trope of the "angry black man" whose expressions of frustration or irritation take on heightened significance and reinforce stereotypes of black men as dangerous (Wingfield 2007, 2012). Ultimately, all of these representations perpetuate the broader cultural message that blacks are essentially unsuited for high-status professional work.

While they do not regularly encounter overt racism from patients, black doctors note that cultural messages about black inferiority have an impact. Black doctors fight hard to offset racial stereotypes and to establish themselves as people who fully belong in the medical profession. Bonita, a pediatrician, states, "I still feel like I have to prove myself a little bit more, like I have to see more patients. Or I have to make sure I'm doing this or make sure I understand this condition the very best. You know, I'm equal, I'm here, I made it, we have the same degree, the same everything. I still feel like I have to prove myself a little bit more." I asked Bonita if she had any idea where this feeling originated, or if she could attribute it to any specific event. She replied, "This is coming from early on, where my mentors

would be like, 'You need to prove yourself a little bit more.' I had two mentors when I started out in medical school, and one was a black female. And she was saying, 'Most of the people here are white males. You need to show that you're just as good.' That means you have to study two hours longer, you need to be the first one there, you need to always answer questions. So I think it was kind of always a thing where we were told to 'stay up on your p's and q's, make sure you're always doing that.' And don't let anyone even come across the thought that, 'Okay, she's not as prepared as someone else.'"

Bonita's account offers important context for how black doctors learn and expect what to encounter in the medical field. An informal part of Bonita's training included the lesson to counter racial stereotypes preemptively by being hyperprepared. She did not necessarily expect colleagues to openly mistreat her, but she did anticipate having to work harder to counter expectations of poor performance that are grounded in racial stigmas associated with black workers.

Davis, an internal medicine doctor, also speaks about the need to act in ways that would preemptively address latent racial stereotypes:

There are negative interactions, right? But that's not the totality of interactions. Being an underrepresented minority has affected how I view the world and how I interact with the world. And those things, I think, are probably very different than probably [the experiences of] a lot of my non–African American colleagues, right? So, things that I don't take for granted, or that I think about, come into the equation when I'm trying to figure out the solution to something. Somebody else might not [think that way]. It might just go way over their heads. They may never think about it. It comes back to this principle of making sure that you are sort of unimpeachable. I don't take for granted that I will always be given the benefit of the doubt.

I was curious about how Davis justified the distinction between "negative interactions ... that [were] not the totality of interactions" and a general sense that racial considerations meant his work had to be flawless. If this broad perception of a higher bar was ubiquitous enough, then it would seem that this racialized atmosphere was, in fact, more pervasive than Davis was describing. When I pressed him for a more specific example of what this meant for him at work, he replied,

> Let's say that I was supposed to do a PowerPoint presentation for a senior-level person who's going to be traveling somewhere, and they were hoping to have my help. Great, we can collaborate— *collaborate* meaning that I'm gonna have to do it. But [my contribution] is going to be great. I think that I have always felt that those opportunities are critically important for me to prove myself, to get the next opportunity. And I also think that if I did a poor job— if there were a lot of typos, if I didn't get to the core of things—the possibility [exists] that conclusions based on predetermined biases based on my race could enter into the thought process in a way that would not happen to somebody who was white. Because, they might also be seen negatively, but it's about them, not about their race. And that's kind of the difference. So, I do think that absolutely affects me. I am always thinking about these things, whether it is conscious or unconscious, and I think it does shape the way I think and act.

Davis offers an insightful assessment here of how colleagues' perceptions may operate in a fluid manner. As he notes, black doctors do not necessarily encounter colleagues who avoid them or refuse to work with them. In fact, he has benefited from collaborative opportunities with senior colleagues whose favor can lead to career advancement. Yet at the same time, he is well aware that these opportunities are conditional, and that

getting them demands exemplary performance on his part. He anticipates that, should he fail to be anything less than excellent, colleagues may rely on racial stereotypes to explain his performance in ways that they would not for his white counterparts. For Davis, racial issues at work are not defined by colleagues who constantly question his judgment or doubt his capabilities. But racial undertones shape the general atmosphere, requiring impeccable performance in all areas in order to avoid triggering racial stereotypes. The specter of racial stigmatization and the attendant stereotypes of black inferiority leave Davis constantly aware that he might have to disprove these unspoken beliefs at any time, even if his routine interactions with white peers and superiors are generally sanguine.

Other respondents describe seeing white colleagues treating one other more respectfully. Akinyele gives one account of this: "I see how my white colleagues are treated differently. Getting chances to speak, attendings agreeing with them more easily—especially with attendings. Like, 'You know I just said that, right?' But they don't hear it until someone white says it. I've noticed that a lot. It's not as bad as it was. Things are getting better; it's not as bad as my forefathers had it." Akinyele describes a phenomenon that is usually described as happening to women in male-dominated settings—the unpleasant experience of stating something in a group setting, only to have it ignored until a man makes the same comment. This type of encounter feeds into Akinyele's general sense that white colleagues subtly treat black doctors with less respect.

The assumption and perception that blacks are less skilled, intelligent, and capable are certainly not limited to the medical profession. Rather, these representations are part and parcel of

American culture and convey that blacks do not belong in high-status work. Black doctors believe that their colleagues are not immune to being influenced by these stereotypes, and suggest that race affects their work as they attempt to distance themselves from and disprove cultural tropes of black inferiority. Though black doctors say that these interactions are occasional, one limitation of this study is that it is difficult to know what sort of racial conversations happen in their absence. Caitlin, a pediatric emergency medicine doctor, provides a window into this when she states,

> Most white doctors don't know that I'm black, so they tell me all their secrets. They'll just say whatever. They say whatever they want to say. So I can remember vividly this white resident who talked about, not another patient, but another African American attending. A neonatologist who was Nigerian. Clearly [she] was born in the Americas, born in Atlanta, had no accent. I think she had dreadlocks, but American just like you and me. And [the resident] said something in reference to her Nigerian heritage, something about her speaking in tongues, and made some clicking-like sound with his tongue, or something like that. And said it to me in a joking fashion, but amongst some other residents.

Caitlin is an extremely light-skinned black woman who could pass for Latina or white. Given that, she has a window into "backstage racism"—the way that whites engage in extremely graphic, overt racist language, joking, and stereotypes when they are in what they presume to be all-white safe spaces (Houts Picca and Feagin 2013). Her incidental exposure to these conversations indicates that while black doctors may perceive only an undercurrent of racial stereotyping by colleagues, they may in fact be unaware of more extreme comments that happen behind their backs.

Race as a Structural Problem

In addition to observing cultural racism, black doctors also note the ways race is enmeshed in the structural processes that shape access to the medical profession. They observe that, in medical school, residency, and eventually practice, race artificially diminishes the number of black doctors, keeps them in the minority, and limits their access to mentors. When they talk about the ways race affects their careers, they are much more likely to define these issues as systemic problems that have more of an impact on shaping the context in which they practice medicine.

For many black doctors, this analysis of structural racial patterns begins with the educational system and the way it fails black students who might be interested in a medical career. Akinyele talks about the ways medical schools fail to recruit students of color and the need for affirmative action policies that could improve their numbers in medical programs:

> I think there are certain things that need to be focused on. One is: How does affirmative action play a part in the progression of students moving from undergraduate to professional school and on to residencies? ... In my particular class and the class before me and several classes behind me, the ratio of the African American students to the entire class was on the order of 1 to 10, meaning 1 black student for every 10. So really, we were actually about 10 percent. So it was really: for every 170 students, there were maybe 10–15 African Americans. But I don't feel as though the schools make enough of an effort to include enough people. There's the obvious political correctness to encourage those who are interested to apply and to say, "Oh, we understand you come from a great background, you have a great undergraduate history. We want to bring in students that shine and that are not just numbers." But when it all boils down, it's still 10 percent.

From Akinyele's perspective, race matters because institutionalized processes in medical school admissions leave blacks underrepresented and isolated. It is not so much that he routinely
encounters direct, interpersonal challenges from colleagues or
from patients. But he does notice that black workers are underrepresented in medicine, and attributes that to larger systemic
patterns that exist outside the bounds of the workplace.

Davis, the internal medicine doctor, also talks about the key
role that affirmative action plays in creating more of a pipeline
of black doctors:

> The reason that I think affirmative action is so important is because
> I can't come up with a better way to allow for the kid who would
> never have thought that this was possible, to think about it.... It's a
> numbers issue, and I think it's a critically bad tool; but I don't have
> a better tool. It speaks to a huge national, institutional problem of
> opportunity, where the opportunity is so different, and then the
> kid is punished for the natural result of that difference. And then
> the fingers point, like, "See, you're not smart enough." And then
> that message is filtered back through the entire community, and it
> starts again. So that's a huge problem. It's a self-fulfilling prophecy.
> So, I think that that's, honestly, the most important thing.

Davis situates the role that affirmative action can play in opening up doors for children of color who may not have the cultural
capital to consider medicine as an occupation. This is an important point, given that early exposure is essential for setting black
children on the path to nursing or medicine. For Davis, racial
obstacles in medicine are not direct barriers that he encounters
on a regular basis in interactions with colleagues or patients.
Instead, they are the bigger, structural patterns that keep blacks
out of medicine in the first place—and they are problems that
can be solved (at least to some degree) by structural remedies.

In other cases, these structural barriers leave black doctors without mentors who could guide their interest in addressing racial aspects of medicine. Alexandria, the geneticist, offers a particularly succinct assessment of this: "I can't say that I've experienced much tension in the everyday work setting based on the fact that I'm a black woman. It's that people don't understand why my interests lie in the areas in which they do, as they relate to genetics and various populations. And there's not an active movement in that field already. So I think that's where race is more of an important factor." Alexandria, like many black doctors in this study, wants to reduce health disparities and to provide care for black populations that have historically been underserved. So for her, the underrepresentation of black doctors in her field is a major structural issue. She does not see an environment where race directly holds her back. But paradoxically, she works in just such an environment, where the low number of black doctors leaves her lacking the mentorship that would allow her to progress in her field.

SEXISM AND SOLIDARITY: BLACK WOMEN DOCTORS

These racial issues are also gendered. Overall, both men and women doctors assert that explicit racial problems are few and far between in their everyday interactions at work, and that while they can remember occasional racial comments from patients or colleagues, these are not commonplace. Yet black women doctors take their analysis a step further. Almost to a person, they note that while race plays a structural role in shaping their work, gender is a much more notable, significant, and consistent factor, an ever-present part of their daily interactions that limits their

occupational success. For nearly every black woman doctor interviewed for this project, race seems incidental enough that gender bias stands out as a major driver of occupational inequity.

In an answer representative of most of my interviews with black women doctors, Angie, an orthopedic surgeon, responds to a direct question about how race affected her work by saying, "As a woman or as a woman of color, I feel like we have to overcome some barriers first to kind of establish yourself. Of course there's the training, and if you're in an institution where that person may not know who you are, you have to kind of get the mind-set: 'No, I'm not the nurse; no, I'm not someone else. I am the doctor.' And I think—because people look at you and don't necessarily see you—I may not be the first person that comes to mind."

Note that I asked Angie directly how she felt *race* affects her work. Yet a question about racial barriers immediately elicited a response about gender-related issues. Furthermore, her experience of being presumed to be the nurse rather than the doctor was so commonplace that I came to expect to hear this from black women doctors. It is not an overstatement to report that nearly every black woman doctor in this study reported this experience.

Jayla, the pediatrician, also believes that gender held her back more than race: "I think the reason I say that is because I can see how even nurses treat male doctors versus me and my colleagues that are female. And how even some fathers versus mothers treat different-gender doctors, and how they kind of communicate with them. It's different. There's a different level of respect [for men]." For Jayla, these differences are not necessarily drawn along racial lines. She does not mention observing patterns where nurses or patients routinely treat black doctors with less

respect. However, she does say that she has noticed that parents and nurses communicate with women doctors in ways that convey less trust, belief, and respect for their authority. This shapes her conclusion that the dominant issue she faces is gendered rather than racial.

Caitlin, a pediatric emergency doctor, offers the same characterization during our conversation:

> In dealing with other physicians, I think that being a female makes things a little bit more complicated. I think that when at work, when I have to call a consultant, say, that's a surgeon, most overwhelmingly the surgeons are male—neurosurgery, orthopedic surgery. And I think that they assume that when they call back and I pick up the phone, I'm going to say, "Hi Dr. Stone, this is Caitlin. I'm one of the ER fellows. I have a patient that has an issue. Do you mind? Do you mind? Do you mind?" No. That doesn't fly. Because then they're going to take their time, do whatever they want to do, get to you when they get to you, not involve you in their treatment plan, [and] maybe you'll disagree or maybe you'll agree, or whatever. So I think that that's always the assumption [for women], that you maybe know less or you have a less aggressive personality. I don't ever feel like they take my knowledge base into question. Maybe sometimes. But it's *always* my personality that they take into question. [They think,] because maybe they're male and maybe they're consulting, that somehow I should just accept whatever they say, and that maybe I'm asking them to do something. But no, in reality, I mean for you to get your ass down here and to reduce this fracture! I've already looked at the x-ray. I'm not asking for your opinion. Although you are a consultant, I'm telling you what to do, so move it!

In Caitlin's experience, doctors who are men generally treat women, regardless of race, as though they should be tentative wallflowers. She describes having to develop a more aggressive personality to break through this, and cites this sort of stereotyping as a

more constant, routine part of her job than problematic racial interactions.

Not only do many women see gender bias in medicine as the more salient issue, but also, importantly, they see it as a factor that creates a sense of interracial solidarity between themselves and white women doctors. Aliya remarks,

> I think you bond with the female doctors because they can relate and they know how it feels. They know how it feels to go through four years of medical school or three years of residency and still be called a nurse. The male doctors will never really know how that feels. So even though the male doctors have respect for you, they can't really understand how that feels. And it's kind of a slap in the face when you have to leave and go get one of your male colleagues to come help you because one of your patients doesn't have any respect for you. So you do bond with your female colleagues, I feel like, more than your male colleagues. At least I do. And [that happens] regardless of the race, I think, because my female coworkers now are all different races and ethnicities and [race] hasn't really come into play so much [among us].

Aliya states point-blank that not only does gender have more of an impact on her work outcomes than race, but it also establishes a bond between women who share this sense of exclusion.

Jayla, the pediatrician quoted earlier, shares this viewpoint. She, too, cites parallels in the ways women of all races are treated: "It is different, but I'm sure there are some similarities. For example, some female doctors may feel like they're having to prove themselves; or sometimes you get called Ms. Flood instead of Dr. Flood. You sometimes wonder if people are questioning you or second-guessing you. In the back of your mind, you always wonder about that; and that type of thing is hard to prove. So it's one of those uncomfortable feelings, like you're

always having to prove yourself." Like Aliya, Jayla describes this as a common phenomenon for women in medicine, and one that binds black and white women together through shared experience.

Even some of the black men interviewed for this study highlighted the challenges women face in medicine. Bart, a black male emergency nurse, states, "I think it's good that there are more women coming into medicine. I like it. It changes the stereotype. It's been too long where people imagine doctors as men. Why can't your doctor be an Asian woman with long hair? I see it happen where people assume that the women working here are nurses and I am the doctor. I know it makes them angry. I like the image being changed." Bart's observations are consistent with accounts from other black men in male dominated professions who are mindful of the ways in which women of all races face sexism and gender bias in these fields (Turco 2010; Wingfield 2012). Though Bart works in nursing, a female-dominated job, he is similar to the black men who are lawyers, doctors, engineers, and bankers, and who, in other research, identify how a "boys club" mentality in these professions curtails women's advancement.

The gender biases in medicine are well documented. In 2005, only 32 percent of US medical school faculty, 15 percent of full professors, and 11 percent of department chairs were women (Kass, Souba, and Thorndyke 2006). Even in pediatrics, where women comprised more than half of the physician population, fewer than 10 percent of the department chairs in these programs were women (Carnes, Morrissey, and Geller 2008). White women doctors note that even though their numbers are growing in these areas, the general "boys club" culture in medicine still means they are seen first and foremost as women and potential mothers rather

than as committed physicians (Boulis and Jacobs 2008). Other women of color cite similar challenges, with both first- and second-generation Indian American women doctors reporting severe and pervasive gender discrimination at work, including instances where women were steered away from the most competitive and lucrative specialties in medicine on the assumption that they would prioritize family over work. These women also encounter racialized perceptions of foreignness and otherness that hinder their opportunities for advancement (Bhatt 2013).

Furthermore, additional quantitative data hint at these perceptions about the ways women are treated in medicine. I submitted survey questions through the American Panel Survey, a nationally representative survey conducted by Washington University in St. Louis. One of the questions posed the following vignette: "You are plagued with recurring headaches, but your regular doctor is unavailable. How likely are you to trust your new doctor?" I varied the race and gender of the practitioner so that respondents were assigned a doctor who was either female, black, a black female, or race and gender unspecified. Social psychology suggests that "woman," without a qualifier, often connotes a white woman, while "black" conjures images of men (Ridgeway and Kricheli-Katz 2013). Based on this, I theorized that respondents who were assigned the "female" doctor likely envisioned a white woman, while those assigned a "black" physician would assume a black male practitioner. Interestingly, more respondents asserted that they were more likely to trust a black doctor (55.67 percent) than a female one (30.15 percent). Even black female doctors were viewed more favorably (46.76 percent) than a hypothetical female doctor. Data analysis, shown in table 3, indicates that of those assigned a doctor from one of the three explicit categories (female, black, and black female),

TABLE 3

Respondents' Trust in Doctor, by Race and Gender

Likelihood of Trusting Doctor (%)	Female	Black	Black and Female	Control
Very likely	30.15	55.67	46.76	8.28
Likely	48.24	25.71	34.48	40.35
Neutral	17.88	10.58	14.44	44.04
Not likely	0.74	3.29	2.37	5.07
Not very likely	2.99	4.75	1.95	2.27
Total %	100	100	100	100

respondents were least likely to report that they were very likely to trust a female practitioner.

Data from the American Panel Survey hint at other findings that are more clearly evident in the qualitative data. They suggest that women may be even less likely than men to trust a practitioner who is a woman. The results of the multivariate analysis suggest that respondent gender "matters" only when the doctor is a woman. When the doctor is a woman, women respondents trust the doctor less than men respondents do ($p < .01$). However, when the doctor is black or black female, men and women respondents are equally likely to trust the doctor. See figure 5.

This quantitative data suggests that black women doctors' perceptions that gender is a significant barrier for them have merit. Respondents viewed both black doctors and black women doctors as more trustworthy than simply women doctors. Thus, this survey data hints at a finding that also emerged in my interviews—namely, that the gender bias in medicine marginalizes women in ways to which black women doctors are particularly attuned. This analysis indicates that when black women interviewed for

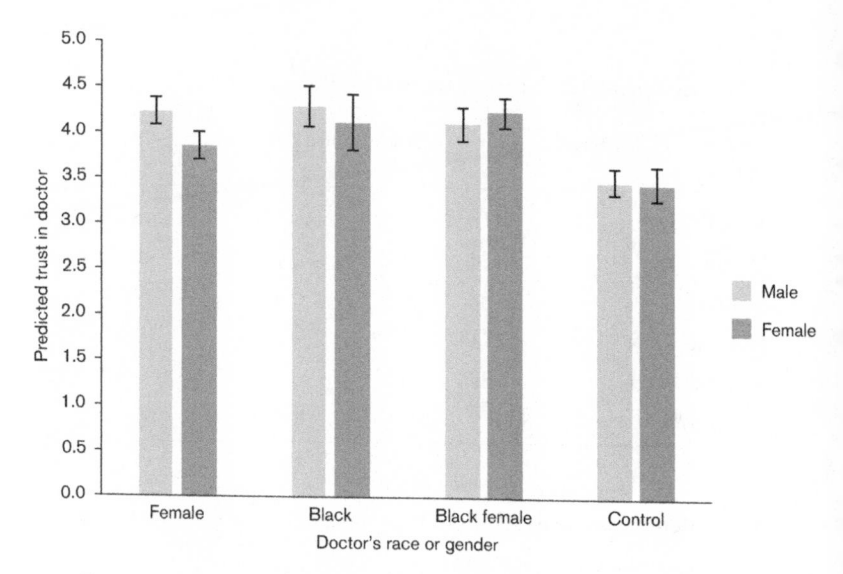

Figure 5. Predicted trust in doctor by respondent gender and experimental condition. Source: The American Panel Survey, September 2016.

this study reported that patients seem to see them as less competent and qualified than their men counterparts, these perceptions may reflect a widespread belief that women, generally speaking, are not trustworthy practitioners.

Black women's interview responses, however, represent a unique intersection of gender, race, and occupational status. Because of black women's status in the occupational hierarchy, racial barriers primarily present themselves with respect to cultural and structural processes—colleagues' lower expectations, educational barriers, access to fewer mentors. Because racial issues are so heavily coded and institutionalized, however, the sort of gender-based obstacles that can occur during routine interactions (e.g., being mistaken for the nurse) become all the more evident and frustrating.

RACIAL OUTSOURCING AND EQUITY WORK:
STRUCTURAL SOLUTIONS OVER
CULTURAL COMPETENCE

For black doctors, race is embedded in the structural and cultural processes that determine their pathway into medicine and establish the general atmosphere for their work. Yet the organizational measures that exist in their workplaces (if any are present at all) rarely acknowledge these issues. Consequently, racial outsourcing occurs when, given the limited organizational attempts to address the racial issues black doctors encounter, this work gets transferred to doctors themselves.

In the medical field, attempts to address racial problems largely take the form of emphasizing the concept of *cultural competence* (Hoberman 2012). This term refers to practitioners' and organizations' ability to offer health care services in ways that can speak to various patients' particular social and cultural needs. Depending on where they work, both doctors and nurses may be required to complete intermittent training and paperwork that highlight the importance of being not only culturally competent but also mindful of how cultural differences can inform patient practices and behaviors. These trainings encourage health care workers to factor these cultural differences into the ways they interact with and treat patients.

I did observe some doctors who took the lessons of cultural competence into consideration. For example, while I shadowed Dr. Ella Chapman, a black woman obstetrician and gynecologist at a large university-affiliated hospital, we led several other doctors in making the rounds of the day's patients. We paused outside the door of a patient who had emigrated to the US from Somalia, and Ella informed us that the patient was a practicing

Muslim. Given that, she instructed the men to wait in the hall-way and give the patient time to replace her hijab. After the women on the team walked in and introduced themselves, Ella said, "We have several men on our team who are waiting in the hall. I'd like them to come in to be part of our discussion here about your treatment. Do you want to take a few minutes to put your hijab back on first?" The patient complied, and when she was ready, we alerted the men physicians that it was safe to enter. This attention to cultural issues and how they can fac-tor into patient treatment was not standardized or required by hospital protocol, but it was a consistent part of this doctor's practice of engaging with patients.

Yet cultural competence is not without its detractions. Train-ing varies by program and rarely tackles the historical underpin-nings that can drive doctors' and nurses' antiblack stereotypes, assumptions, and beliefs. Cultural competence training generally does not address the long history of medical racism or implicit bias (Hoberman 2012). Furthermore, studies that evaluate the effectiveness of cultural competence training emphasize the extent that it leads to improved patient outcomes, not its ability to resolve racial tensions for practitioners of color (Govere and Govere 2016). As a result, most of the doctors in this study told me they are underwhelmed by what they see as lackluster attempts to address the racial issues they encounter. Randy, an emergency medicine doctor, actually rolled his eyes when I brought up cul-tural competence, replying, "It's the right idea, but that stuff doesn't mean anything. Nobody takes it seriously! The way they do it, the trainings and modules, it's just one more box to check. They just want quick fixes. Doing the hard work, really changing the profession to get more black and brown people in here—that's not sexy." The racial challenges Randy encounters in medicine—

insidious racial stigmatization that lowers expectations for black doctors, educational processes that eliminate aspiring black physicians, lack of mentors—are not solved by cultural competence modules that encourage practitioners to be mindful of how cultural and social differences can influence patients' responses to medical care. Ella, the obstetrician-gynecologist, agrees: "It's just a box to be checked. Right? So maybe there's a lecture you have to go to, or a module you have to complete online, but it's a box to be checked more than an institutional commitment.... Once a year we have to do a billion computer modules that are annoying, and you're trying to figure out what the shortcut is to complete them as quickly as possible. I feel like cultural competency falls into that realm." Left to themselves, organizations may offer cultural competence training that highlights ways social factors inform patients' interactions in the health care system. But they do little to address the ways racial processes affect practitioners.

Since doctors do not observe any institutional measures that seriously address the racial dynamics they encounter, they instead do the equity work of addressing racial issues themselves. For black doctors, this involves pursuing structural solutions to the racial issues that plague the medical profession and thereby affect communities of color. Given that the issues they are most attuned to occur at the structural level, it is perhaps not surprising that this is where they concentrate their efforts. Black doctors like Ella routinely engage in mentoring and training young doctors of color in an effort to offset the isolation they encounter in their professional work—isolation that she has experienced firsthand. She notes, "The problem is that when you get past your first two years of medical school, everything is completely subjective. And so, in terms of you getting into the best residency or the best fellowship, it's largely based on your ability to have good

social interactions with people. If you're marginalized from the very beginning, you're kind of screwed. So I'm always trying to do what I can to be there for young students who contact me, because you don't want them to have the experience you had." By taking these steps, Ella seeks to offset the disadvantages that black students encounter in medical school and then later upon graduating, when their status in the numerical minority keeps them from accessing the mentorship and social networks that are critical for advancement in the field. She does this without institutional support or recognition, essentially trying to challenge systemic processes that handicap aspiring black doctors.

Other doctors attempt even bigger, more far-reaching changes. Randy, the emergency medicine doctor mentioned above, collaborated with several other black male doctors to start a nonprofit organization designed to address the systemic inequalities that can contribute to violence in poor, urban, predominantly black areas. Randy was motivated to start Brothers Stopping Violence because "working in the ER, I see so many black men from my neighborhood come in with injuries, who've been victims of violence. It just made me ask, 'What if we created an environment that pushed back against the impetus to create violence? Something that bridged the hospital and the community?' I really want to help provide increased opportunity to the people we're working with." Randy recasts the violence that is all too common in impoverished communities as a public health issue. In that context, he envisions violence prevention as a health care initiative that he can champion and support through his work in the medical industry. For him, it makes more sense to attack the structural causes of violence and to put his energy behind transforming those.

Lance, the retired doctor whose story opens this chapter, had thought extensively about the structural aspects of medicine

and how they adversely affected black physicians. He notes that the enormous debt that physicians take on to complete medical school has a measurable outcome on black doctors:

> Something like 80 percent of black medical students now come from families in the top third in terms of income. And only something like 3 or 4 percent come from families in the lower third in terms of income. So we're setting up an aristocracy almost in medicine, which, again, was not the picture when I went to medical school. Because by and large, if you got into medical school, there was sufficient scholarship support available that you could go. But that's a real problem. And you see this all over higher education. I think it may be more striking in medicine because the cost of going to medical school is so much higher.

Lance goes on to note that seeing this emerging pattern was the impetus for many of his efforts to create institutional changes that, he believed, would offset the disadvantages black students encounter in their attempts to enter the medical profession. He sought to implement these changes by taking leadership roles at the medical school where he worked and by using his platform and his connections to a past president to push for legislative action that would increase opportunities for minority physicians:

> From a larger perspective, blacks are terribly underrepresented in medicine. That was one of the rationales [for the addition of medical schools to some historically black colleges and universities]. In 1950, 2 percent of the nation's physicians were black. After all of the efforts in the second half of the twentieth century, [black doctors now constitute] about 4, 4.5 percent, whereas blacks have moved from 10 percent of the population to 12 percent of the population. If we were represented in medicine proportionately as we are in the general population, [that number would be much higher]. We have one-third the number of black doctors that we should have. And I maintain that because, as a society, we still have bias and unequal

opportunity, that in the same way that often women are more comfortable seeing a female doctor, you also have minorities who are often more comfortable seeing someone from their own group. You want to have someone you trust. So for all those reasons, we argued that we should have diversity as well as the other one—that we should have equal opportunity.

Most respondents in this study are not positioned as highly as Lance and were not able to push legislation and bend a sitting president's ear. However, while few respondents share his level of influence, most share his belief in the need to change systemic processes that curtail black doctors' advancement. The depth of commitment Lance exhibits in addressing the structural factors that keep black doctors underrepresented in the medical industry is quite common among the physicians with whom I spoke, even if his reach in doing so is unusually vast.

Individual attempts to enact structural solutions, however, can meet with failure and frustration. Jayla Flood, another doctor who believes that race primarily affects black physicians through structural and cultural processes, also feels that in that context gender is the bigger impediment to her work. Interestingly, as a partner in a private practice, she is theoretically in a position to help enact specific measures to address the low numbers of black doctors in their employ. However, her partners in the practice have not supported overt measures to attract more workers of color. Indeed, she shared a story with me that illuminates how even her individual efforts to draw in minority doctors were thwarted. One day during lunch, we were chatting in the break room when I asked her about the process for hiring new practitioners. As she was the only woman of color in the partnership, I wondered if there had ever been opportunities to hire other racial minority doctors. She sighed and said,

As a matter of fact, that actually touches on one of the few things that have frustrated me about being here. We did have to hire a practitioner a while back. And we had all these discussions and conversations about how it would be good to have a more diverse practice. We *all* agreed to this before we started looking at candidates. So then what happens? We're considering candidates, and there's this Latina doctor in the pool who I think looks really good. She met all the criteria we wanted, and she was even bilingual! But then people start saying, "Oh ... she speaks Spanish? Is that going to be a problem?" Like that's a bad thing! Now, granted, we don't have a huge Spanish-speaking patient population, but why would that be a disadvantage? I was so irritated with everyone. And we did not hire that candidate.

Though Jayla's story here is about a Latina candidate, it nevertheless highlights the toll equity work can take, as well as the fact that doctors are not always able to create structural changes. Despite agreeing that they wanted to diversify their practice, Dr. Flood's partners opted to forgo that commitment once faced with the prospect of acting on it; and an attribute that could have been a qualification became recast as a liability. In the absence of any organizational attempts to address racial issues, Jayla found herself doing the work of trying to hold her partners accountable given their stated goal of bringing in more minority doctors. Yet her example shows that transferring this work to black doctors, even those in positions of power, has its limitations.

SUMMARY

Black doctors' work experiences are an interesting window into how race affects high-status professionals working in a culturally masculinized occupation. These doctors argue that their daily workplace routines are rarely marred by overt, intentional

racist acts. This finding runs counter to studies that document extensive racist aggression directed at blacks in predominantly white spaces (Evans 2014; Feagin and Sikes 1995; Moore 2007). It also challenges prevailing stereotypes that indicate blacks are quick to blame race for everything or to use race as a crutch to avoid hard work. The fact that black doctors explicitly state that racist interactions do not characterize the daily dynamics of their workplaces provides empirical evidence that many black professionals do not always see race first and foremost as a driving factor that explains their hardships. The irony here, however, is that even though they do not encounter racial hostilities on a daily basis, the more systemic and cultural ways that race operates at work means they are still subject to its effects.

Black physicians acknowledge that race informs their work by shaping important structural and cultural processes that are critical for success in the medical industry. Educational pathways disadvantage black students, leaving them underrepresented in medical schools and largely bereft of potential mentors. Additionally, cultural beliefs about black inferiority create subtle biases that black doctors challenge through a commitment to excellence and high performance. This a gendered process as well, as these institutionalized mechanisms make the forms of overt sexism black women doctors encounter all too visible and noticeable. As a result, understanding black professionals' racial experiences requires considering the ways these experiences are also informed by gender and occupational status.

Yet few black doctors find that the organizations where they work have invested time, energy, and resources in addressing the structural or cultural ways that race does seem to have an impact on their work. At best, some facilities may require cultural competence training, which lacks attention to systemic issues, medi-

cal racism, and racial stereotypes. However, doctors are largely skeptical of, if not annoyed by, cultural competence training that is not designed to address their racial realities. When this sort of organizational effort seems lacking, racial outsourcing means that the work of correcting these issues is left for black professionals. Black doctors thus do the equity work of trying to create structural solutions to the racial issues they encounter. As a result, equity work leaves black doctors with the added responsibility of seeking structural change and attempting to address the systemic processes that keep black doctors underrepresented and that disproportionately affect black patients.

When "That One Time" Is All the Time

One morning I arrived at University Hospital as the physicians waited to begin reviewing the list of admitted patients, their progress over the night, and their recommendations for treatment—a process they called "running boards." Since we had about ten minutes before the shift formally began, most of the doctors sat around chatting about their weekends. I took a seat in the rear of the room near Dr. Erin Jessup, a white woman resident with wide brown eyes and brown hair covered by a surgical bonnet. We greeted each other and began discussing the local news of the day—a winter storm projected to hit the area that afternoon. Near us, two other doctors were discussing one's upcoming vacation, while I overheard two others gossiping about a patient from the day before.

The nurses had their own table in the same room. While their table was not far away from the doctors', there was very little mingling. The nurses did not run boards with the doctors, and since the shift had not yet started, they engaged in their own small talk. I couldn't hear exactly what the nurses were

saying from my place in the room, but their conversation clearly grew increasingly boisterous and was punctuated with frequent bouts of laughter.

After a few minutes, Erin got up to begin running boards. The doctors quickly snapped to attention and began to listen intently as she started explaining which patients remained in the hospital. The nurses stayed at their table and continued their conversation, but I noticed that now several doctors began to throw them annoyed glances. The nurses were not quite so loud that they drowned Erin out, but it wasn't possible to forget they were in the room, either. Finally, Dr. Emily Martin, a white woman, turned away from Erin and said, "Hey! Hey guys, you've really got to quiet down. You're too loud." Her tone was not rude, but it was direct, and several other doctors sitting near her nodded in agreement. The nurses immediately hushed, and Erin continued running boards.

Perhaps more than any others I observed, this example illustrates the stark status differences between medicine and nursing. It would have been virtually impossible to witness that scene in reverse, with nurses admonishing doctors for creating a mild interruption. While the two professions are interdependent, doctors are clearly at the top of the health-care food chain. This hierarchy is inescapably gendered, with women comprising the majority of nurses and men overrepresented in medicine. But black workers are underrepresented in both nursing and medicine. Does this lead to different outcomes? How does race affect black nurses differently than black doctors? What do these status differences mean for racial outsourcing? For equity work?

These fundamental variations between nursing and medicine mean that race informs nurses' work differently. While doctors argue that race affects their work in primarily structural and

cultural ways (e.g., racial stigmatization, limited educational opportunities, and constrained access to mentors), nurses assert that race shapes their work through both structural *and* interactional processes. Like doctors, they note that similar aspects of their educational training systemically disadvantage black candidates. But unlike doctors, nurses recount explicitly racist statements and acts that are commonplace in coworker interactions. Organizational initiatives do little to resolve either structural or interpersonal challenges, so racial outsourcing means that nurses assume responsibility for dealing with these issues. For nurses, however, equity work means seeking both structural and interactional change to protect patients of color from the types of overtly racialized experiences they routinely encounter.

STRUCTURAL BARRIERS: SCHOOL AND SCHEDULING

School

What structural issues most concern black nurses? From their perspectives, educational reform and scheduling processes have racialized outcomes that affect their work in this field. Janet was the first nurse who drew my attention to the way changing educational requirements actually worked to black nurses' disadvantage. During our interview, she stated,

> You also have the difference between the LPN, the licensed practical nurse programs, or the diploma nursing programs, which are more like community college nursing, versus the bachelor-of-science nursing programs, which are college- or university-level programs. And the push is to have, [for] all nurses, the entry level be a bachelor of science in nursing and not community college or

diploma programs. So those nurses who do attend community college or diploma programs actually may find that they struggle a little bit more to obtain a job than those with a bachelor's degree. Which also kind of makes me think about the fact that I don't know how many of our nurses that go to community colleges are black nurses because the tuition is less expensive; or maybe it's a little bit easier to get into the program in terms of just the numbers of people that they accept, or the feasibility of having a family and going to a community college.

Janet notes that the changing expectations in nursing may inadvertently discredit or disadvantage nurses of color, black nurses particularly. She observes that, as the profession turns toward requiring a bachelor of science in nursing as a minimum qualification, this can potentially adversely affect black workers in the field who, for economic, cultural, or social reasons, find it simpler to pursue a nursing degree via community colleges or diploma programs.

Emma, a registered nurse, also speaks about this increased educational requirement:

> Of course they're always pushing for more RNs to have their bachelor's degree. And maybe now, the women that I work with—a lot of them have their associate's degree as a registered nurse, so most of them are back in school actually, now, going to get that BSN credential [added] to their RN license.... Also, I've heard [that] if anyone's interested in getting in their master's program—I'm not sure if it's set in stone or not, but I know it's coming into play, where you have to go straight to your doctorate. You cannot stop at a master's level. Speaking for myself, the biggest thing is the financial piece of covering school. Many of us, unfortunately—or those that I know—are working moms with families, or single moms. And nursing is very good for job stability. But then having to add on a whole 'nother two years of schooling whether you want it or not, and having to financially figure out how that's going to get covered—it can be a strain. And I feel like it's an unnecessary strain. It can be extra stress.

For Emma, the increased educational requirements seem needlessly burdensome. Like Janet, she notes that these can put a financial burden on black women who may be interested in the profession but do not necessarily have the economic resources (or the personal interest) to pursue a master's degree or doctorate in the field. Given that black women are much more likely than other racial and gender groups to return to school later in life, additional barriers are likely to have an outsize impact on them (Denice 2017). These efforts to professionalize the field further, then, may indirectly screen out black workers interested in pursuing nursing.

Lindsay makes a similar assessment of how changing educational requirements can have an adverse impact on black men and women pursuing nursing:

> But the nursing school issue, that may be an issue. It's actually harder to get into nursing school nowadays. That may be an issue with black nurses, because I have a lot of people coming to me—I went to a two-year school. I didn't go to a four-year school. Only have an associate's. But to be honest, that school was way tougher than any four-year school—I swear—in the world! Because they have to cram all of our things into a two-year program, just like a four-year program. So it was very hard. Now, to get into that two-year program, you basically have to have a 4.0, and all your sciences have to be A's. It's a waiting list for different schools. So I can see that being a problem.

Lindsay reiterates that the more restrictive standards for two-year programs could potentially be problematic for black women entering the field. As the field becomes increasingly professionalized, the pathway to nursing can become narrower for workers of color.

Theresa speaks about this process in very blunt terms. She argues that this thinning-out process is not an accident:

The education portion—that's another place where they have to address the nursing shortage, because they weed a lot of black nurses out in nursing school. They target them. First of all, a lot of times black people don't test well. And that's not to say that all black people don't test well, but it's been said that sometimes they don't test well. They're harder on them in terms of: how do you look, what ways are you wearing your hair, what colors are in your hair, those types of things. And they'll put little demerits and points and stuff here and there and take off for these things. I had one girl that was in my nurse practitioner class, and she had a gold tooth. She was going for her master's. She had a gold tooth. They picked and picked and picked and picked and picked at her until they finally got her out of the program. And it was right before graduation. She was [at the] end of semester and needed to graduate, and they got her out of the program. She had a gold tooth. To this day she's still not a nurse practitioner.

From Theresa's perspective, it is not just the increased educational requirements but also the social practices and occupational culture of nursing schools that create problems for black nurses. She believes that, in addition to facing heightened standards, black women in particular face racial and gendered expectations that become additional burdens. In the particular example she cites, these added barriers are construed through class-based and cultural coding that render a gold tooth unsuitable for the nursing profession.

The increased educational requirements that these black women nurses cite also have to be situated in the broader context of work and organizations in the new economy. Today, public financing in the form of grants, loans, and other credits has gotten more scarce, while higher education has only gotten more expensive. Earning a BS in nursing can cost approximately seven thousand dollars, excluding room and board, with costs

for a master's or doctorate running thirteen thousand dollars or twenty thousand dollars, respectively.[1] Furthermore, the rise of for-profit universities means that a growing number of institutions capitalize on this persistent inequality, leave students with more debt than they do career options, and in fact disproportionately enroll black women (Cottom 2017). When respondents discuss the ways these added educational requirements can disproportionately penalize black applicants, they highlight the fact that these innocuous attempts to further professionalize nursing can actually exacerbate the racial disparities the profession seeks to minimize.

Scheduling

Black nurses also identify structural problems that perpetuate racial inequality when it comes to scheduling. They argue that the way in which schedules are decided and allotted produces racial divisions. Many observe racial differences in how nurses are assigned to shifts, and they contend that these variations put black nurses in a suboptimal position when it comes to scheduling, opportunities for advancement, and networking. Theresa, the nurse practitioner mentioned in the previous section, told me, "Most of the time they weed black nurses out on the hiring end. They hire you into the floor that nobody wants to be on, the floor where you're going to get eight to twelve patients each shift, and you'll run around like a dog all night; whereas they take the white nurses and put them on the floors that I've worked on where I've only had two to three patients

1. Source: "Tuition and Estimated Cost," UTHealth, https://nursing.uth .edu/prospstudent/applresources/progcost/default.htm. University of Texas projected estimates of the costs associated with nursing programs.

at a time." From her perspective, there are differences in where black nurses are stationed relative to their white peers. She argues that black nurses routinely are given the less desirable shifts with higher patient loads.

Sela, a nurse on a mother-baby floor, made the same observation. She had recently moved to the East Coast from a large midwestern city. When I asked her if she felt there were ways that race made a difference in her work, she commented,

> I will say this: I did find a big, noticeable difference. It started back at home. I work night shift. I worked night shift when I worked back [home]. And it was one night [when] I just looked around, and I was like, "The majority of the population on night is black." I was like, "That is weird." And if we did have a white coworker, they were soon like, "I want to go to day shift." And that was very odd. And even where I am now, I think I have one white nurse on nights, out of everybody that's on nights. I'm just like, "That is really odd." I don't know what the correlation is to that, but it's just really odd.

I asked Sela how this sorting process happened. She replied,

> It's funny you ask that, because everybody that I talk to who's a nurse noticed that and pointed that out. They've said that they feel like black nurses often get the night shift. And that the day shift, I guess, is the more desirable one because it's daytime and you can go home and have your evening. But usually that's not what happens for the black nurses. Plus, [day shift nurses] feel like, working night shift, we don't do anything. They just feel like the patients sleep all night, [that] we sit at the nurse's station, when it's the total opposite. I mean, regardless, we don't have [all the nurses] there. We still are doing something. So it's: We deserve respect, because it's a bunch of pressure. We're up all night with patients. So it's still a lot going on. We don't have everybody there, but it's still a lot going on. Patients are up all night because they have babies.

Sela's response is an interesting one that touches on several important points. She notes that the pattern of black nurses being assigned to the night shift has not escaped other black nurses' attention. Furthermore, the night shift is stereotyped as the easy shift, despite the fact that nights on a mother-baby floor are not necessarily a time for rest and relaxation, much less sleep (as any parent of a newborn well knows). Thus, when black nurses are slotted into the night shifts, this not only can perpetuate a sense among them that they are being treated differently but also can feed into perceptions that they are not gaining the same type of valuable experience as their peers who are granted day shifts.

Callie, a patient care technician on a mother-baby floor at a large, prestigious hospital on the West Coast, also notes that there seem to be racial aspects to how schedules are assigned: "I notice even in the scheduling, as opposed to some of the other girls that are going to school, I feel that—well, a few of us feel that [white nurses] get accommodated much better with their school schedules, as opposed to the black ones on the floor." Callie requires a somewhat flexible schedule because she has returned to school to pursue her nursing degree. But even in a technician's role, she, too, notes that her white colleagues pursuing their degrees appear to be allowed much more flexibility when it comes to scheduling hours. Callie's experience suggests that, in addition to the ways scheduling can be an unintended barrier for black nurses in the profession, systemic processes, too, may limit black workers' ability to enter the field at all.

These results show that there are some minor similarities in the ways black doctors and nurses believe that race affects their work. Specifically, both groups identify structural patterns that operate to their disadvantage. Both also highlight education as a common barrier. For nurses, structural barriers in nursing

education eliminate them, while systemic processes in scheduling contribute to a form of occupational segregation. Recall that in the new economy, networking and social connections are a critical form of occupational advancement. Thus, when institutional processes channel black nurses into shifts that are essentially racially segregated, this impedes their opportunities for occupational mobility and advancement by limiting the nurses with whom they can form critical ties for sharing information. Inasmuch as whites tend to reserve leads and advice about potential jobs for other whites, clustering black nurses together on the night shift can potentially lock black nurses out of key opportunities (Royster 2003).

WHEN "THAT ONE TIME" IS ALL THE TIME:
RACE AND EVERYDAY INTERACTIONS

While nurses share doctors' belief that race affects them through structural patterns, their perceptions of interpersonal accounts are quite dissimilar. Recall from the previous chapter that for black doctors, explicitly racist interactions are rare and characterized as infrequent incidents that happened "that one time." This is decidedly not the case for the nurses in my study. Most nurses shared numerous, much more overt examples of the ways that routine interactions with colleagues and patients include racial stereotypes, biases, and hostility. For nurses, inflammatory statements and behaviors are a routine part of work, not isolated incidents.

Emma describes this in general terms as happening as early as nursing school. Describing a white woman nursing professor whom Emma believed treated black and white students differently, she states,

I guess it would just be her reaction to questions. Just general questions. It would kind of come off like: "Why are you asking me that?" Or just her responses were very snooty. It's like she had an attitude, and she didn't want to be here. Or things of that nature. But then [with] the Caucasian students, she would love to laugh and joke, and they can ask any type of question or be funny, be silly, and she was like, "Oh, you just so crazy." Or she would just laugh, like in general conversation. But then, let it come from an African American, or somebody in particular that maybe she just wasn't too fond of, [and] it would be a totally different response.

This difference in interpersonal interaction left Emma with the clear impression that this professor was biased in favor of her white students. This is not farfetched, as teachers' racial perceptions shape their interactions with students (Ferguson 2000; Lewis-McCoy 2010; Tyson 2013) and could possibly be a factor in black nursing students' educational outcomes.

Janet, a nurse in the mid-Atlantic region, recounts an environment where racial tensions were constantly high:

They would challenge my knowledge. They would give me these really menial projects to do—like, for instance, I was on my shift and I was being trained by one nurse who was just a mean person. Mean-spirited person. She would say little nasty things, and she was not very talkative. She wasn't social. It was very hard to spend twelve hours, three to four days a week, with somebody who doesn't want to talk to you. And so she would basically just treat me as her assistant as opposed to actually trying to train me to do anything. She would just kind of use me as her assistant. I particularly learn very quickly, and so I get things done very quickly. And I would get things finished, and they would be looking as if I probably did them half-assed; or they would go back and check my work, and then they would be shocked to find out that I actually did get it done, and [then they] would find other things.

Here, Janet describes a generally uncomfortable atmosphere where her training nurse establishes a relationship that casts Janet in the role of personal assistant. But I wanted to find out more about what this meant in practice, so I pressed her for more specifics. She said,

> I can recall one night, this woman—she was white, she was kind of late forties. Had been a nurse for probably twenty years and had probably been nursing at that particular hospital for a good twenty years. I was finishing up some work that she had asked me to do, and she came back into the office where I was and she said, "Here, I have this stack of papers that I want you to enter into the computer." And this is months into my orientation. I had already been using the computer. I said, "Ok, whose work is this?" I was asking her whose work is this and what is it, what's the purpose of it, etcetera. Come to find out, she had gone and collected up charting from other people and decided that she wanted me to enter all of this stuff to get "practice" using the computer. And I told her I wasn't going to do it. I told her no. I said, "I have used this computer, I know how to use the computer, you have seen me use the computer. I don't understand why you would want to then go around and collect up work for me to do, just busy work." It was things like that. We kind of had a little bit of a head-butt. Of course she started crying. Why, I don't know. *[Laughs.]* I looked at her and said—you know, when you get really calm and you start saying things in a very calm manner, I think people get scared. And so I was very calm, and I just said, "You are not my mother; you are not going to curse or talk to me this way. I am not going to do what you asked me to." And I walked out.

Janet rattled off a number of examples like these. They all involved white women nurses who actively created what she experienced as a hostile work environment.

Lest we think this experience was exclusive to Janet, we can look at other black women nurses who have similar accounts. Mindy, another nurse, offers a particularly egregious example:

There was just kind of this demeanor of: how dare *you* be in intensive care, because—basically, because of your race. It never starts out as things that they say right out. They start—some nurses, some white nurses, will kind of not say anything. They don't come right out and say it. It's the way that they look at you when you notice these subtle differences. But long story short, someone actually said to me—we were talking about after work getting together, hanging out, and [she] said, "Oh, you can come to my house, but you'd have to be carrying a pail and wearing a rag on your head to come to my home."

Mindy described this to me as just one of many incidents that happened to her while working in a prestigious hospital in a major urban location. She did not characterize this instance—in which a coworker openly and derisively stereotyped her as a cleaning lady—as an infrequent experience or as out of the ordinary. Rather, she went on to tell me that this sort of experience happened frequently, and she followed up with another story:

This one particular lady, I was leaving the same time she was leaving. Not the same lady who made the comment, a different lady. I was leaving the same time she was leaving, and I noticed she had a Confederate flag in the back of her car, hanging up. So we were talking about this whole race-relationship thing, because you've got to start the conversation, like, what's going on. And she was like, "Yeah, I have the Confederate flag in my car. But to me that means family pride, and that means that's who I am." And being the only nurse of color here at the time, I'm like, "But that means your family owned my family. That's offensive to me." And she looked me right in the face and she said, "Well, how is that my problem?"

Note that this is the same urban, metropolitan hospital, but that this account involves a different white woman colleague. As Mindy notes, interactions like these set the stage for various racial outcomes: how she perceives her workplace, the relationships she

has with colleagues, and how she sees race shaping her work even in a field that is openly seeking to become more racially diverse. As she puts it,

> These are the people I'm working alongside of. I'm a young, new nurse. I'm looking to them—one, to [show] respect and, two, for guidance. And, you know, it's just those deep-seated issues: that they look, they smile, they keep going. But you can't help but think that it has to be the reason that it takes somebody longer to do something for you. Or, when your pump goes off and beeps, that that person, or those people, who walk past your room, go in another room and do the little small things. It's those types of things, [so] that you're like, "Okay. I see what's going on here." It's never anything that's direct, as far as patient care. I've never said that I asked someone for help and they didn't give it to me. It's nothing that I could go and be like, "Oh, they're refusing to help me." But it's those subtle things that they do that make you feel like you're in a racist environment. That's just one example. There's so many of those things.

Mindy pointedly notes that the challenges she describes do not directly impede her ability to give patient care. They do not create a work setting where she cannot get assistance when she needs it. But they do establish a context in which overt racial stereotyping by, and distance from, white coworkers have given her the sense that she works "in a racist environment."

Theresa describes ways that innocuous encounters at work facilitate social exclusion:

> There's always a comment about what is it like to be black: "Well, this doesn't bother you, does it?" or "Does that bother you?" or "Well, you're not like *them*." Those comments. "You're not like *them*." "You're not like the other black people." I'm like, "Yeah, but I am." *[Laughs.]* I am. "No, no, you speak well." Or just having to hear stereotypes—them lumping everybody into one bigger stereotype and saying, "Well, since you don't meet that stereotype, that's why

we like you." But even that didn't mean anything. If you go on social networks, social networks like Facebook and such, you see where they hung out after work and had drinks, or hung out over [at] somebody's house, or whatever. And of course I was never invited to any of that, but I could see the pictures on Facebook.

Theresa's workplace accounts resemble the theory of tokenism and the way that groups in the numerical majority engage in processes that highlight the contrasts between themselves and those in the numerical minority (Kanter 1977). Coworkers repeatedly highlight how she differs from the ways they imagine blacks behave, talk, and interact, but even these perceptions are not enough to stop them from excluding her from social gatherings and outings.

Given these accounts, it is perhaps not surprising that Theresa closed our interview by stating,

> The one thing I can say is that I've always been aware of my color. It's not an occupation where you can just work and think about your job. You're always aware of your color, you're always aware of yourself. As a nurse practitioner, there were times when I first started working in this affluent clinic in the middle of this hoity-toity city where I felt, "Ugh, I have to touch these people in the face. I have to touch to see what's going on with you." And so there were times when I felt very aware of my blackness. I'm touching this white person under their chin, or whatever. I was always cautious to make sure that I wash my hands, [that] they see me washing my hands or sanitizing. Go overboard to make sure that they see that I'm clean. That I'm clean and I'm not one of *them*.

The racial stereotyping she encounters clearly has an impact on the way that Theresa does her job. Nursing, for her, is not just about providing care. It becomes a profession in which she is constantly aware of potential racial stereotypes and works constantly to undermine them.

RACIAL SOLIDARITY ACROSS GENDERED LINES

Again, gender matters in understanding black professionals' racial encounters. In the previous chapter, I noted that since black doctors assert that race affects them more through institutionalized mechanisms, black women doctors' experiences with everyday sexism seem all the more obvious and damaging to their professional careers. To a degree, the opposite is true for black nurses. Given that both black men and black women nurses encounter pervasive, overt racism from their white colleagues, this has the effect of minimizing perceptions of gender differences between black men and black women in this field. Regarding this point, when I asked Janet if she felt there were differences between her own racial experiences and those of her black male counterparts in nursing, she replied,

> I think it's the same for black men in nursing. With white men in nursing, because the nursing unit is full of women, a lot of times the women kind of kiss up to the male nurses or flirt—and I'm sure some of them go way past friendly—but flirt in a friendly way. They will let the male nurses get away with more. And by that, I mean longer breaks or what have you. But a black male nurse? No. I haven't seen that happen. I think they experience types of situations very similar to what I do.

Janet's observations are consistent with studies showing that white men working in female-dominated jobs enjoy social and cultural advantages that are not necessarily extended to their black male colleagues (Williams 1995; Wingfield 2012). Her comments also suggest that, for black women nurses, there is more of a sense that they have a common racial experience that collapses gender differences. This is an important counterpoint to situations described in the previous chapter, where black women

doctors reported greater solidarity with their white women counterparts than with black men physicians. The perception that racist interactions are commonplace among black nurses suggests that in this profession, black men's gendered advantage seems minimal or even nonexistent.

Black men's accounts of their experiences in nursing certainly echo those of their black women coworkers. They, too, experience routine acts of unmistakable racial animus that occur simply as a daily part of their work lives. Steven, an orthopedic nurse, reports, "The nights that I worked in the ICU, the staff wouldn't talk to me the whole night. They would not. The charge nurse gave me my assignment. They had a nurse's station, and in the nurse's station they had a desk there. It was a long desk, and it had the tall chairs and everything. And everybody sat around and did their charting and that type of thing. When I came out to do my charting, they all got up and left. And they would not talk to me the whole night." Steven, like Mindy, works in a racially diverse urban location. However, even in this population, he encounters overt racial hostilities, where white nurses openly exclude him and, in this case, deny him even basic social courtesies.

Kendrick is a physician's assistant but offers a comparable account from his own work:

> One of the surgical assistants actually used a derogatory term that I wasn't familiar with. I don't know if you ever heard this term, but they sometimes will say "Mondays." The guy made a comment, saying he hated Mondays. And me not knowing—it was actually a Monday that day! And my reply was: "Yeah, I don't like Mondays either. The day after the weekend, you're trying to get back into the flow of things with the week and whatnot, and I'm usually tired." And then his response after that—because I wondered, when he said it, why the physician was looking at him strangely.

And I didn't pay any mind to it, especially after I made my comments. But yeah, he said, "Fucking Mondays." Excuse my language, but that's exactly what he said. And I had seen [another colleague] get pissed, and there was another surgical assistant in there, along with my preceptor, who also was a PA [physician's assistant]. And that surgical assistant actually started to cry because, at the time, they understood what he was saying. But I didn't necessarily. But I was starting to catch on to it. And then finally they just said to him, "You know what, [the other assistant] can have this. You leave the OR." And then the physician actually asked me, "Do you understand what he was saying?" I said, "I didn't initially, but I do now."

The term *Mondays* is a pretty common, recently devised derogatory term meaning "black people." The thinking behind this is that no one likes Mondays, hence they are comparable to black people. While accounts this extreme were not commonplace, this was one of a few racial accounts that Kendrick shared that inform his perception of how race affects his work.

Kendrick's account is also significant given the directness of, and the hostility embodied in, the surgical assistant's statements. Essentially, this assistant explicitly used a racial slur in his presence. The assistant was removed from the operating room, and I was unable to determine if there were any other consequences for this behavior. When it happened, Kendrick opted to let it go, deciding that he did not want to be troubled with the issue any further, so he did not know if this surgical assistant was ever reprimanded more formally.

Ultimately, the fact that black men and women nurses are subjected to routine cases of racial harassment means that the sort of interracial, gendered solidarity that black women doctors report is not replicated among their counterparts in nursing. Both black women *and* men in the nursing profession report

being on the receiving end of harsh, demeaning racial comments from their white coworkers. In the face of such consistent hostility, cross-gendered racial ties are much more pronounced. This suggests not just that occupational status matters in shaping black professionals' racial workplace experiences but also that these factors intersect to create gendered outcomes as well.

BEING A "CHANGE AGENT": RACIAL OUTSOURCING AND EQUITY WORK

When I spoke with nurses about the ways, if any, the organizations where they work sought to address these issues, they often reacted with derision. Although there is a general campaign under way to bring more men and racial minority women into nursing, in practice that effort amounts to empty words, according to most of my respondents. Black nurses note that in many cases the organizations where they work have statements on their websites or in their paperwork affirming their commitment to diversity. However, they have not observed any specific interventions or efforts designed to translate this commitment into measurable outcomes. Consequently, black nurses that I interviewed generally feel that diversity initiatives are limited to face-saving statements that are not supported by actions. Steven, an orthopedic nurse, told me,

> When you look at the settings, the more people say that they're diverse, the more they are not diverse. They're diverse on paper because you have to be. But if you're diverse on paper, you ought to be diverse in practice. One cannot go without the other. And when I say that, I say that to mean that when you're stating that you are a diverse program, your nursing staff should reflect that. I know one school where in the fall of 2011, they admitted fifty students into the

nursing program and none of them were African American. And they had two African American professors there in the department of nursing at that school. So that was not very representative of what their mission is. And then they said, "Well, they just didn't qualify." But they can't show you the data to indicate that they didn't qualify, when they admitted four white people who didn't have the GPA to get in.

From Steven's point of view, organizations' statements that they are committed to bringing in more workers of color are just window dressing. He believes that nursing schools and facilities put out statements to indicate that they support diversity while doing nothing to achieve it. This allows them to be diverse "on paper" without allocating resources to changing the structural practices that exclude nurses of color. At the same time, he notes, rules are bent to allow white students who do not meet stated qualifications to access nursing programs.

Janet, a nurse affiliated with a university hospital, also harbors serious doubts about the intent to bring in more nurses of color:

> One of the things that I would like to see—and I'm not sure if this change is coming soon enough—but there are limited numbers of diversity scholarships for more nursing faculty that come from various backgrounds. They're few and far between. And [they are] one of the things that I know a lot of nursing schools *say* they are pushing toward. And a lot of schools in general are diversifying their facult[ies]. That said, I think if that actually does happen, in more of a real way as opposed to kind of on paper as it is happening now, I think that that will really benefit black nursing students. In terms of hiring, from the employer side, I don't know that they're really putting in the effort that's required to try to get more black faculty. I think it's an "on paper" kind of thing.

Janet shares Steven's impression that support for diversity happens on paper but not in practice. Consequently, she has doubts

about whether her colleagues are genuinely committed to diversifying the nursing faculty.

Given black nurses' beliefs that the organizations they work for are insufficiently committed to redressing the systemic and interactional racial biases they encounter, racial outsourcing means that this work shifts to these nurses. Thus, they do equity work when they seek to address these issues themselves. In some cases, nurses aim to enact structural changes similar to those sought by doctors. After seeing many black teen mothers at her hospital, Sela told me, "My ultimate goal is to open up a guidance center for these teen girls, because I just feel like they are really lost. They are just out here, just lost. And so that's my thing. I want to work with that population. To me, it helps to see that, okay, this is what I need to deal with." Sela believes that seeing and working with black teenage girls would give her the tools she needs to change social conditions for that population:

> It really helps me to see them. You try to talk to them, but I find that a lot of them are kind of closed off. They're so used to being judged for being a teen mom that they are closed off a little bit. But some of them will open up to you, and it helps. That helps. But being in the setting, dealing with them, it helps me to see what exactly they need, because some of them are clueless. Clueless about life, let alone motherhood. So they need more, and that's awesome that I get to do that, because that's my ultimate goal.

Sela's goals are similar to those of some of the doctors mentioned in the previous chapter, who respond to racial outsourcing by doing the equity work of trying to address systemic inequalities. Note, however, that Sela's focus is not on addressing the structural problems that create disadvantages for black nurses. Instead, she is more concerned with creating an institutionalized solution

for patients of color, with particular attention to the vulnerable population of black teen mothers.

Another nurse, Katie, argues that working as a staff nurse inhibits her ability to make the major structural changes she wants to bring about in her workplace, but that it cannot stop her from working to improve conditions for her patients. After witnessing some patients being mistreated, she remarked,

> I knew I had to do something, and being a staff nurse was not going to allow me to advance or initiate any real changes. Staff nurses don't have power—or more importantly, they think they don't. Whereas it's been drilled into me: you are a change agent. You should be a change agent. I've seen women of color really mistreated, and in one case I left because of it. But about a year later it came to me. It was like: "No, no, no. You can't be a part of this, and you can't allow it to happen."

Like many other nurses in this study, Katie encounters explicitly racist statements and actions from her white colleagues. She also chafes at the ways educational requirements and scheduling processes work against black nurses. Being a staff nurse offers only limited options for changing these conditions, but redefining herself as a change agent gives her a way to create better opportunities for the women of color she sees at the hospital. When her organization can not create satisfactory change, she turns to equity work as a means of doing so herself.

Steven similarly described how he views his role as a nurse. In light of the fact that he encounters routine racial discrimination, he sees himself as someone who can intervene on patients' behalf to prevent them from having the same troubling experiences: "[Patients] need someone like me who is going to advocate for them when they need someone to be a mouthpiece for them, when they can't speak for themselves. They need someone like

me to do that." While many nurses of all races may view themselves as committed to patient advocacy, this statement takes on a different tenor when it comes from black nurses. A primary reason why black nurses are so dedicated to this sort of work is because they doubt that organizations are prepared for, and capable of, protecting patients of color from the sort of overt racism they encounter. Inasmuch as black nurses' experiences with race at work are significantly shaped by both structural and interpersonal processes, they observe that the organizations in which they work are singularly unable and unwilling to do more than offer platitudes about the importance of diversity. In that context, racial outsourcing means that black nurses take responsibility for fighting their patients' battles and being the "change agents" who help patients "when they can't speak for themselves."

While many black nurses engage in equity work by trying to create better outcomes for their patients, it is noteworthy that very few seek to improve their own workplace conditions. Recall that doctors' equity work involves attending to the structural processes that artificially minimize the numbers of blacks in medicine (e.g., educational disparities, racially exclusive social networks). Helping to open the field to more black physicians could, at minimum, address some of the challenges black doctors encounter as a result of being underrepresented in the profession. However, black nurses' equity work is focused more on improving conditions for patients than for themselves.

This may be a result of nurses' intermediary position in the occupational hierarchy. As the story that opens this chapter illustrates, nursing is a white-collar, professional occupation, but, within the health care hierarchy, nurses are unequivocally in a subordinate position relative to doctors. Thus, while black physicians may perceive that race inhibits their occupational

advancement, their high status may empower them to seek ways to engender beneficial structural changes in their workplaces. Katie's earlier comment that "staff nurses don't have power—or more importantly, they think they don't" could explain why these nurses are more confident about advocating for equitable treatment for their patients than they are about pursuing measures that would fundamentally change their work conditions.

SUMMARY

Black nurses' experiences provide another look at how professionals deal with race in ways that are informed by gendered and occupational status. They also highlight forms of equity work that are different from those undertaken by doctors. Black doctors believe that race mostly affects their work through structural and cultural processes, and black nurses note that these systemic factors create racial inequities for them as well. However, black nurses also report routine expressions of racial hostility that simply are not present in black doctors' accounts of their everyday interactions.

Black nurses' racial encounters are classed and gendered in ways that have important implications for racial solidarity. Whereas black women doctors cite gender as a more significant factor in their work and profess a sense of commonality with white women physicians, heightened racial tensions in nursing mean that black women see black men more as allies than as colleagues who share racial status but have a fundamentally different experience. Indeed, black men nurses do not describe having access to the "glass escalator" that white men ride to higher-status supervisory positions (Wingfield 2009). Thus, this finding suggests that for black professional men, race and occupational

status may intersect to negate or at least minimize some gendered advantages in certain work settings.

Black nurses, like black doctors, believe that the institutions where they work fall far short of addressing the systemic and interactional racism they face. They observe that organizations adopt politically correct language about diversity but do little to make it a reality. As a result, racial outsourcing leads these nurses to do equity work—they take steps to address the racial problems they note in their workplaces. But their occupational status means that they have to take different routes than black doctors. Believing that they have limited agency to change workplace structures, they recast themselves as change agents who can prevent patients from encountering the same sorts of overt racism that characterizes their work.

CHAPTER FOUR

Sticky Floors and Social Tensions

Callie is a black woman who works as a patient care technician on a mother-baby floor in a university hospital on the East Coast. She describes it as a "*very* prestigious hospital," and it is in fact affiliated with one of the best universities in the United States. Most of the patients she sees are white and well off, and though some patients of color are admitted to the hospital, they are in the minority. After working there for several years, Callie, like many other technicians in this study, came to view her work as a stepping-stone in her career progression. She really wanted to move into nursing and was taking classes that would go toward her nursing degree. She saw this as a way to have more of an impact and to focus more fully on patient care.

At the close of our interview, I asked Callie if there was anything else she wanted to add or any points she wanted to emphasize or reiterate. She replied,

> I just want to say that I think most hospitals are really on board
> with the diversity training, and I think that's such a wonderful

thing that these companies are doing. I think that is helping out a lot in the workplace. I think it stands for what we're not tolerating. You've got to respect one another and people's cultures and backgrounds. And I really think that it's a good start. It's a start in the right direction. Like I said, in my hospital, if you get dinged for something—like, if you get in trouble for something like that—they go hard on you. Because it's like, "No, we spent all of this money to send you to diversity training, and you know better."

Callie is one of the few with whom I spoke who offered this enthusiastic perception of how organizational efforts to address racial issues had an impact on her work. And it is worth noting that part of her support for these initiatives stems from her belief that her hospital was not just instituting training but also holding workers accountable. Employees were no longer allowed to use racial slurs or make ethnic jokes without consequences (both of which had happened on her floor in the past). This sort of enforcement led to Callie's positive interpretation of her organization's attempts to acknowledge and resolve racial issues, and contributes to her viewpoint that initiatives like this one create a measurably more equitable workplace.

Most of the other black technicians I interviewed, however, do not share Callie's optimism. Instead, they take a more measured approach that in some ways parallels that of the doctors and nurses discussed in the previous chapters. They observe that race affects their work; and once again, their position in the occupational hierarchy informs how this manifests. Yet for technicians, organizations' racial outsourcing is more likely to include both explicit and implicit mandates. Managers openly task black technicians with additional work not assigned to their white peers. Of their own accord, however, black men technicians also do equity work when they use their cultural capital to

connect with black patients and help them navigate a complex health care system. In contrast, black women technicians constantly tasked with additional work not assigned to their white peers are more likely to pursue other employment options.

TECHNICIANS' RACIAL CHALLENGES: INTERACTIONS WITH PATIENTS AND NURSES

What are the racial realities that black technicians encounter in the workplace? As I have noted, these are largely tied to their position on the occupational ladder. In many health care systems, technicians are charged with basic duties that entail collecting information on which doctors and, to a lesser degree, nurses make their diagnoses. They may be the first workers to see patients and, in that role, can gather vital statistics, ask pertinent questions, and monitor equipment. Nurses may assign routine tasks to techs or delegate assignments to them. Given techs' position, it is perhaps not surprising that when they cite the ways in which race affects their work, they describe interactions with two parties: patients' families and the nurses with whom they work.

Patients' Families

Part of Callie's enthusiasm for her organization's efforts to address racial issues stems from the fact that she has encountered many race-related incidents and offenses during her time at the hospital. Doctors are rarely the source of these tense encounters; in fact, her interactions with doctors are minimal but typically cordial and professional. Patients' families, though, seem to feel completely comfortable treating her with open suspicion, contempt, and hostility. She describes a recent case:

Not too long ago I had this patient, and I came to her room to get her baby. It was time to do the baby vitals, and to do the PKU[1] on the baby, and her family was in there. Her dad was in there. So when I came in, I did her vitals, and then I asked her could I take the baby, and I told her I would be back in about ten minutes. And her dad started going off because she was handing me the baby; and he was like, "What are you doing?" And she was like, "Oh, Dad, please don't start." And he was like, "You don't know who she is. She's just coming in here, grabbing the baby, and she could be anyone. Look at her!" I looked at him, and I'm like, "Well, here's my badge." My badge had flipped around, so I turned it around, and he was like, "That's the problem here. They'll let anyone work here. You people are lucky to be here!"

At this point in the diatribe, Callie simply turned and walked out. She decided she had had enough and did not need to stand there being insulted. She informed the charge nurse on duty—a white woman—of what happened, and that nurse later went into the room to take the new baby for its test. Notably, this patient's father did not object to the charge nurse taking the baby, but he did use the opportunity to follow up with his questions and doubts about Callie's qualifications and right to be there. While this was one of her worst recent encounters, she let me know that this sort of disrespect from patients and/or their families is not at all unusual.

Michael, an emergency room technician, has similar stories. White patients' families react to him, too, with suspicion.

Someone higher up will basically give me an order, and then I'll go in to take care of that patient. Sometimes when I go in—say the patient will need a laceration repair because the kid got bit by a

---

1. *PKU* stands for phenylketonuria, an amino acid disorder. It is standard practice for hospitals to test newborns for this shortly after birth.

dog. And [with] most of those patients, the parents come in. It's a white family. They don't want to see me. They want to see someone else. I explain to them, "I'm a trauma tech. This is what I do." The physician comes in, explains it to them, [that] I'm a trauma tech, this is what I do, and they still demand to see a plastic surgeon. So sometimes we would call the plastic surgeon who was on call. It would take maybe twenty-five minutes to an hour for a real reply. Then they'd reply, and they'd talk to the family on the phone, explaining that this is what I do as well, and sometimes the family will allow me to go ahead and repair, sometimes they would not allow me to repair. They can change their demand, or then we just have to wait until plastics is available to deal with it.

To some degree, it is probably fairly common for technicians of all races to face questions about their work, given that patients generally expect the doctor to be the person who performs important procedures. But from Michael's standpoint, these doubts are more frequently applied to him and other black technicians. As a result, he is simply resigned to the second-guessing that is commonly encountered by many black professionals.

Working in jobs that afford them lower status relative to doctors and nurses means that technicians routinely encounter situations where patients' families openly question them. Their experiences are more similar to those of nurses rather than doctors, in that they are accustomed to being second-guessed in ways that evoke their racial standing and occupational status. However, their position as technicians means that interactions with nurses also are a source of racial tensions.

Interactions with Nurses

Most of the techs interviewed for this study could cite examples of challenging interactions they had with the nurses on their

floors or in the practices where they worked. Fractious relationships with at least some nurses were common. In this context, racial stereotyping, misjudgments, or tensions are more likely to emerge during daily routines of interacting with nurses than with the patients, given the regular and close proximity in which techs and nurses find themselves.

Jackson, the emergency technician, encounters this in pretty typical circumstances. He notes that nurses—and occasionally doctors—assume that he does not understand technical procedures that are actually in line with his job.

> A lot of times, you walk into a situation and they want you to do something, and then you're like, "Oh yeah, not a problem, I know what you're saying, I understand the big words, I've been around the block, I've seen this." But they look at you and they just go, "Oh, he's not going to know that, because he's a person of color and he's just a technician, and he hasn't said that he's going to medical school or anything like that." A lot of times they'll look at us technicians and go, "Oh, are you preparing to go to medical school or whatever?" [He answers,] "No, don't want to do that." But then they start scaling their vocabulary down, and I'm like, "You don't have to scale your vocabulary down. I've been around here long enough to know most of the procedures you guys do, and how you do them, and I could probably assist you with them, if I had to." So yeah, you do get some of that. And then when they realize, "Oh, yeah, you do talk our language, oh, okay"—then it changes, you know? Then they remember your name and everything else. But not until.

Assumed incompetence is one of the issues that most frequently dog black professionals across the industry, workplace, and occupation. Note that while black doctors characterize their racial interactions as generally pleasant and unremarkable, even they observe that they have to combat the presumption that they are not as skilled and capable as their white colleagues.

Jackson's experience as a technician thus has some similarities to what doctors encounter, in that the stereotype of blacks as less qualified than their white counterparts runs constant. There is a notable difference, however. While black doctors describe this as a relatively minor annoyance, akin to background noise, black technicians find these perceptions more commonplace and more likely to come from those in positions of greater authority.

Melvin, a certified medical technician for a nonprofit organization, speaks of similar experiences. Since part of his job entails reaching out to troubled youth, he often works closely with one or two other technicians to pick up and treat kids who will be admitted to the facility where he is employed. But as one of the few black men affiliated with the organization, he often feels closely scrutinized by coworkers and supervisors. In one case, while Melvin was on a call, a young woman asked him if she could contact him directly. He thought she might have been flirting with him, but gave her a business card with his contact information anyway. He paid for this decision later: "My supervisor had come to me and said—because it was a situation where it was a white female and me in the car—so it was like, 'Oh, it's unprofessional to give your number to someone.' But the entire situation, I thought, was kind of colored wrong. I didn't approach the woman, she approached me, just for conversation. And then there was flirting going on, but I was remaining professional up until the point where she said, 'Well, can I contact you directly?' Can you? Yes, you can. Yeah, you can. Why not?"

When he had met the young woman in question, Melvin was at a train station but not with any of the teens connected with his organization. He did not initiate conversation, but simply gave his contact information to a woman who requested it. Thus, from his perspective, his coworker and supervisor cast him—

inaccurately—as the aggressor in this situation. This can be a fraught position for black men, given the ways they are frequently depicted as hypersexual, dangerous, and threatening, particularly to white women. For black men navigating professional workplaces, this perception of black men as sexual predators can inhibit their ability to fit into these settings (Wingfield 2012). Coworkers and supervisors seeing him in this role, then, could have serious consequences for his job.

Amber, a cardiac monitor technician, also describes challenging interactions with the nurses at her facility. Because her work mainly requires "watching heart rhythms," sometimes for up to fifty people at a time, she has minimal engagement with patients. She does, however, routinely interact with nurses, which frequently is trying and exhausting: "The nurses are *always* full throttle. When they answer the phone, I can guarantee you, there's always an attitude. I've been hung up on. You know, they'll be so busy, and they have a five-minute time period where they have to get the patient back on the heart monitor, and if they're not then I automatically have to call their charge nurse. And then that starts more of an attitude and a little bit of animosity." Dealing with nurses is the part of her job that Amber finds the most stressful. In some ways, this is due to several circumstances beyond her control. For one, the hospital established this "five-minute rule" because of an incident in which a patient died when he was not placed back on a monitor within that time frame. Yet despite the fact that this policy is completely out of her control, technicians like Amber can become the object of nurses' frustrations with these guidelines.

As other technicians indicate, nurses' treatment of them can have major employment consequences. Amber told me that she usually could smile in the face of nurses' hostilities and rudeness, but not always.

One time it just turned flat-out ugly. She wrote me up, apparently. She told me that I had an attitude. So I wrote her up because I said she wasn't really complying. She was not answering her phone. So once we write someone up, we put an incident report in—[that] is what the write-ups are called. Then both of our bosses have to review. So they were both investigating, and she ended up looking kind of silly because I had a phone record of calling her and her not answering, where she said she did not receive a call from me and said I had an attitude.

Despite following hospital protocol, Amber was still subject to retaliation after the nurse filed a written complaint against her. It is important to note here that the details of this incident parallel the ways black professionals are likely to experience differential treatment at work that leads to discriminatory outcomes (Roscigno 2007). First, Amber found herself subject to a possible punishment for following written rules. Second, the nurse in question alleged, not that Amber committed concrete errors relating to her job performance, but rather that she "had an attitude." Racial and gendered stereotyping of black women as difficult, rude, and ill-tempered is pervasive and has adverse consequences for them in many workplace settings (Harlow 1997; Kennelly 1999; Kirschenman and Neckerman 1991; Wingfield 2008). Luckily, Amber had a paper trail to support her version of events, but it is worth noting that her account parallels many other accounts of the more covert, subtle forms that modern-day racial discrimination takes in the workplace.

"EXPAND YOUR HORIZONS": OPTIMISTIC VIEWS OF ORGANIZATIONAL INITIATIVES

With the exception of Callie, whose story opens this chapter, most technicians I talked to did not perceive their organizations

as invested in addressing the racial problems that they encounter personally. This is not to say, however, that they find their organizations completely indifferent to these issues. Instead, they believe that the hospitals and health care facilities where they work are in fact attempting to address racial issues—but primarily in ways that would alleviate these challenges only for higher status workers, like doctors and nurses. In other words, technicians observed that their organizations do talk about the importance of making doctors and nurses aware of the need to acknowledge racial issues. The technicians are optimistic that these initiatives will improve the ways practitioners relate to patients, but they do not expect that this improvement will trickle down to themselves in any way.

Amber, the cardiac monitor technician, works at a facility that does require cultural competence trainings for doctors and nurses. She asserts that these efforts have some value even if they do not affect her work directly: "I don't think that it'll impact the work that I do, just because of my minimal patient contact that I have. But as far as everyone else, I do believe that it'll impact them. I'm thinking of the nurses and doctors that are being trained. It might make them go a little bit more of the extra mile to make sure everyone is comforted and kind of on the same level. Of course they always go the extra mile, but now it's just adding another key role." Cultural competence training geared toward doctors and nurses will likely not improve the racial conditions Amber encounters. These efforts probably will not prevent nurses from going "full throttle" or stop them from treating her with disdain or disrespect. But she believes they do have some utility in terms of how they might affect patient outcomes.

Jackson also agrees that this sort of organizational action primarily helps nurses interact with patients outside of their cultural frame of reference. He notes examples of this in which nurses treated patients who had cultural practices very different from their own.

We get a lot of immigrants here from war-torn countries that have been through what we call genital mutilation—especially from some of the countries in Africa, from where their genitals are sewn shut. You know, their husbands sew their genitals—they get their genitals sewn shut until they come back from war or wherever, and then they cut them open. So if you weren't culturally competent, you wouldn't know about that. That [surprise] generally happens more to the nurses, when the nurses—or when the doctors—have to go in and do a Pap smear or just a general pelvic exam. And usually I catch it when they come back into the staff area and they're talking about it. And some of the Caucasian nurses say, "Well, I never heard of that" or "I never saw that." It's out there. And these are nurses that have been around for ten or fifteen years, you know? I go, "No, it's out there, it exists. You just got to expand your horizons."

As Jackson sees it, if organizations enact cultural competency training that makes doctors and nurses more attuned to the minority populations they serve, it can only help provide more nuanced, effective care. But this attentiveness, if directed only to patients, will do little to remedy the racial stereotypes and mistreatment that technicians like him endure from patients, their families, and nurses.

Technicians, then, find that race affects their work in ways determined by their position in the occupational hierarchy. As relatively low-status workers (compared to doctors and nurses), they can be, and frequently are, subject to openly racist statements and

behaviors by patients, their families, and the nurses with whom they most commonly interact. Furthermore, they are well aware that when organizations do focus on workplace racial issues, they do so for higher-status workers like the doctors and nurses who are required to complete cultural competence or diversity training. Yet even though these initiatives overlook their own experiences, technicians are hopeful that they will achieve some success in helping mid- and high-level practitioners better serve patients.

Technicians' belief that diversity work is not tailored to their experiences is consistent with the way this work has developed over time. Many private-sector corporations and industries seek to diversify their high-status workers, with little attention to those in lower-tier jobs. This is, in part, how organizations maintain a "sticky floor" that keeps women workers and men of color trapped closer to the bottom of the organizational structure— the focus on the top levels of organizations means that racial minority men and women of all races stay concentrated at the bottom (Shambaugh 2008). While high-status occupations are frequently the subject of campaigns to create more racial/ethnic and gender diversity, this is rarely the case for occupations at the bottom of the organizational hierarchy (Berrey 2013). What this means is that many of these occupations stay predominantly filled by workers of color, and that there are rarely campaigns to increase diversity among them or address the issues these workers encounter. It may be that in the new economy, higher-status workers seem more important (and thus more likely to be subject to diversity-related campaigns) because of the economic value they can bring to organizations. This focus on high-status, profit-generating workers means that the overt racial incidents that lower-status professional workers encounter can continue to be completely unacknowledged.

RACIAL OUTSOURCING, EQUITY WORK, AND
BLACK TECHNICIANS

Organizations still engage in racial outsourcing in ways that have specific implications for technicians. Again, this is incontrovertibly linked to their position in the organization. As health care has become increasingly commodified, many companies seek to boost profits by cutting labor costs and requiring practitioners to take on larger patient loads. The tendency to compel practitioners to assume heavy loads is exacerbated in some areas by a shortage of mid- and high-level practitioners, particularly nurses and primary care doctors. But it is also important to note that in some cases, this shortage is compounded by the taxing and stressful workplace conditions that practitioners must navigate. Indeed, many of my respondents argue that they do not believe there really is a nursing shortage at all in the areas where they live. They echo nurse Kimberly's blunt assessment that hospitals cannot—and in fact do not really want to—keep workers, because "they can save money when they have one nurse doing the work of two."

Ella, an ob/gyn, agrees with Kimberly's perspective that the oft-lamented labor shortage really has more to do with workplace conditions:

> I don't believe there is a shortage, to be honest with you. I feel like they don't pay people enough. On the labor floor that I'm on, the charge nurse, who should be assigned no patients, will often be assigned three patients. The transport nurse, whose job it is to get on the plane or the helicopter and go out and get patients and bring them back—and who is on for twenty-four hours—when she's not out in the field, they're so short [of] nurses that they make that person take on patients. So, we have a revolving door. I would say that if you paid those people well, and you had them with

safe nursing ratios when they were at work, that I don't think we'd have a shortage.

While the prevailing wisdom is that these labor conditions exist because of the shortage, Ella actually makes the opposite argument—that the tendency to overwork nurses and pay them poorly is what creates the shortage. Nurses' skills allow them to transition out of hospitals and into other settings (e.g., working for insurance companies, in schools, or other locations), and Ella contends that they do so because the lack of labor protections induces burnout and turnover.

Callie, the technician on the mother-baby floor in a major city, has already observed the effects of the labor shortage in her own hospital.

> When I first started in that department, the max, the ratio, was like four to one. So a nurse could have four patients, which really is twice that, because, of course, if you include the baby, you're looking at eight. So the max was four. Which was a lot. But of course, you had the tech there aiding and assisting you with the baby and the mom, too, so it wasn't bad. Well, now they're up to six. Oh, it's crazy. And I'm telling you, [nurses] come for about six months to a year and then they're gone.

Perhaps not surprisingly, Callie sees that having nurses in short supply is stressful. Even with the technicians to help, assigning six patients (and their babies) to one nurse can be exhausting and leave nurses depleted.

Significantly, Callie argues not only that this makes more work for technicians but also that their subordinate position means the nurses are able to take out their stress on them:

> There used to be two techs at night, so one would be for one wing and one would be for the other wing. Now it's just one tech for

the whole floor, so we fill it. We totally catch it. And that's what leads to [high turnover]. Someone's been a tech for ten years or more, and now all of a sudden [nurses act like that tech] doesn't know how to do their job. [That tech] is one person. You could only do so much. And then so much is passed on to you. But if you're not performing the way some nurses feel you should perform, then of course there's your job. There goes your job. So trust me, we're feeling it. It trickles down.

This shortage not only creates more work for Callie but also leaves her at the mercy of frustrated nurses who can call for her termination. Given that hospitals are already laying off workers, a confluence of organizational and occupational dynamics means that the nursing shortage puts Callie and other technicians in a vulnerable position.

Amber, the cardiac monitor technician, also connects the shortage of available nurses to challenging experiences she faces in her work. She mentions that nurses react antagonistically to interruptions (even those that are required by hospital policy): "We're so short-staffed in our hospital. In five minutes they feel like they have a big patient load; they're in the middle of a med pass or doing blood transfusions, and they just feel like, 'Really? Why'd you just call me?' Basically, they take their frustrations out on us. All the time." Understaffing thus has predictable consequences for nurses, in that it makes it harder for them to do their jobs effectively. However, it also has unintended effects for black technicians like Amber, who find themselves subjected to nurses' ire and frustration.

When organizations do not invest in their labor forces and instead expect workers to "do more with less"—and often, *for* less—this situation creates stress, frustration, and anxiety (Cooper 2013; Chen 2015; Silva 2013). But for black technicians, it

also leads to an environment where managers task black workers with additional assignments that are not similarly delegated to their white counterparts. In this context, racial outsourcing occurs when managers openly require black technicians to do certain types of labor that white technicians are permitted to avoid.

Johnnetta is a technician on a mother-baby floor at a midwestern university hospital. She agrees that "the short staff makes it busier. It makes it more chaotic, more hectic. It's just busy and stressful because you're ripping and running, and nobody knows which way you're—it's just stressful. It's a stressful situation." But she also observes that one way her hospital deals with the nursing shortage is for managers to assign black technicians additional work that falls outside the bounds of their job description.

> They will be like, "Hey, do this, do this." They will ask people of my race to do more stuff versus, you know, white people. Like turning over rooms or cleaning a room or taking a patient somewhere, things like that. If we're in the OR all day, that's what we [are supposed to] do within the OR. And then the patient care techs are supposed to clean the rooms and everything. So, if we come out of the OR, we're not supposed to do the rooms. But sometimes you have management that'll be like, "Hey, go do the rooms." And that's not how it's supposed to work. But they do it anyway.

Johnnetta was not thrilled with these extra assignments, and her displeasure is compounded by her observation that they seem to be delegated only to black technicians. Her assessment suggests that as health care organizations prioritize free-market outcomes and generating profits, cutting labor not only leaves workers economically insecure but also gives organizations another means of engaging in racial outsourcing. Yet in this case, managers explicitly task black employees with a different sort of equity work,

requiring technicians to do the physical labor of making the facility ready for patients (even though this is outside the bounds of their job descriptions). Notably, this sort of overt racial outsourcing is more prevalent among professionals at the lower end of the occupational tier (technicians rather than doctors), who do not enjoy the protection and insulation of high-status work.

Michael is a military veteran in his fifties who has worked as an emergency technician for nearly two decades. He shares a story that is somewhat similar to Johnnetta's, noting that, given his position in the health care hierarchy, nurses with less experience are able to pass undesirable tasks on to him.

> When I look at the people who actually delegate more work to me, I look at it from the perspective of: the physician will assign the work, and that's within the scope of practice. The nurse will delegate work to me, as well as assign the work. And the people who are within this nursing field, the bulk of them who I deal with, are white. So, when I look, I look at the delegation of duties, as opposed to the assigning of duties. If it's my assignment, I don't care who you are, okay? But when it comes to delegating the work, it comes to: this is what I don't want to do, so I'm gonna let you do it, have you do it. And that's, for me, where the issues really come into play.

Michael feels that nurses, who are disproportionately white, take undue liberties in delegating work to black technicians. Additionally, short-staffing makes them more likely to leave technicians to do work alone, even if the task at hand requires more than one person. He gives the example of having to catheterize a child to make this point:

> I know it's not a one-man procedure. It's a two-person job. Either I'm going to have to get you, the parent, to help hold your child while I catheterize her to get the urine, or I'm going to have to go back and get assistance from someone else. And when I go back to

get the assistance from someone else, the nurses are never available to help me, because they talk about the stuff they need to do outside of that. Now, I'm getting a technician to come help me. So, another black person is going to come help me. Whereas the nursing staff, the majority of nurses, are white. They're delegating the tasks. Now, what happens when, say, I'm tied up, repairing a laceration, so I can't do the catheterization of the patient? Now, the nurses have to do it themselves. Well, two of them will go in and do it together. So they automatically go in as a couple, when doing a two-person procedure, whereas when they delegate it to a tech, they send you in alone.

At Michael's hospital, as at Johnnetta's, nurses are in short supply. From Michael's standpoint, they take this as an opportunity to delegate more work to technicians. However, they do so in ways that compromise patient care and technicians' ability to work effectively. He contends that nurses do not do this to each other, and that they make sure they give each other the necessary support. Once again, racial outsourcing happens when white professionals can allocate extra, racialized assignments to black workers, who do not share the same status and protections.

OPTING OUT VERSUS DOUBLING DOWN: GENDER DIFFERENCES AMONG TECHNICIANS

Black women technicians discussed in this study have responded to this form of racial outsourcing by seeking other work. If and when they deem the demands on them, as a result of equity work, too great, black women technicians seem comfortable pursuing other options. In some cases, this means transferring laterally out of one job into another that they hope will provide some relief from racial outsourcing in the form of additional, racialized labor. Amber informs me that she quit a previous job

for exactly this reason: "These patients were older. Their minds were still back in the day, like when everyone was segregated and all that. So for many of them I became 'that colored girl.' They would call me that. Or they would think I was their house-maid, because that's where their mind would be. They would see my skin color, and that's what they would think."

Amber reports that the management at this previous job indulged this mind-set to the point of encouraging her to comply with patients' demands that she cook their meals, run errands, and complete other tasks well outside of the bounds of her job description. This sort of additional service work was simply too much, and she quit. She adds,

> The director of nurses, a lot of times she would pull [aside] more seasoned people and ask what can she do, how can she help. And they'd pull [aside] people who had been there for a long time, and they would say, "We don't want to lose y'all. Can y'all tell us what it is—like, why is our turnover rate so high?" They would pull me [aside] oftentimes, because I would just tell them like it is. I'd be like, "Well, this is why." And they would just appreciate my feed-back. It didn't really help as far as keeping people, but they asked a lot of times for my feedback.

Faced with management that seemed unwilling or unable to make the concrete changes that would have stopped this sort of racial outsourcing, Amber simply left this job as soon as she was financially able to do so. This required working two jobs simul-taneously for a while—she started her current job while still employed at this one—but once she was hired full time, she was able to leave this position for good.

Johnnetta, the surgical technician, intends to leave her posi-tion, too, and try to move into nursing: "I am interested in nurs-ing. I am, but I haven't started school yet. I'm still trying to figure

out what schools I want to go to and stuff like that. Right now I don't have time; I have too much going on. But I really want to start, hopefully sometime next year." Johnnetta actually pursued nursing school in her twenties, but she recalls "partying too much" and ultimately leaving before completing her degree. But from her viewpoint as a technician, nurses have more autonomy and are better paid. Thus, moving into that line of work offers a route away from the sort of racial outsourcing technicians typically encounter.

The accounts here provide an important counterpoint to the concept of "opting out." Usually used to refer to upper-class, well-educated women who leave the workforce to become full-time caregivers, this terminology generally highlights the limited occupational opportunities, workplace sexism, and cultural expectations that push some women towards full-time parenthood over paid work (Stone 2007). Black women technicians' experiences, however, indicate that the process of opting out occurs differently depending on the women in question. These women also confront institutional and organizational challenges that make their jobs unsustainable. It is simply that these obstacles are constructed by gender, race, and class in ways that make their workplaces problematic and leaving the labor force unrealistic. The technicians I spoke with did not have the economic security necessary to opt out of the labor force entirely, but they certainly could and did opt out of specific jobs if racial outsourcing made their working conditions too unpleasant.

Black men technicians are less likely to mention leaving for other positions. Like black women, they encounter a more formally institutionalized type of racial outsourcing that involves being tasked with assignments that are outside the bounds of their job descriptions and which seem to be relegated only to

black workers. However, they also describe doing equity work that is not specifically required by their institutions, but which still helps improve their organizations' ability to connect with minority communities. In this way, the equity work they do is shaped by both extrinsic and intrinsic motivation.

While black women technicians talk of quitting when racial outsourcing becomes too much, racial outsourcing for black men technicians means that they do equity work by going out of their way to assist minority patients. Many black men technicians contend that one of the uncommon skill sets that they bring to their work is their ability to connect with and understand patients of color. Being able to communicate with black patients who do not have much exposure to the health care system, or who are uncomfortable being treated by predominantly white doctors and nurses, is a skill that enables technicians like Jackson to relate to and understand patients in critical ways. As he puts it,

> A lot of times it's just with terminology. We work predominantly in the inner city. The level-one trauma center, we're predominantly in the inner city, and a lot of the folks that staff the place live further out, in second- and third- and fourth-tier suburbs, and even further out, you know? So there's a bigger tendency for the cases that do present, they tend to show up using a lot more street slang. The verbiage is more, I would say, inner-city geared, and things like that. And a lot of times the nurses don't pick up on it, and I just go, "Oh no, he meant that, but he said that, you know?"

Understanding patients' language and slang could in fact be considered a form of cultural capital that black technicians bring to their work (Bourdieu 1986). This particular skill benefits them when it allows them to connect with patients and improve their treatment. However, in the context of a short-staffed hospital

setting with fewer nurses and doctors available than needed, this takes on a different meaning. Jackson's ability to relate to black patients means that one consequence of the high turnover and short supply of practitioners is that he ultimately finds himself doing more of this type of work. He cites one of the challenges of his work: "Folks that got newly acquired health care, they don't know how to use the system. So we spend a fair amount of time having to educate them on how to use the system—you know, how to navigate it." When this is coupled with the fact that technicians like Jackson are also serving as intermediaries between black patients and white practitioners, who may be culturally unfamiliar to each other, then having more work because of a shortage of nurses and doctors takes on a heightened racial dimension.

Melvin, the technician working for the nonprofit organization, also mentions how cultural capital can help him relate to patients better than some of his white colleagues: "What's the best way to put it? ... There are cultural differences that definitely come up in the professional environment. So we work in tandem—usually it'll be two of us going to pick up a child in a company vehicle. So that can be—not awkward, but you definitely notice differences in communication when it's me or my white female colleague going to pick up a fifteen-year-old black inner-city youth." Again, keep in mind that in the context of an environment where technicians are already doing more work to compensate for the shortage of doctors and nurses, this particular equity work takes on greater significance. Not only do black technicians have to step up to help fill in the gap this labor shortage causes, but also racial outsourcing means they are doing equity work in the form of additional unseen labor that is intended to make black patients feel more comfortable.

A presumed familiarity with black patients is not isolated to workers at this level of the occupational hierarchy. As we will see in the next chapter, black doctors and nurses also feel a sense of familiarity with and connection to the black patients that they treat. This sense of connectedness drives arguments for diversity in health care, as advocates of this "racial realism" perspective suggest that black practitioners' commitment to communities of color can make a measurable difference in reducing health disparities (Skrentny 2014). The logic is that black practitioners are much more likely than their white counterparts to want to practice in predominantly black areas that may be medically underserved; thus, it is a legitimate, compelling interest to try to attract more blacks into medicine and nursing. What I show here, however, is that as organizations do less and less to address internal racial issues or connect with communities of color, their reliance on black men technicians to fill this gap becomes a form of racial outsourcing. Organizations, then, do not have to establish strict guidelines or structures to become more accessible to minority communities, because they have black men who, apart from meeting their stated job requirements, not only perform equity work when they leverage their cultural capital but also do this work for free.

SUMMARY

For black technicians, race affects their work and shapes their experiences with racial outsourcing and equity work in distinct ways. Lacking the status and protections that mid- and high-level providers enjoy, black technicians describe a work environment where explicitly racist sentiments come not just from patients' families but also from the nurses who are situated above

them in the organizational hierarchy. Unlike doctors, who argue that they have only occasional experiences with overtly racist behavior, technicians are much more akin to nurses in their descriptions of racial stereotyping as a common feature of their everyday interactions. Yet, with the exception of a few technicians who note that understaffing contributes to the racial differences in allocating workloads and responsibilities, technicians rarely highlight structural processes that perpetuate racial inequities at work. Thus their assessments of race in the workplace do not completely parallel those of nurses, who note that both structural and interpersonal dynamics disadvantage blacks in that profession.

Perhaps as a result of the microaggressions (and macroaggressions) they encounter, technicians are more hopeful than other workers that organizational attempts to address racial issues and tensions will at least help doctors and nurses be more attuned to their patients of color. They do not expect these attempts to change their own racial experiences, but believe these organizational efforts have merit. Ironically, of the three categories of workers studied for this book, technicians are the ones who have the least-direct exposure to diversity initiatives in the settings where they work; yet they are the ones who are most optimistic that these efforts, broadly speaking, can engender substantive change. These findings might suggest that among various categories of black professionals, diversity policies may be best received by those with the most distance from them.

Black technicians' position at work also plays an important role in shaping the equity work that they do. While racial outsourcing both compels doctors to do the equity work of seeking structural solutions and drives nurses to become change agents, when it comes to technicians this process occurs differently.

In an environment where organizations routinely cut labor costs but still attempt to function efficiently, managers overtly engage in racial outsourcing when they direct black technicians to do equity work in the form of tasks and assignments that fall outside the bounds of their job descriptions. Equity work also happens when, in response to this short-staffing, black men technicians draw on their cultural capital to encourage and assist black patients who are unfamiliar with or intimidated by navigating the complicated terrain of health care. Black women technicians, however, respond to racial outsourcing by seeking other employment options or, in other cases, changing careers entirely.

The differences between black men and black women technicians highlight important considerations for how race, gender, and occupational status intersect to create varied outcomes. It is telling that black women technicians, unlike black men, do not report that racial outsourcing compels them to do equity work in the form of utilizing cultural capital in order to assist patients of color. This may be a function of the areas where black women techs in this study were situated. For instance, Johnnetta, as a surgical technician, largely assists doctors with surgeries and does not interact with patients frequently, since they are under anesthesia during this process. But these findings complicate some of the gendered assumptions about women's propensity for caring, nurturing behavior and their willingness to assist others. Black women technicians are more likely to take stock of their occupational options and pursue other choices rather than simply accept racial outsourcing and the attendant equity work it creates. Black men do not mention quitting, but do speak with some satisfaction about the ways cultural capital aids their ability to do their jobs effectively. Thus it may be that, for black men, work is still linked to self-identity (and remains enough of

an economic necessity), so that even the process of racial outsourcing becomes an opportunity to prove their effectiveness and skill at work; whereas for black women, explicit forms of racial outsourcing are sufficient justification to pursue work elsewhere under what they hope will be better conditions.

CHAPTER FIVE

It's Not *Grey's Anatomy*

Of all the health care workers I interviewed for this project, perhaps none spoke as passionately about their commitment to working in the public sector as Dr. Randy Goodwin. While Randy attended a private, highly selective, historically black college, after graduating he went on to a public medical school in his home state. Since then he has been affiliated only with public medical facilities that serve predominantly poor black and Latino communities. This is not an accident. For Randy, providing high-quality care to poor minority patients is about making a small step toward broader, more comprehensive social change. But it also reflects his way of connecting his own background and personal story to the professional route he has chosen.

During one of my visits to City Hospital, Randy and I stepped outside to get some fresh air and decompress while he was on break. Standing under the awning and shading our eyes from the bright sun, we looked around the neighborhood surrounding the hospital. Randy sighed as he noted the abundance of fast food restaurants across the street, and explained that it made it

hard to promote healthy eating when patients were surrounded by cheap, unhealthy food options. Then he pointed to a squat brick building situated a few streets over.

"That's where I went to elementary school," he said. "I've actually been back over there to talk to the kids. And sometimes I'll see kids who are in school there now in the hospital. It happens. I remember once I gave a young lady my business card. You know, taking care of one of her relatives, we got to chatting, she said something about she wanted to be a doctor or whatever. I'm like, 'What school did you go to?' 'Oh, I go to such and such high school.' I'm like, 'Wow, that's where I went. You know Ms. So and So?' It's just a real connection."

For many black health care workers, especially those in the public sector, it is clear that the hospitals where they work are inextricably linked to the often black, frequently urban communities in which they are located. It is not uncommon for them to treat people from these neighborhoods, or uncommon to hear black doctors and nurses emphasize this as an important facet of their work. But the work black professionals do in public facilities also offers an additional example of racial outsourcing, of how organizations rely on black employees' equity work to appeal to, service, and interact with black patients in ways that cut across occupational lines. Black practitioners' labor in the public sector is a critical form of equity work that allows these facilities to serve patients even while dealing with declining resources.

PUBLIC-SECTOR PERCEPTIONS

As a result of decades of budget cuts, privatization, and dwindling tax revenues, the public sector is struggling (Thistle 2006; Wilson, Roscigno, and Huffman 2013). Most black health care

workers are well aware of the challenges inherent in working under these circumstances. Bonita, a pediatrician, has had experience in both public and private facilities. At the time of our interview, she was employed in a private practice. She found the public sector too demanding:

> When you're in the hospital, you work twelve-hour shifts. Sometimes seven days in a row, depending on how you worked it. But you do them back to back, and it just got to be a lot. And at the time I had just gotten pregnant, and I was like, "Oh yeah, I can't be here for twelve hours." And in the morning, overnight, I was there, and it started to be too much. So I wanted a regular schedule, I wanted the basics, the nine-to-five—and then I do my notes; then I come out. That's it. It was the time constraint, it was stressful.... I was in a rural area in North Carolina. We were seeing a lot of people who didn't have insurance, who would come into the hospital, and if they had another doctor they probably wouldn't be in the state. Not taking care of themselves. And they end up in the emergency room with a whole host of issues. And so I felt the need to go back to [private practice].

From Bonita's perspective, work in the public sector comes with multiple challenges that she was able to avoid by joining a private practice. She identifies the unrelenting hours and exhausting demands of caring for patients with irregular health care as key components of public-sector work.

Emma, a nurse, cites a litany of issues that arise from working in a public hospital owing to the budgetary constraints that are always present.

> I think they're even cutting more of the budget, to where you're not allowed to get as much overtime as you once were. The way my floor works, you can sign up for being on call if you're needed on that particular shift that you signed up for. And when you get called into on-call, that's double pay. That's [additional pay] for you. But it is now to a point where the management will search for another

nurse that may be available on another floor, to cut costs. And then if they're not available, they'll go to the pool that we have, because they don't have to pay them as much. Then they'll go there. And if they can't get someone there, then they'll call in a PRN nurse,[1] because, again, even though their rate is higher, they don't have to pay them as much because it's not double time. And then you're the last resort, but you're required to sign up for on-call for a certain amount of hours per pay period. But there's no guarantee that you will get on-call, because they will try to get anybody else before they call you in, due to money issues. *[Sighs.]* Budgets.

Emma went on to list other issues associated with the funding challenges that accompany work in a public hospital. These include pressures to clock out on time regardless of patient needs, abrupt scheduling changes that affect nurses' work hours, and the push to have each nurse care for more patients per shift to avoid having to hire more staff. Given the ways in which public hospitals are frequently underfunded, Emma's frustrations are likely representative of many of the challenges associated with this work.

Kent, another nurse at a publicly funded urban hospital, also compares the public and private sectors. He told me, "The under-resourcing here is so frustrating. I work at [County] Hospital too, and it's so different. Here, the resources aren't there. City hospitals don't have a good legal team; patients assume they'll get bad treatment *here.* Other hospitals silence workers with gag orders so the news doesn't get out. [Workers] don't talk, so [people] have a better perception [of the hospital]. People come here expecting the worst, and because it's under-resourced, what they get is not ideal. Here, three nurses may do the job of six. I make $120,000 [at County]. I make $84,000 here." For Kent, there are concrete

---

1. *PRN* stands for *pro re nata* and indicates a nurse who is doing short-term or contract work rather than full-time work.

financial differences between his job at the privately managed County Hospital and his work at City Hospital. He also argues that, at City Hospital, people come in with lower expectations, which the hospital, with fewer resources, is less able to offset.

Against this backdrop, black health care workers occupy a somewhat unique position among black public-sector professionals. Despite the tightening budgets, economic constraints, and other challenges and issues associated with public-sector work, many black health care workers still make a conscious choice to pursue employment here. Nurses like Sela stay for the racial diversity and the ability to interact with a wide variety of people: "Personally, for me, I like the public [sector] more so. I guess because it's more relatable. But what I don't like is how it's run. That's the thing. I don't like how it seems to be a difference in treatment, but I like the diversity of it. I do. We get Hispanic, black, Asian—I see more of that. We do get white patients. They are the minority, but I get to see some of everything; whereas at my old job I rarely saw even Hispanics. Even with that, it was like—white. And that was it." The old job Sela references was at a private facility in a large midwestern city, where most of her coworkers and patients were white. Based on her experience, the multicultural setting she seeks cannot be replicated in the private sector. Working in the public sector gives her the opportunity she prefers, even if she must also contend with the frustration of seeing patients being treated differently.

For health care workers like Darius, the public sector offers a way to give back. Darius, a physician's assistant, works at a university with a top physician's assistant program. But he also does community service hours, providing health care to poor populations. He speaks about the importance of doing work in the health care industry because of the possibilities it offers to serve

black communities: "My passion has always been free care. I grew up poor. I got health care through Medicaid and always wanted to go back to my community and give back. I never forgot where I came from. My family is still there. So I always wanted to serve the poor." For Darius, the ability to do work that specifically targets underserved poor, predominantly black populations is a driving force in his career.

Technicians also discuss wanting to give back and find opportunities to help those in need. Callie, a patient care tech on a mother-baby floor, is in fact pursuing options that will help her do this more effectively than tech work can allow:

> My whole goal is to work my way up to possibly being a director or even higher, and the reason why I say that is because I would love to push for more—I guess you can call it pro bono? But more free care. Like, for instance, my hospital, they have funds where they cover patients that are having financial troubles and stuff. But the thing is, I would love to be the person, to be the advocate to try to find more programs and bring them to our particular hospital or whatever hospital where I'm working. That way we can help more people. There's money out there. There's funding out there. We just have to find it. We just have to get that. We have to find it and help people.

Technical work is not going to allow Callie to achieve her ambitious goals, but her account shows that among black workers, this desire to give back and help others transcends occupational category.

Steven, a nurse, shares a similar viewpoint with me. He, too, has had experience working in private facilities, and says,

> It was very easy [working in private settings]. *[Laughs.]* Because, like I said, they were all about the almighty dollar. Most of my career has been in public hospitals like Charity, and I've done some PRN work at University Hospital, where the standard is,

they raise the bar, keep it up there, and they keep raising it. So I could very easily be a nurse and work there and actually fit into the culture. Because it's a different culture in every setting, and you have to be able to embrace that culture, number one. And you have to be able to engage yourself in the culture. But I choose to stay in public facilities because I felt like that's where the greatest need is.

Steven offers some important framing here that situates his decision to stay in public-sector work. He notes that he can acclimate to the culture at University Hospital—an elite, predominantly white institution—and has experience there, and would be a cultural and professional fit should he seek employment there. But for Steven, other factors are more significant. It is more important for him to use his nursing training to work in a public setting that treats mostly poor and uninsured patients of color, so that he can help them get the best care possible.

This perspective is present among black doctors as well. Joel, an emergency room doctor at a public hospital, compares the challenges faced by the staff there to what he believes are easier experiences at private, more affluent hospitals:

There are places where private emergency departments can get MRIs that aren't for emergency reasons. For instance, spinal injuries. Someone with knee pain, or appendicitis, a kid who you don't want to expose to radiation. We can get other scans involved, but if the hospital had the resources like Midtown Hospital in the city, we could get more staff support, CAT scans, etc. We could better serve patients. City Hospital is city funded, so we feel the effects on both sides. But at the end of the day, I'm living my dream, I feel blessed and positive. Growing as a leader, I want to be someone who does so much for the community. At the end of the day, as much as we complain, we have the best job in the world. The challenges we face are just opportunities to grow.

Joel is frustrated by the lack of resources available to him at City Hospital, but characterizes this as a price to pay in order to do the bigger, more important work of caring for poorer residents. Randy, whose story opens this chapter, speaks of this benefit eloquently and at great length. Here he discusses how his background and his commitment to caring for disadvantaged populations make the public sector the best choice for him:

> When I was in medical school, I spent a lot of my time at County Medical Center. I happened to go to General County for residency. I'm at City Hospital, where I work right now. So I've always kind of had this affinity to working in the public sector, because a lot of my family members have gone to public hospitals, and so there's a sense of familiarity. My neighbors go to public hospitals. Public hospitals tend to be your level-one trauma centers, and so that's where you see a lot of the high-end traumas come in through the emergency department. But I did know that early on—it wasn't like I just decided to take a rotation at the public hospitals early on. It's where I was assigned to. And so I always noticed a big difference in how I felt and how patients were taken care of in the public hospitals, compared to in some of the private hospitals, especially with people who didn't have those same resources. In private hospitals, you have a homeless person that comes in, or if you've got somebody that doesn't have any money, the care is limited, and how people treat them is pretty variable. And the public hospital staff— I don't have to worry about that. I know they're going to get good care, and I know we're not going to turn somebody away, regardless of their ability to pay or their socioeconomic status. So I've always kind of gravitated toward that environment.

Randy's statements underscore the link between this commitment to caring and wanting to serve the black community, and the appeal of public care facilities. Note that he has spent virtually all of his training period and career working in publicly funded

hospitals, all of which wrestle with major funding and equipment shortages. But for Randy, this is the only way to give care to members of his community and the people with whom he identifies.

To be clear, there is a racial dynamic to this commitment as well. Practitioners talk about the importance of caring for the poor, but they are by no means oblivious to the fact that a disproportionate number of poor, uninsured patients are black. Alexandria, a geneticist, told me,

> In the near future I plan to move into a realm where I'm more engaged in research and working more closely with medically underserved minority populations and helping to educate them about the resources so that they can make informed decisions. That's where my passion lies, and I think a lot of it has to do with my upbringing and my graduate school training. I trained at Hampton University, where our mission is to be of service to our surrounding community. So I would really feel as though everything I did was in vain if I did not go back to helping the populations that are near and dear to my heart and the populations that helped get me through my graduate program. That interest has always been there.

For Alexandria, this racialized concern for black communities is the primary force that drives her ambitions. This specifically race-conscious approach to medicine means that, for her, even a highly accomplished career would seem less successful if it did not also include a way of reaching out to and serving black communities.

Mindy, another nurse, also talks about specifically choosing the public sector in order to serve communities of color: "[Blacks] are culturally a higher percentage of the poor, and so I just feel I take personal responsibility in making a difference. I'm really focusing on the culture that needs it the most and figuring out ways to reach them. And I look at this opportunity [to be a nurse

practitioner], and it's really about being able to bridge the gap."
This focus on serving poor black patients shapes her occupational
goals and makes the public sector worth the financial trade-off.

> I would love to work at a [federally qualified health center] or
> something like that. I do still want to provide care for low-income
> women, just because I feel that being who I am, being—I was tell-
> ing you about the smile that I get when I walk into a black patient's
> room and they see me; and they can identify with me and they
> trust me. I feel that sometimes low-income women may get the
> short end of the stick, or [that] from life experiences, they don't
> trust a white provider as much, or [they] feel like the system has
> done them wrong for whatever reason. And that can get in the way
> of them being as healthy as they can be. So it's only fair that they
> have access to providers that they can trust, that they feel they can
> talk to, that will listen to them. Private sector does pay better, but
> the private sector comes with its own issues. You get entitled peo-
> ple and folks who think that just because they say so, it is so. But
> yeah, I'll probably stay in public sector.

Mindy is unequivocal about the fact that a key part of her
work involves being a deterrent to the kind of adverse experiences many low-income women, particularly women of color,
encounter in the health care system. It is important to her to be
a corrective to the ways that poor minority women have been
exploited through the health care industry or other institutions.
She also recognizes that her very presence as a caregiver of
color not only can help her reach these patients but also can possibly improve their health outcomes. As a result, she is willing to
forgo the greater financial rewards present in the private sector
so that she can make a more personal difference in public health
care facilities.

This desire to give back to black communities crosses gendered and occupational lines. Doctors, nurses, and physician's

assistants all speak of wanting to help members of a black community that, by and large, has been underserved and subject to poor medical care and health outcomes. This commitment to the public-sector challenges some of the prevailing ideas that this arena is no longer a space where blacks can find stable, rewarding work. While it is true that public-sector employment is down, and that blacks are disproportionately affected by its growing privatization, it nonetheless remains a draw for blacks seeking professional work (Greenstone and Looney 2012; Laird 2017; Wilson, Roscigno, and Huffman 2013). Indeed, data from the 2015 American Community Survey show that blacks comprise 18 percent of those working in the public sector (*African-American Labor Force in the Recovery* 2012). They thus form an indispensable part of what remains of the public-sector workforce.

In this context, then, working in the public sector helps fulfill a noneconomic, more sociocultural mission. Yet the shrinking resources allocated to the public sector means that these institutions are increasingly reliant on black professionals to keep running. This puts black health care workers in a position where, when they are driven by the desire to provide better care to poor black communities, their very presence and willingness to work in the public sector becomes a form of equity work. Organizations can capitalize on black professionals' firm commitment to the public sector and the black patients who rely on it for care, making black professionals' labor a form of equity work that allows the public sector to function in spite of dwindling resources and support.

EQUITY WORK IN THE PUBLIC SECTOR

While they are well aware of the costs and limitations of working in the public sector, black health care workers generally

seem comfortable with the trade-off they are making. It is important enough to them to provide care for black communities that they make peace with the fact that this means sacrificing financial rewards (to a degree). However, they are still aware that the organizations where they work rely heavily on them to provide respectful, high-quality care to communities of color. Many public-sector hospitals in particular describe themselves as focused on and fiercely dedicated to meeting this community's health care needs. But even as organizations bill themselves as institutions devoted to providing high-quality care to diverse populations, black health care workers note that they often have to be the ones who offer this care in an efficient, personable manner. This is particularly evident as black health care workers compare their own treatment of black, often poor patients to the ways their white colleagues interact with this population.

Why Equity Work Matters: Stereotypes and Patient
Care in Public Facilities

Because of their shared racial status and commitment to the public sector, black health care workers usually feel a sense of kinship and solidarity with black patients. This does not appear to be true for their white peers. To the same degree that black health care workers feel personally obligated to treat black patients with kindness and respect, they note that many of their white coworkers apply racial stereotypes to the patients they serve. Given black health care professionals' commitment to caring for these populations (even at their own financial expense), they find that seeing white coworkers dismiss or shame black patients becomes extremely frustrating. It also illuminates the ways racial outsourcing requires black professionals to do the equity work of assuming an outsize

role helping organizations meet their stated goal of providing care for racially diverse populations.

In many cases, equity work is done subtly, without a lot of fanfare. Ella, the obstetrician/gynecologist, for instance, makes it a point to stand close to and even touch some of her patients as she completes her rounds at the hospital. She is especially likely to do this for patients whom she expects will not receive the same level of care and concern from her white colleagues. In one case, we had to deliver some very bad news to a young black woman patient. Before going in, Ella explained the patient's history to me, and said, "She's going to take this hard. It's not an easy situation to be in, and there's really no right answer as to what she should do." When we entered the room, Ella greeted her patient warmly, stood next to her bed while explaining the situation, and touched her arm reassuringly as she shared what would need to happen next.

At the end of that day, I talked with Ella a little bit more about this patient. When I asked her if she thought her manner was common among other physicians, she laughed outright and replied, "Girl, please." Comparing her own approach to patients to her colleagues' approach, Ella notes how her own attitude about treating patients evolved when she transferred to a hospital that served a poorer population.

> In my old practice, I served patients who are on Medicaid, but a lot of my patients were really kind of middle-class or affluent suburban patients. And so, if you were late, they penalized you. Right, I could still see you, but you were going to be seen after every other single on-time patient before you.
>
> Here, I don't do that anymore. Patients sometimes have to catch two buses to get to me, or they have to get their kid to school and then get here. If they don't have transportation, they got a ride. I mean, the social situations are so complex that I will see you

whenever you get there, because I realize that the average patient goes through a lot.

Yet Ella continues on to point out that most of her colleagues do not share this sentiment about patient interactions. Instead, they are likely to assume ill intent:

> A lot of [my coworkers] don't see that, and they're just like, "These patients are always late. They have no respect for time." Or, we admit patients who are pregnant, a lot of times not because admission changes anything but because they are so high risk that a bad thing could happen at any moment and we just want to be there to catch it. But for the young mom who is single and has five kids, who's going to take care of her kids? Yet, when she decides to leave, we make her sign paperwork that says she's leaving against medical advice. And it's, "I can't believe this woman would go home with this condition, and she is willing to kill her baby. And I advised her that all these bad things could happen, including death." All true. But, I mean, we'd also say she was a bad person if her five kids who are under the age of ten are at home by themselves. So, [it's easy for them to] forget the human aspect and the complex situations that our patients have and just operate as if our patients have the same lives we do. Which is unfair.

While Ella takes pains to be cognizant of the social context in which her patients make decisions about health care, compliance, and treatment, her observations indicate that her coworkers do not necessarily make such efforts as commonly as she does. Her perception is borne out by some interactions I witnessed between white practitioners and patients of color. During another visit to her hospital, I was heading back to the room where doctors and nurses convened for their morning meetings when I heard someone speaking loudly. I noted, farther down the hall, a young white woman nurse in conversation with an older black male patient who appeared to be in his seventies. I hesitated long

enough to discern that the gist of the conversation involved the nurse's frustration with the patient for failing to follow her medical advice. Before I ducked into the central room, I overheard her angrily ask, "Why are you standing?! I have told you so many times that standing is *not* good for your lungs or your abdominal muscles! You *do not listen!*" The patient simply hung his head and bore this scolding silently.

I did not say anything to Ella or any of the other doctors about what I overheard, but I did note that the tone and approach this nurse used was starkly different from the ways I heard black practitioners talk to black patients. To be sure, black health care workers sometimes expressed frustration with the patients they treated. They noted that some patients use the ER for routine care rather than emergencies, or they described feelings of irritation with patients who ignore their professional advice and refuse to vaccinate their children. However, I never heard black practitioners express these feelings directly to patients. They were exacting and careful about treating all patients, but particularly black poor ones, with the utmost respect, and often did so in ways that offered a sharp contrast to the interactions I witnessed between white practitioners and black patients in public care facilities.

Akinyele, the anesthesiologist mentioned earlier, argues that some of these differences are rooted in white practitioners' racial stereotypes of poor black patients:

> Here's the deal on the care. When a patient walks through the door, they're there for help. Now, there are people who do take advantage. Or attempt to take advantage or try to get the most out of their visit, but the bottom line is: we are there as service providers. The detractors say, "This person has no insurance; this person's a frequent flier; this person only wants narcotic medication, they don't really have a problem." But that notwithstanding, it shouldn't

determine or shape your care for them. You should care for them the same. There were many times when I saw patients shunned simply because of their skin color and what problems they presented with that may or may not be prevalent in our communities, but that our community can't help. But [you can] tell that, over many years of time, we began to change our own lifestyles. But that's not something that can change tomorrow. So having a physician—if you want to use [that for] lack of a better term—taking it out on the patient because of who they are or what environment they're from, I thought was very unfair. Without considering that maybe it's not the fact that they're black or that they're poor or—maybe they just don't know. Maybe they don't have education. And from my colleagues' perspectives—I've seen where they administer care and, hopefully, they administer it in the best way possible, regardless of how the patient looks or sounds. But there's all sorts of anecdotal conversation about "I know how *these people* are when you give them medication" or "I see this all the time with *this* population." Where is that research? Where is that evidence?

Akinyele is careful to note that he hopes and believes his colleagues still administer the best care they are able to offer. But his comments also highlight his sense that seeing white practitioners stereotype and denigrate black patients makes it all the more important for him both to monitor colleagues' actions and to offer care that is thoughtful and considerate, in contrast. This racial outsourcing has multiple consequences. It leads to equity work for Akinyele, as he watches coworkers to ensure that they are in fact treating black patients the same as others. This then creates dissension, frustration, and social distance from white coworkers who seem comfortable viewing black patients through derogatory racial stereotypes.

Katie, a nurse, also shares a particularly egregious example of seeing a black woman patient mistreated by white medical staff. She states,

I heard someone screaming, and my patient became very frightened because the screams were horrible. And I said, "Oh, I think it's
someone in the last stages of labor." But it was disturbing to me, the
new young nurse [shadowing me], and the patient. We were very
disturbed. And in the afternoon when I left the room, I came out
and the residents and the head nurse of the unit—she was a very
flirtatious-type woman—she was flirting with the physicians and
they were all laughing. What had happened—it was such a busy
day in the labor birth unit that anesthesia was in short supply. And
this woman [whom we heard screaming] was not in labor. She had
a tubal ligation under local anesthesia. And she said [that] when the
physician finished, he looked down at her and said, "Oh, that wasn't
so bad, was it?"

Katie recalls that she was aghast at this scene, and describes it
as one of the defining encounters of her entire nursing career.
Indeed, her account of seeing this black woman condescend-
ingly and cruelly treated evokes gynecology's earliest roots
in the US, when Dr. Marion Sims experimented on slave women
while they were fully conscious, given no anesthesia, and obviously unable to give their consent. Equally horrific was the way
Katie's white colleagues reacted indifferently to this patient's
pain. Even today, white doctors still have pernicious racial
stereotypes about blacks, believing that they are biologically
different from whites in many ways, including having a higher
pain threshold (Hoffman, Trawalter, Axt, and Oliver 2016).
When white doctors can treat black patients in this fashion—
and face few consequences for doing so—black workers find
themselves stepping up to do the equity work of offsetting this
type of care.

Later on, Katie shared with me her experience of finding herself in need of care and seeing, from a different vantage point,
how women of color are treated in the health care system.

Very briefly, something happened to me, a major accident almost five months ago. And when I arrived at the hospital in the trauma ward, they didn't know—and it shouldn't make any kind of difference—they didn't know who I was in the community. And I received very poor treatment for about fifty-five minutes. And then someone noticed my name, and they went to see who I was. This was in a major inner-city urban hospital. When I arrived, I was just an overweight, middle-aged black woman. And not terribly overweight, but you know. Overweight. And I'm on a board. And I said, "You see me, as we would say, phenotypically." They just see who I am by looking at me, and they made a judgment.

Katie is in the uncommon position of having seen firsthand how her hospital treats women like her when they arrive as patients, and her impressions were not favorable. Having this personal experience with the ways that people of color can be treated in care facilities makes black professionals feel even greater distance from their white colleagues.

Ainsley, an obstetrician-gynecologist, has had a very similar experience of being in her patients' shoes.

I've also been a patient in my health care system. So now I understand more of why black patients have a distrust of the system. I think, as a person of color in the health care system, I do believe that you are treated differently. I remember I was scheduled for a procedure as a patient, and the nurse is referring to me as "sweetie" and "honey," just kind of talking down to me or talking over me as if I weren't there. [At one point,] we were having a conversation, the nurse and I, about a nanny. Another nurse came in, and she was like "Oh, are you a nanny?" And [the other nurse] was like, "Oh no, she's a physician here." And suddenly, the entire timbre of the conversation changed. During that same encounter, I'm in the procedure room undergoing anesthesia, and when I have a patient going under anesthesia, I will hold her hand. Anesthesiologists are usually trying to talk and comfort people. It's scary, even if it's for

something minor. They had music blasting. They were speaking over me. Their procedure was going to be late, so I'm lying there in a pretty vulnerable position for a long time, and everybody is just kind of talking around me as if I am a car that they're working on and not a person. I feel like they just made some assumptions about me. As soon as people realized I was a physician, the entire encounter would change. But it shouldn't matter, should it? I mean, every patient should be treated well, regardless.

Ainsley, like Katie, saw for herself what the experience of being a black woman patient in her hospital entails. This not only gave both of them greater empathy for the patients they encounter but also added to their feelings of distance from their white colleagues, who they see, firsthand, treating black patients dismissively.

Note that these findings add greater depth to black doctors' characterizations of racial interactions, discussed in chapter 2. When asked how they believe race affects their work, doctors note that there are few overt cases where colleagues (or patients) mistreat them openly and directly. The narratives doctors share in this chapter are consistent with that claim, but develop it in an important way. While black doctors do not routinely encounter colleagues who openly stereotype or belittle them, white coworkers' biases manifest when they interact with black patients, particularly poor black patients in public hospitals who are easily stereotyped when observed through the lenses of class and race. Thus, black doctors' occupational status and prestige may allow them to avoid direct expressions of racial bias. But they still see white colleagues' racial prejudices toward black patients who do not have the same level of economic and social privilege. This is particularly pronounced for black doctors who work alongside their white colleagues in the public sector

and treat patient populations who are disproportionately poor and black.

Consequences of Equity Work

In the public sector, black health care workers are able to fulfill certain occupational and personal goals that transcend simple financial rewards. But black professionals also do equity work when, in the absence of organizational efforts to ensure that patients of color receive respectful care, they step in to make sure this occurs. This form of equity work takes a toll, however. It frays relationships with both white colleagues and the larger institutional structures in which black professionals work, leaving black health care workers feeling frustrated and alienated from coworkers and the institutions that they believe are exploiting their racial loyalty.

In many cases, this sense of distance emerges when respondents discuss their reaction to the Affordable Care Act. Though this legislation further shifts health care out of the public sector (by requiring citizens to purchase a product sold in the private market), black health care workers appreciate the end result—that it allows more people to have access to health care. Given this outcome, black health care workers generally regard the ACA, despite its flaws, as a good start to fixing some of the deep-rooted problems of the health care system. Yet they believe that for many of their white colleagues, this aspect of the ACA is lost. Instead, they argue that their white coworkers are more likely to see the ACA as an example of government overreach that undermines their individual freedoms, a belief that fosters a sense of distance that can erode camaraderie.

Katie, a nurse practitioner, spoke to me about the distinctions she saw between the online comments of black public-sector

workers and of white practitioners in private practice, all of whom took an online course she teaches on this topic:

> I would say to you there's two schools. Lots of people, significant numbers of health providers, think that the Affordable Care Act is a horrible thing. I try to teach that it's not. It's a policy, and it's not health care reform. It is insurance reform. So some of the things we need to do about health and health [care] delivery and outcomes haven't happened, but it's a start. Before it was going to be instituted, it was passed March of '10. That very year, I was teaching the doctoral policy course. And I forget the topic, but it was something related to that. I had it online, and [my students] had a discussion forum. I had maybe forty-three doctoral students in one course. And there were three cohorts throughout the day. Some of them were online, [and] they talked about: "This thing is horrible that's coming." And "we don't need it." And "we have the best health care in the world." Oh, and they loved one of the code words we use when we want people to feel a certain way: *socialized medicine*. I was online that day for eleven hours.... So in the early afternoon, evening, I got the two other groups, and the tenor of their conversation was different. And one of them said, "I don't know about the Affordable Care Act. But I know we need a change. We need something." And they would talk about how their patients didn't have access to certain things. So I went back and I said, "What is the difference? What am I seeing here?" Well, the folks in the first of the three groups were all private practitioners in the cities. Those are the people who are making good money for being providers in a private setting. The ones who were saying things aren't good are the people who were serving the rural population, primarily. The private practice people were more likely to put it down and say it was terrible and socialized medicine, but the people with the underserved saw the potential for it.

Katie astutely notes the ways that class and race matter in shaping the response to how privatization shapes health care. While

the mostly white private-practice nurses rail against the ACA, those in public-sector work are more exposed to the need for reform that would improve access and care.

Curtis, an oncologist, also speaks about the ways that white colleagues' public disdain for the ACA can have a silencing effect:

> I know one colleague for sure who is very, very, very conservative, very anti–Affordable Care Act. And there are several things that the Affordable Care Act makes you do which are painful, kind of onerous. You've got to do this X, Y, and Z, and it's another check box that you've got to deal with. And you'll get the email from one of our colleagues, one in particular who [will say], "Oh my God, ACA stuff, blah, blah, blah." He will ramble on about it for a few minutes. And for a while my other colleague would engage him, and they'd get into these sort of email shouting matches. It's been very positive from a research standpoint for me to be able to get patients on studies. My politics are probably more toward social liberalism than anything else, and I don't go into that, but there are people within our group up here who will.

For Curtis, the ACA has been helpful in identifying patients of color who may be willing to participate in clinical trials. This sort of representation can be crucial to ensure that medical research is done in a way that includes and benefits people of color. However, Curtis's colleague's vehement denunciations of the ACA lead him to keep his opinions to himself and curb his connections with this colleague in particular.

David, another nurse, also hears these sorts of sentiments from white doctors in his practice:

> The only thing I hear is the complaining from the doctors. They complain every day. And that is the big problem. That's the only thing that I wish they would do, is stop complaining, because ... I

guess it's my personal view. I think that everyone should be afforded the right of having health care. And that's what I feel. Now some people don't believe that. Some people believe other things: like any other thing in this world, you've got to pay for it; and it should be just like any other type of insurance. But I just think if you don't have it, you should still be afforded the right to have health care. I think that is something that our country should be giving to everyone. So the only thing that I have a problem with is their complaining about it. For these guys to be on the higher end of the spectrum of prosperity in our country, I just feel that they should have a little more grace for those who do not have it. They complain about [how] it's ruining—and my side is that there's only twenty-two million Americans that receive it—but what they're saying is that it's ruining the payment system as far as the repayment of the insurance. They state it within the operating room. They'll talk about the reimbursements and their tax dollars. [Because of my position,] I can't disagree with them. They're part owners of our facility, so I let them state their position on it, just like who they will back politically. They state that, which is kind of interesting. They talk about their tax dollars, but they're thinking of voting for someone that doesn't pay taxes.

To a degree, David's silence on these matters reflects his position as a nurse within the health care hierarchy. When the doctors who have an ownership stake in his facility are critical of the ACA, it is impolitic to challenge them publicly. However, the perception that white (mostly male) doctors are hostile to legislation that can help underserved communities (even if they still get care from public hospitals) contributes to distance between black and white workers.

It is important to connect this to the racial stereotyping overlaying the ACA. When opponents, especially conservative ones, criticized this legislation, some described it as welfare, reparations, and indicative of Obama's socialist inclination to take

money and resources from well-off whites and redistribute them to poorer, less-deserving blacks, who were believed to be his core constituency (despite the fact that this is not how socialism actually works). These are all terms that are consistent with the sort of coded racial discourse that marks blacks as lazy recipients of government handouts rather than as people who want and are willing to work for economic and social rewards. Thus, when black health care practitioners in the public sector see their white colleagues castigating the ACA—a major legislative achievement that benefits black populations and that was passed by the first black president, no less—it serves as a powerful symbolic reminder of their racial difference and distance.

"IT MAKES ME FEEL LIKE MAMMY": GENDERED CONSEQUENCES OF RACIAL OUTSOURCING AND EQUITY WORK

Racial outsourcing creates subtle cleavages between black and white professionals at all levels of the occupational ladder. However, it also produces specific gendered reactions from black women, particularly those working in medicine. Recall that as a result of their occupational status, black women physicians work in jobs that are unquestionably at the top of the health care status ladder. As a result, they have more latitude than nurses and technicians to attempt to enact far-reaching, structural changes. Racial outsourcing means that they do the equity work to reach communities of color when their organizations do not, and they do so by trying to develop clinics, special programs, and other initiatives that have the potential to create significant systemic changes.

One consequence of this, however, is that it leaves black women doctors particularly frustrated and annoyed about the

ways racial outsourcing evokes racial and gender stereotypes about black women's labor. Black women doctors express very strong feelings about the ways that racial outsourcing exploits their commitments, empathy, and concern for people of color. They share the emotions of anger, weariness, and mistrust of the colleagues and institutions that they believe take their herculean efforts on behalf of black patients for granted.

I heard one particularly forceful expression of this during an exchange with Dr. Randy Goodwin and two of his colleagues at City Hospital. When I first arrived, Randy took me around to introduce me to other doctors and nurses in different sections of the hospital. At one point, he introduced me to two women doctors, one white and one black, in an adjacent department. "This is Adia," he said. "She's a sociology professor and she'll be shadowing me for a research project she's doing."

The two women welcomed me warmly and introduced themselves. Dr. Ashley Davis-Jackson was tall with a wide smile and freckles. I later learned that she was biracial, though she identified as black. Dr. Rebecca Plies was white, appeared to be in her fifties, and was of average build with a blonde bob. After introductions, Rebecca asked me to tell her about my project. I replied, "It's a study of how work transformation affects black professionals. I'm really interested in how a lot of recent changes to how work is done affect black professionals, especially when they're employed in a rapidly changing industry like health care."

Ashley and Randy nodded. After all, Randy had heard my spiel about the project already, so this summary was not new to him. Rebecca nodded her head thoughtfully. She said, "That's interesting. You know, I wonder if maybe whites really have the same outcomes as blacks, though. I mean, I think it's probably understudied, but it's probably pretty much the same for

whites. Don't you think? Would health outcomes really be that different?"

Without even glancing at Ashley and Randy, I had a feeling that the subtext of the conversation had just changed. Before I could answer, Randy spoke up. "Not really. I mean, everything—there's so much research that shows that blacks have worse health outcomes. Even across income levels. It's not even just a class thing." I added, "Besides, my project is more about health care professionals. So I'd be more focused on how changes to the way we work affect black doctors, nurses, and if there are racial differences there." Ashley said nothing.

After a few more minutes of small talk, Rebecca went off to check on a patient. When she left, it quickly became clear that my suspicions that the atmosphere had changed were correct. Ashley immediately turned to Randy and me and said, "See? That is so typical of white people. And there's an example for your study! We all know that blacks have worse health outcomes across every measure. Shit, we work in this hospital where we see this type of shit every day!! But there it is. White people always want to act like, 'Oh, it's not *really* race. *That* doesn't matter anymore!'" Randy laughed and agreed.

When Randy left, I asked Ashley more questions about her work at the hospital. She echoed some of the comments I had heard from other black women doctors and nurses, saying,

> It is frustrating how under-resourced we are. And [administrators] will overwork you. It's crazy. But it's because they know that we're here because we're committed to these populations. So funding gets cut, we don't have the things we need, but they know we'll still come in and work our asses off to get our patients what they need. It's kind of bullshit. It makes me feel exploited. It makes me feel like Mammy, honestly. Because we empathize—*no one* has more

empathy than black women. But that's not rewarded in the structure of how medicine works. So we just keep on working and working with less and less.

Ashley's comments are important for several reasons. For one, she emphatically stresses how white colleagues' willingness to ignore racial differences and outcomes, even in a hospital that serves a predominantly minority patient population, can engender social distance. Second, she underscores how the shrinking public sphere engages in racial outsourcing as it discreetly relies on black professionals' equity work to continue providing some level of care to underserved populations. Even though they are employed in severely under-resourced environments for lower pay than they know they could earn in the private sector, black professionals remain determined to compensate for the negative treatment that they know black people can receive in the health care system. But they also sense that this loyalty is exploited when administrators rely on their dedication to providing care under bleak circumstances. Furthermore, this can create a particularly racialized and gendered outcome for black women, who may be subjected to enhanced pressures as a result of the ways they connect with patients (particularly other women of color) and their wish to improve the system.

Ella, the obstetrician/gynecologist, speaks about this as well. When I shadowed her at work, she was in the midst of a particularly busy week as she was back "in service" (serving as the attending for the week), as well as preparing for an unusually taxing procedure the next day. Importantly, she also was hosting a special group for low-income mothers (mostly women of color) to emphasize the necessity of regular health care, nutrition, and wellness.

I sat with Ella in her office for about an hour at the end of her day. Most of her time was spent on the phone calling her clinic members to remind them of their group meeting the next day. I wrote in my field notes, "Ella's phone stays ringing! Who knew so much of a doctor's time was tied up in phone calls, texts, etc.?" When she got off the phone for a few minutes, I told her I was surprised to see that so much of her job involved this kind of work. She said, "Well, this is somewhat atypical because of all the things that are happening this week. But if I were in private practice, or had patients who were more well off, this wouldn't be happening. There would be a whole infrastructure in place to attend to these sorts of details."

I was curious about how Ella saw this aspect of her work. After all, she had trained at some of the top universities in the country. It seemed to me that she'd made a conscious decision to immerse herself in work with poor, predominantly black mothers, providing high-quality care despite the complications entailed in doing so. When I prodded her about this, she replied, "I feel a commitment to these women. My colleagues don't get that. I'm always explaining to them that patients aren't just being difficult or stubborn, but they're making real choices about food, child care, and being compliant. Given where we are located, these are the patients that we are going to have. Our mission is supposed to be about providing care. But we do so with half the resources that we need, because they know they can rely on black women to do the work."

Again, Ella makes an insightful point about how organizations rely on black health care workers, and black women specifically, to go above and beyond and pick up the slack when organizations state that they appreciate diversity but do not devote specific resources to reaching minority communities. It is also worth noting that these women see this as a decisively

raced and gendered arrangement. Indeed, social institutions from nuclear families to civil rights organizations have long relied on black women's labor in order to function smoothly and effectively, so the raced and gendered patterns Ella and Ashley identify have an established historical precedent in America (Collins 2000; Robnett 1993). These black women doctors show that one of the downsides to racial outsourcing and the resulting equity work is the frustrating sense that, not only do their institutions exploit their labor, but they do so in ways that tap into black women's long-standing experiences with being taken for granted by the organizations in which they work.

These feelings provide a new twist to the concept of emotional labor, a term initially coined to refer to the ways that organizations commodify and exert control over workers' emotions (often in ways that perpetuate gender inequality). Emotional labor is complicated by the relationship black workers have to predominantly white organizations (Evans 2014; Hochschild 1988; Wingfield 2010). For black women in these settings, emotional labor may not be explicitly mandated by organizational structures, and it is racialized in ways that Hochschild (1988) did not anticipate. In contrast to (white) women working as flight attendants (Hochschild 1988) or in the legal field (Pierce 1995), where emotional expectations are both gendered and embedded in the occupations in which they are employed, these black women do a sort of emotional labor that is driven much more by the experience of being a racial minority than by occupational or even organizational dictates. This leaves them concealing their frustrations about equity work because they know, as black workers, that this is expected— not because that is part of the physician's job.

Addressing this point, Aliya, a neonatologist, speaks about the need to hide her feelings: "It bothers me a lot, yeah. It does

bother me. In the position I'm in as a trainee, and not the department chair, and I'm not the medical director, ... there's not much I can do about it. Other than complaining. But yeah, there's not much I can do. You just cover it up." Black women physicians like Aliya find themselves in a contradictory position. They know that organizations rely on their commitment, dedication, and empathy in order to meet their patient populations' needs, and are attuned to the ways this evokes gendered and racialized implications. Yet despite their status as doctors, being in the racial and gender minority means they still feel they have to work to hide their feelings of frustration and discontent at this arrangement. Hospitals do not establish specific guidelines for black women doctors' emotional performance, but the intersections of race, gender, and occupational status structure the sort of emotion work they do all the same.

Even Suzanne, a geneticist in a high-ranking role in a public hospital, makes the same calculations about the emotional labor that stems from her feelings of being taken for granted by her institution: "It's trying to take a toll. Yeah, I think I've just become more jaded. I've become more jaded. I've become just ... not nearly as open as I used to be with my colleagues. I used to be very, incredibly, open; and now I'm just a lot more guarded, because I just ... it's not even being hurt, it's just [that] you tend to become apathetic about it." For Suzanne, the negative emotions associated with feeling taken for granted drive her to become cynical and guarded. Her relatively high-status position even among doctors at her hospital indicates that for black women in medicine, the disturbing sense that organizations take advantage of their commitment is enough to prompt the emotional labor of concealing these emotions, even if doing so results in apathy.

The American Panel Survey data bolster these women's arguments about the gendered costs of medicine. In figures 6 and 7, I show the predicted trust in doctors, conditional on an individual's income, when the doctor is female, black, black and female, and when the doctor's gender and race are not specified (i.e., the control group). These results are based on a multivariate linear regression analysis that allows me to account for the individual's gender, race, educational level, and age. When the doctor's race and gender are not specified, there is a hint of a positive relationship between income and trust in doctors inasmuch as individuals with lower incomes show less trust in physicians. However, the trend that jumps out is the lack of trust in *women* doctors among low-income individuals. People with very low incomes (relative to very high) do not trust women doctors ($p = .101$), and they especially do not trust black women doctors ($p < .001$).

For black women working in these public facilities, where patients are often low-income or uninsured, these gendered biases may compound their sense that they encounter a uniquely racial and gendered experience in these settings. The American Panel Survey data are consistent with many other studies showing that women of all races face specifically gendered challenges in medicine. They struggle to get patients' and colleagues' respect, confront the stereotype that women simply are less capable than men in science and math, and navigate grueling work environments that leave little to no time for a work/family balance (Boulis and Jacobs 2008; Cassel 2014; Pololi, Conrad, Knight, and Carr 2009). The American Panel Survey shows that patients who believe that women doctors are less capable are more numerous among the low-income populations who are disproportionately present in public facilities. Women physicians already work harder to gain patient trust. For black

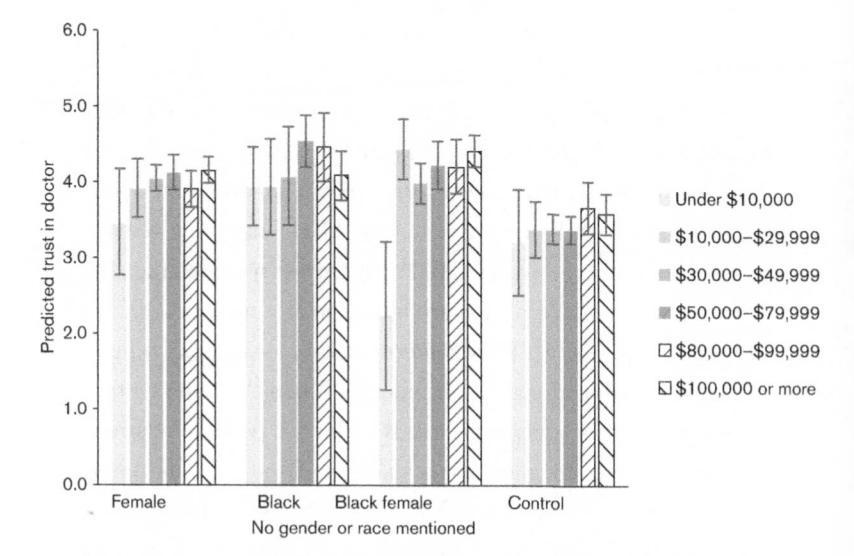

Figure 6. Predicted trust in doctor by respondent income and experimental condition.
Source: The American Panel Survey, September 2016.

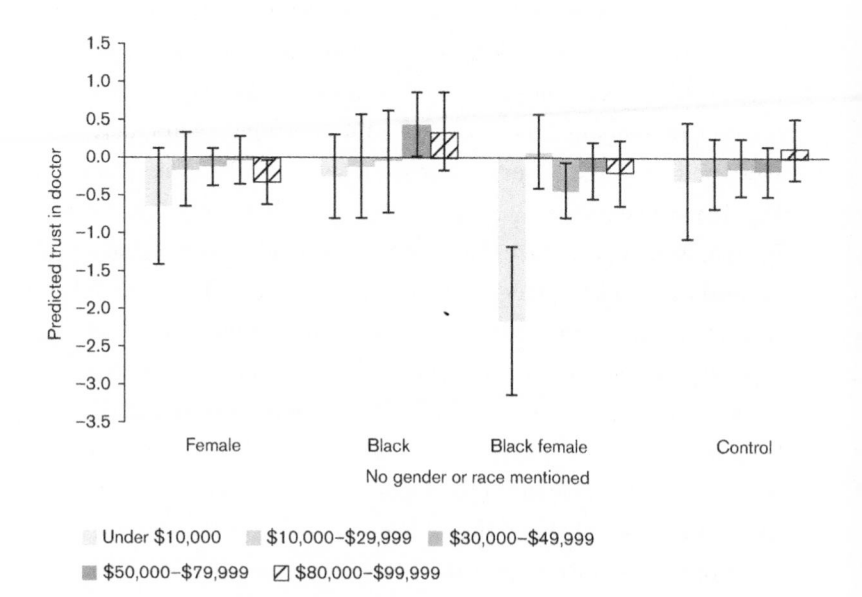

Figure 7. Average marginal effect of respondent income on trust in doctor. Source:
The American Panel Survey, September 2016.

women, this additional work may exacerbate their frustration with institutions that they believe exploit their work with little acknowledgment or reward.

Black men doctors do not offer these same gendered and racial perceptions of being taken for granted, but this should not be taken to suggest that their commitment to public-sector work is any weaker than that of their women colleagues. As we know, some of the black male doctors in this study had also established programs that allowed them to reach underserved populations, in excess of what the hospital expected or required. Interestingly, though, while they also express frustration that institutions take their labor for granted, they do not put it in the same racial and gendered terms that black women use. It may be that the long history of black women providing unacknowledged, uncompensated services makes these black women doctors particularly attuned to the ways that this pattern is unfolding in their own lives. And given the well-documented pay gap between women of color and everyone else, black women doctors may be especially aware of the lack of financial rewards attributed to their efforts relative to those of their counterparts. Race and gender, then, intersect again to shape not just how equity work occurs but its consequences as well. This is particularly evident when the process of racial outsourcing leaves both black men and women feeling as though their labor is being appropriated, but creates specific feelings of resentment for black women.

SUMMARY

Work in the public sector is complicated for black professionals. On the one hand, it offers a direct opportunity to have an impact on the communities to which they are most committed. As

health care becomes increasingly stratified, the public sector suffers from the effects of privatization, disinvestment, and underfunding. Yet for many black patients, this under-resourced public sector is their only option for health care. Consequently, health care workers who are determined to be a resource for black patients find that the public sector offers a place to do this.

However, the demands of the public sector mean that racial outsourcing puts black health care professionals in an uncomfortable position. They work for organizations that often claim a dedication to providing care to diverse populations. Yet their white coworkers in these settings frequently rely on racial stereotypes and judgments as they assess and treat black patients. Racial outsourcing then occurs as black health care workers do the equity work of both keeping these organizations running despite a shrinking allocation of resources, and assuming an outsize responsibility for stepping up to compensate for the ways that they see white colleagues interacting with black patients.

Not surprisingly, racial outsourcing has stark emotional consequences for black professionals in this context. It leaves them frustrated, alienated, and distant from their white coworkers, because they see them stereotyping black patients as drug users or noncompliant patients. It also engenders mistrust and anger at the organizations in which they work, because they see the ways that their important labor goes unacknowledged and unappreciated. For black women doctors, this is an especially bitter pill to swallow, as it evokes long-standing racial and gendered patterns in which black women's work is exploited and appropriated without compensation or reward.

Conclusion

In the new economy, the relationship between organizations and workers is distinctly different than in previous generations. Today, many organizations recognize the need to acknowledge and respond to growing racial diversity. At the same time, they balance this with growing pressures to improve profit margins and meet a financial bottom line. Simultaneously, the public sector—where many communities of color access education, transportation, and other basic needs—suffers from declining attention and support. The current state of the health care industry provides a particularly illuminating look at this situation. Professional organizations representing doctors and nurses now openly accept that their professions simply must become more racially diverse in order to provide care effectively to a population that is steadily becoming less white and more black, brown, and Asian. At the same time, health care has become increasingly commodified in ways that have led to a stratified system of privatized care for a privileged few and publicly funded, under-resourced care for most others.

I argue in this book that this tension creates a process of racial outsourcing. As health care becomes more and more of a market-based commodity, it leaves the organizations attempting to serve diverse populations ill equipped to address the needs of minority communities. In the absence of specific, tailored programming targeted to this end, organizations today are increasingly reliant on black professionals for this labor. As a result, black professionals do the equity work of reaching out to and serving the needs of communities of color. This happens through both overt and implicit processes: in some cases, organizations tacitly accept black professionals' equity work, while in others they explicitly assign it. Either way, in a broader economic context where organizations cut labor costs, shift more responsibilities onto workers, and prioritize profit margins over employees, racial outsourcing allows them to address and engage minority communities without expending extensive institutional resources.

The results of this research also show how racial outsourcing and equity work are inextricably linked to workers' positions in the occupational hierarchy and to the racialized, gendered, and classed encounters they have in that setting. Doctors see race as something that primarily affects their work through structural and cultural processes. This is gendered to the extent that these institutionalized processes make the everyday sexism black women doctors encounter on a routine basis all the more apparent, creating more of a connection between them and white women doctors than between black women doctors and black men in the field. Organizations' efforts at cultural competence are not effective in addressing these challenges. Consequently, black doctors take the initiative of doing the equity work of pursuing systemic solutions to racial issues.

Nurses find that race shapes their work through explicitly racist interactions as well as structural ones, and the ubiquity of this collapses gender differences that might otherwise persist between black men and black women in the profession. In the face of both overtly racialized interactions and structural processes that disadvantage black nurses, their organizations' statements in support of diversity seem weak and ineffective. Nurses thus do the equity work of pursuing both structural and interpersonal changes that can protect their patients from the types of harassment they themselves face.

Finally, technicians encounter racial mistreatment by nurses, who are situated above them on the occupational hierarchy, and patients' families. Perhaps because of their lower status in the organizational hierarchy, technicians rarely see any initiatives designed to address the racial challenges they confront. Owing to technicians' relatively vulnerable position, managers explicitly engage in racial outsourcing when they task them with equity work that is outside the bounds of their job descriptions and not required of their white colleagues. Black women technicians respond to this by quitting, while black men do additional forms of equity work when they leverage their cultural capital to help black patients navigate complicated new health care systems.

Though occupational differences exist, there are some similarities between how both racial outsourcing and equity work affect black professionals. These show up most clearly when examining the efforts of black workers in the public sector, where institutions rely very heavily on black employees' equity work in order to fulfill their basic missions. Black health care professionals are drawn to public facilities that tout their unique capacity to meet the needs of diverse communities. Once employed in these settings, however, black health care workers often observe that

their white colleagues rely on racial stereotypes and prejudgments of the black patients they see. As a result, black professionals do equity work when they compensate for their white colleagues by ensuring that black patients get the respectful, thoughtful treatment they are often denied in the health care industry. This occurs across occupational lines, leaving black doctors, nurses, and technicians frustrated and alienated from their white coworkers and the institutions that they see as exploiting their labor. It is also a gendered process that creates heightened feelings of irritation in black women doctors, who note that the appropriation of their labor is consistent with ways black women's work is frequently taken for granted, uncompensated, and unacknowledged.

The US economy has changed, and these changes have implications for organizations, occupations, and workers. For blacks doing professional work, these broader economic shifts inform the ways they encounter explicit racial slights and insults. We see this in the way that short-staffing stresses nurses, who then take out their frustrations on black technicians. Yet these changes also lead to organizational practices that create new forms of racial inequality, such as the creation of racial outsourcing and equity work. These broader structural changes, and the forms of racial inequality that result, have implications for health care, for black professionals working in other fields, and for how organizations can do a better job meeting workers' needs in an increasingly multiracial America.

IMPLICATIONS FOR HEALTH CARE

Health care now represents one-sixth of our nation's gross domestic product. It has been the subject of contentious battles over

reform, as policy makers debate whether to make it more of a right available to all or a commodity purchased by those who can afford it. Often ignored in these discussions, however, are the ways that current organizational practices may be creating a health care model with racial dynamics that are unsustainable. As hospitals and other facilities continue to engage in racial outsourcing, they run the risk of burning out the workers who are providing critical care to a growing segment of the population. Part of the reason the medical and nursing industries finally acknowledged the importance of attracting more workers of color was that patients of color show higher levels of physician trust when matched with same-race doctors (Sewell 2015). This is perhaps not surprising, given the long history of medical racism and contemporary white practitioners' stubborn reliance on racial stereotypes (Hoberman 2012; Hoffman, Trawalter, Axt, and Oliver 2016). However, if minority practitioners enter these fields only to be tasked with doing the equity work of connecting organizations to communities of color, this will likely undermine their long-term ability to provide quality care. Burnout is high for practitioners who are largely motivated by altruism and caring; this stands to be exacerbated as organizations rely on black employees' equity work (Dill, Erickson, and Diefendorff 2016).

The results of this study point to an additional way that the current health care system is headed for crisis. The Affordable Care Act can now boast of some successes, having reduced the number of uninsured Americans, allowed people with preexisting conditions to afford medical care, and sought to curb medical bankruptcies. However, constant threats to the Affordable Care Act mean that these trends are far from permanent. As legislators debate whether to impose additional changes to health care (and fail to reach agreement over what those changes should

look like), one likely consequence is that they will miss how further commodifying health care contributes to racial outsourcing that weighs most heavily on black workers. In other words, health care is already at a point where the push both to extract profits and to champion diversity leads to many adverse outcomes for black practitioners. Moving toward a more stratified health care system will likely worsen these effects.

Finally, the results of this research suggest that cultural competence and mere statements in support of diversity in health care are not only failing to improve workplaces for professionals of color. They are also shifting the relationships between organizations and workers, particularly when it comes to black practitioners. Recall that many health care workers were skeptical at best of these programs because they did not seem able to address the racial challenges black professionals encountered. Organizations rarely enact diversity initiatives that have a proven record of creating actual change; indeed, many current diversity programs cushion employers from lawsuits but do not address systemic, institutional processes that disadvantage women of all races and men of color (Edelman 2016; Edelman, Fuller, and Mara-Drita 2001; Embrick 2011; Kalev, Dobbin, and Kelly 2006; Moore and Bell 2011; Williams, Mueller, and Kilanski 2012). The findings from this study suggest that the limited and unevenly applied attempts to establish cultural competence trainings or official statements in support of diversity are not making workplaces more attractive to black practitioners. Not only that, they are restructuring relationships between organizations and workers in ways that leave black practitioners doing often unseen, always uncompensated, forms of equity work.

Racial outsourcing is only exacerbated by certain labor practices that are becoming increasingly common in the new econ-

omy and having a particular effect on the health care industry. Private-sector union membership is at an all-time low of 6.7 percent. Public-sector employee union numbers are higher, at 35 percent, but unions lack much of their former power to address wage disparities and protect workers' rights (Rosenfeld 2013). Indeed, none of the respondents I interviewed for this study mentioned their unions as organizations that could challenge the ways hospitals exploited their labor. Thus, if unions continue to decline in influence and power, black health care workers will likely have few organized allies that can help them push back against racial outsourcing and its effects.

Organizational practices that encourage turnover and labor shortages in various health care occupations also stand to exacerbate racial outsourcing in this industry. In a 2016 report, the Association of American Medical Colleges noted that between 2016 and 2026, the US is projected to fall short of doctors—somewhere between 61,700 and 94,700 doctors.[1] With many nurses nearing retirement age, and nursing schools forced to turn away qualified applicants because of a lack of training facilities, faculty, and instructional space, the nursing shortage has also become acute. However, the responses from practitioners in this study suggest that this shortage is not simply due to a lack of workers, but that organizational attempts to cut costs contribute to high turnover and low numbers of available practitioners, particularly in nursing. When organizations hire fewer workers than are needed and establish stressful conditions for employees, this

1. Association of American Medical Colleges, "New Research Shows Increasing Physician Shortages in Both Primary and Specialty Care," press release, April 11, 2018, https://news.aamc.org/press-releases/article/workforce _report_shortage_04112018/.

means that black technicians, in particular, will continue to encounter racial outsourcing.

IMPLICATIONS FOR OTHER BLACK PROFESSIONALS

Though this book focuses on black workers in health care, I expect that racial outsourcing and equity work are likely present for black professionals in many other fields. Health care is far from the only industry that struggles with seeking more diversity, on the one hand, while, on the other hand, only limited resources are allocated to the institutions that serve minority populations. It is also just one industry where attempts to commodify and privatize services have contributed to widening inequality and stratification. Public education, for instance, has also long been a target of privatization efforts that have had a notable impact on worsening racial disparities in access to education (Lewis-McCoy 2010; Newfield 2008). It is useful to consider whether the racial outcomes black health care workers describe also extend to black educators. Do they pursue education out of a dedication to caring for underserved black populations? Does this drive them to go above and beyond for their students? And perhaps more critically, do organizations rely on this commitment in ways that exploit black teachers, creating social distance and a sense of separation between them and their white counterparts? My hypothesis is yes, but additional research is necessary to say for sure.

The racial experiences black professionals describe, and the ways they are shaped by gender and occupational status, also likely apply to black workers in other professional contexts. Based on this study, I theorize that black workers in other high-status

professions (e.g., law or finance) similarly find that they do not necessarily encounter daily, overt expressions of racial bias. However, these professionals may be attuned to the ways structural and cultural processes work to their disadvantage, and may do equity work through their resulting pursuit of systemic changes. For instance, it is not difficult to imagine that while black lawyers may not encounter explicitly racist assaults on a daily basis, they might be highly attuned to the structural and cultural barriers that keep blacks underrepresented in this profession, and this might be gendered in ways that have distinct consequences for black women lawyers. It is also not hard to conceive that these racial experiences vary at different levels of the occupational ladder, with black paralegals and legal assistants encountering incidents that parallel those of nurses and technicians (see, for instance, Moore 2007; Pierce 1995).

These findings suggest that when it comes to understanding race, black professionals' experiences cannot be divorced from their occupational and organizational status. Sociologists have yet to theorize extensively how race is embedded in organizational structures in ways that have concrete outcomes for people of color (for exceptions, see Ray 2019; Wingfield and Alston 2014). The results of this study indicate that race is built into organizational processes, determining nurses' scheduling outcomes, technicians' assignments and responsibilities, and doctors' ability to avoid overt expressions of racial bias. Further, this study indicates that some of the racial experiences commonly attributed to black professionals—presumptions of incompetence, explicit stereotyping—are connected to organizational status and economic patterns. (Recall, for instance, that organizational efforts to cut costs by hiring fewer nurses leave black technicians particularly vulnerable to their frustrations.) Sociologist Joan Acker

(1990) wrote that organizations are not neutral but are actually gendered institutions that perpetuate women's disadvantaged status. I show here that organizations are similarly racialized constructs that yield divergent processes of racial inequality depending on the worker's status.

Finally, the results of this research are crucial for pointing us in new directions for thinking about black professionals at work. All too often, discussions of racial inequality focus on what is done *to* blacks—discrimination, stereotyping, differential treatment. But this is not the only story to tell about black workers, and to remain locked in this paradigmatic framework risks missing the ways black professionals respond to living in a society that remains highly racially stratified. The findings from this research highlight the ways black professionals work both within and outside of organizational structures to try to offset the effects of racial inequality. They do this by dedicating themselves to communities of color even to their own financial detriment, and by committing themselves to creating opportunities for other workers of color in the absence of institutional support.

The issue here is not that they do this work but that this becomes a core component of how organizations reach minority constituencies in the absence of formally institutionalized efforts. In the immediate post–civil rights era, some organizations integrated their workforces by hiring blacks in managerial roles, where they were responsible for community outreach or urban development. Yet these managers predicted that when the political economy shifted, their jobs would become much less secure (Collins 1988). While their work has solidified into diversity offices that remain present in many organizational settings, I argue the lack of explicit attention to issues of racial stratification, coupled with organizational changes in the new economy,

created the climate that allowed racial outsourcing to develop (Kelly and Dobbin 1998).

Today, racial outsourcing puts black professionals in a position where they attempt to change systemic and interpersonal racial dynamics without explicit organizational support, resources, and in many cases, acknowledgment. Thus for some black professionals, particularly those in extremely high-status occupations, workplaces may look much different from those of their predecessors in earlier generations. These particular workers are much less likely to face overt racial hostilities that characterize the daily routines of their workdays. But the processes that perpetuate racial inequality are inextricably linked to basic organizational functions that rely on black workers' labor and racial agency.

It is also useful to think about how occupational status may mediate the difference between encountering the more overt, direct expressions of racial bias and subtler, ambiguous ones. Many of the processes that perpetuate racial inequality today are largely covert, hidden, and shrouded by an "anything but race" rhetoric that belies persistent racial disparities (Bobo and Smith 1998). For a time, this was particularly true when it came to public discourse about affirmative action policies, residential racial segregation, or interracial marriage (Bonilla-Silva 2001). But when it comes to how racial biases are expressed or perpetuated in the workplace, the degree to which these are shared openly or covertly may be linked to occupational status. It may be useful, then, to be a bit more circumspect about the extent to which whites have adopted colorblind, or postracial, language when it comes to their public discussion of racial matters. As the nurses and technicians in this study can attest, for workers at their occupational level, blatant racial stereotyping has hardly disappeared behind the polite veneer of colorblindness.

The conclusions here also have important implications for how we think about the intersections of race, class, and gender in the workplace. These overlapping factors push black women into low-wage work and inhibit their pathways into higher-status occupations (Branch 2011; Browne and Misra 2003). However, this study suggests that occupational status can also maximize gender solidarity or minimize gender differences between black workers. Recall that black women doctors' experiences with overt sexism and institutionalized racism leave them with the sense that they have more in common with their white women counterparts than with black men physicians. For nurses, accounts of racist interactions are so widely shared that black women see black men nurses as key allies in the profession. Black women technicians choose to "opt out," while racial outsourcing means black men technicians utilize their cultural capital both to help initiate uninformed patients of color into the health care system and to excel at their jobs. These findings offer more detail about how these intersecting categories inform work for different groups. They also reveal both nuanced views of how black professionals identify barriers and obstacles to their work, and shifting perspectives about who experiences comparable challenges.

WHAT SOLUTIONS MAKE SENSE?

Now that we know more about racial outsourcing and equity work, what should be done about them? One critical and obvious step that organizations can take is to put more effort and precision into their attempts to engage with communities of color. The results of this study show that in the health care industry, these initiatives often take the form of cultural competence

training or broad statements supporting an organization's commitment to diversity; but black health care workers believe these to be particularly ill suited for addressing the racialized aspects of their work experience. They also note that these efforts do little to affect patients, hence these workers' attempts to do equity work that will change systemic and interactional aspects of how black patients engage with the health care system.

Organizations that do not want to perpetuate racial outsourcing should have intentional, evidence-based initiatives in place that are designed to create both a racially hospitable workplace for employees of color and a racially hospitable place for the minority communities they serve. Recall that programs explicitly designed to address systemic racial and gender inequality show the most success in creating more occupational diversity, and that formal mentoring programs yield modest successes for some groups (Kalev, Dobbin, and Kelly 2006). Additionally, institutions that take an "integration and learning" approach that values the ways diverse groups can challenge and contribute to the organization's mission can help achieve long-term goals (Ely and Thomas 2001). Thus, establishing formal programs that move past cultural competence or public statements, are overtly color-conscious, and are intentionally designed to improve the pipeline of underrepresented workers into these professions might be a viable start.

At the same time, these institutions must keep in mind that occupational status shapes the racial issues that their workers will encounter and structure their solutions accordingly. Broad-based, one-size-fits-all solutions will not work, as workers at the bottom of the occupational hierarchy will likely have different racial experiences than those at the top. To restructure work-places so that they foster support, appreciation, and inclusion of

workers of color, organizations can and should be open to changing their cultures, daily practices, and routine norms in ways that reduce racial inequalities.

Organizations can also assume responsibility for the equity work that black professionals are already doing as a result of racial outsourcing. Recall that black workers engage in systemic and interactional efforts to try to make workplaces more palatable and hospitable for minority communities. For doctors, this means not just mentoring but also actively sponsoring medical students and younger physicians of color who otherwise would be more likely to miss out on the critical relationships that facilitate success in medicine. They also work with or even launch their own community organizations that can rectify racial health disparities. Nurses do some of this as well, while also acting as patient advocates for the most underserved. Technicians are given assignments that are not required of their white counterparts, but they also use their cultural capital to help patients navigate an unfamiliar health care system. Ultimately, black professionals do equity work when they utilize an array of strategies intended to address racial issues.

However, these strategies are all things that organizations can and should be developing so that black health care workers do not have to assume this work on their own. Institutions can establish organizations, or partner with other organizations, dedicated to resolving racial issues. They can found sponsorship programs for women, particularly women of color, that are designed in ways that actually create more multiracial teams at top leadership levels (Ibarra, Carter, and Silva 2010). They can be more mindful of the ways social networks that determine hiring practices frequently exclude black practitioners, leaving black doctors to do the equity work of mentoring potential

minority physicians. Moreover, organizations can both enact consequences for managers who reserve additional tasks for workers of color and refuse to tolerate a culture where high-status workers rely on racial stereotypes to make assessments of minority communities that use their services. If institutions take responsibility for this work, rather than leaving it up to black professionals in their employ, it could potentially send a clear message that organizations really are serious about reaching diverse constituencies, and that they are committed to undermining the racial issues that still affect workers of color.

Organizations can also help minimize equity work by paying particular attention to the practices and processes that affect women working in male-dominated professions. Women of all races note that work experiences in high-status, culturally masculinized jobs can be extremely hostile, and this problem is compounded for women of color (Williams 2015). These issues can manifest through many processes—cultural dictates that value overwork (Cooper 2013), rampant sexual harassment (Zippel 2006), or entrenched stereotypes and perceptions of women as mothers rather than workers (Kitzerow 2014). The responses I received from black women doctors suggest that black women doing high-status "men's" work would particularly benefit from policies targeted at improving conditions for women workers. These could include zero-tolerance policies for sexual harassment, hiring more women in management roles, instituting mandatory paid parental leave, and addressing the culture of overwork that dominates many high-status, male dominated professions.

Organizations should also pay attention to how occupational hierarchies create racial outcomes for workers with lower status. Diversity policies are rarely designed with lower-status workers in mind (Berrey 2013). This can leave these black professionals

coping with racial issues that not only differ from those of their higher-status counterparts but also are not even acknowledged by any institutional policies. One way to address this might be to develop strict protocols for lower-status professionals' work and to establish consequences for higher-status workers who violate these guidelines. Recall that part of the reason Callie, the technician whose story leads chapter 4, was optimistic about diversity initiatives was that she believed there were now penalties for workers who created a racially inhospitable work environment. Organizations can spell out these professionals' exact responsibilities so that workers with more authority cannot add to these in ways that perpetuate racial inequities.

Policy makers, too, can help eradicate racial outsourcing and equity work. When it comes to health care, one way to address these issues would be to establish payment models that take into consideration the sort of social factors that can affect patients. Under value-based care models, which are gaining traction as a more equitable way to assess care and compensation, practitioners can be rewarded or penalized based on patient outcomes, costs, and the quality of care provided. Thus a practitioner may see higher payments for care that results in patients' lowered blood pressure or rates of obesity. Yet without a pay policy that acknowledges that social factors can also affect health, these models can disincentivize physicians from caring for those for whom poverty, discrimination, or other related issues preclude optimal health outcomes.[2] From a purely economic standpoint, why seek out patients whose poverty, lack of access to healthy food, or recurrent exposure to discrimination will likely mean

2 Dhruv Khullar, MD, "Is It Getting Harder to Care for Poor Patients?" *New York Times,* June 26, 2018, www.nytimes.com/2018/06/26/well/is-it-getting-harder-to-care-for-poor-patients.html.

difficulty reducing blood pressure, consequently lowering a physician's pay?

Yet those very patients are the ones that black health care workers are most committed to treating. More importantly, we now know that this dedication also leads many black practitioners to do essential equity work in the public sector, often at great financial cost to themselves and at the expense of their sense of trust in and support for the institutions that employ them. Policy makers can help address this issue by pushing for value-based care models that factor in the ways that social *and* medical considerations affect providers' ability to give care. Tying bonuses to caring for socially disadvantaged patients, for instance, could be a way to offset the disillusionment and isolation that is associated with black doctors' equity work in the public sector.

Outside of the health care industry, policy makers can also address racial outsourcing and equity work by resuscitating the public sector. The growing privatization of this sector of the economy has had disastrous consequences for some groups, black men in particular (Wilson, Roscigno, and Huffman 2013). Despite this, the public sector continues to provide important services, particularly to populations who may be the neediest. But this happens because of dedicated professionals who operate out of a sense of racial responsibility to fill the gaps left when resources are withdrawn. Furthermore, their work comes at a consequence—a sense of distance from their white colleagues, and feelings of resentment when they believe that their labor is being exploited and taken for granted. Restoring the resources that will allow public-sector workers to thrive and to offer important services, care, and support to poor and racial minority patients can potentially play a vital role in reinvigorating

black health care workers who do much of the labor in this realm.

Policy makers can also play a major role in addressing racial outsourcing and equity work if they enact public policies that support unionizing and collective bargaining. The number of public- and private-sector workers who belong to unions has declined to record lows, due in no small part to local, state, and federal government policies that make it much harder for workers to join. Unfortunately for black professionals, unions began to decline in power and scope just as many jobs began to be integrated, so black workers have largely not benefited from the glory days when unions could exert pressure on organizations to improve conditions (Rosenfeld 2013). However, resuscitating unions could offer a means through which black professionals could push organizations to enact policies and set guidelines that take their issues into consideration.

For unions to succeed in this way, though, it is imperative that they do a better job of incorporating workers of color. Historically, black workers in particular were denied access to unions because of both occupational segregation and the exclusionary practices of unions themselves. Stronger, more racially inclusive unions could theoretically work to address the concerns that black nurses and technicians have about racial discrimination and inequities in their workplaces. Black nurses work in a profession that has a relatively large union presence, but none of the respondents in my sample suggested that unions were a viable source of protection against the racial issues they encountered, or that they might offer assistance in pushing back against racial outsourcing. I speculate that this may be due to the very low numbers of blacks in the nursing profession. Consequently, robust unions that are responsive to minority members' needs could potentially

pressure organizations to address the structural and interpersonal racism black health care workers confront.

Active, multiracial unions could be particularly beneficial for black technicians, given that they encounter forms of racial outsourcing that are externally imposed. Inasmuch as black technicians note racial disparities in how work is allocated, collective action might help them to pressure organizations to enact rules that preclude this sort of differential treatment. Additionally, unions could also push health care facilities to establish policies that protect technicians from racist abuses by patients. Thus, policy makers who support multiracial, robust unions can enable workers to advocate for more racially equitable workplace policies.

While few physicians belong to unions, they do have several professional associations that represent their interests. These may be the organizations that can best advocate on behalf of black physicians, especially since many have already noted the need for more diversity within the profession. For instance, the American Medical Association now openly concedes that attracting more physicians of color to the field is critical in order for medicine to meet the needs of an increasingly multiracial population. The organization has a Minority Affairs Section that engages in outreach to improve the numbers of students of color interested in medical careers and offers support to minority doctors working to reduce health disparities. However, the medical association might consider also using its clout to push for other solutions that can help address the systemic problems that black doctors identify as adversely affecting their medical careers—the lack of federal and public support that can help defray the high costs associated with pursuing an MD, long-term racial disparities in education, and the ways social networks can exclude and isolate black practitioners.

Many of the suggestions here run counter to contemporary neoliberal economic tenets that push organizations to focus on profits and market values. However, at this point it is pretty clear that these principles are failing many Americans. They are increasing stress, worry, isolation, and alienation among large swaths of working citizens (Chen 2015; Cooper 2013; Silva 2013). Often, these consequences are framed in economic terms, but in an increasingly multiracial society we cannot afford to concern ourselves only with economic divides. It is imperative to consider racial consequences as well.

Institutions, organizations, and workplaces are eventually going to have to adapt to a changing, rapidly diversifying society. By the year 2020, most children born in the United States will be children of color. Asian Americans are the fastest-growing racial minority group, Latino/as are now the largest group of color, and by the year 2044, according to projections, the US will cease to be a majority-white country. Thus, it is essential that workforces begin to transform to meet the needs of the population who, by and large, will become a growing segment of the labor force. As more blacks move into professional occupations, workplaces will have to assess how they can restructure to become more accommodating. As long as black workers navigating the new economy encounter workplaces where racial outsourcing means this work is delegated to them, then organizations will be unable to benefit fully from their talents. That result would be our society's collective loss.

Appendix

I collected data for this project by using three different methods: intensive interviews, field observations, and survey data. This mixed-methods approach allowed me to generate a wealth of data from a variety of different sources. Interviews were valuable because they allowed respondents to speak candidly and in detail about the particulars of their work in the new economy. It also gave black respondents an opportunity for discussing the ways that they believed race had an impact on the work that they did, and to think through specifics about how this occurred. Fieldwork provided a means of observing health care workers in action, so to speak, and allowed me to see firsthand the manifestations of some of the issues they described. It also offered a handy way to meet additional respondents who might be willing to be interviewed for the project. Finally, survey methods provided quantitative data that gave a broader picture of some of the issues respondents described.

INTERVIEWS

Interviews were conducted from January 2014 to July 2017. I collected interview data from seventy health care workers, fifty-five black and fifteen white. Respondents were employed as doctors, nurses, physician

assistants, and technicians in any field of health care. Interviews generally lasted ninety minutes and took place in my office, respondents' offices, or in a neutral location, like a coffee shop. In cases where respondents and I could not be in the same location, interviews were conducted via telephone or Skype.

I began interviews by asking respondents for general demographic data. They then were asked how they first became interested in health care in general and in their careers specifically. After that, I asked about their pathway into their current career and the length of time they had done this work, and to describe their daily routine. With this established, I followed up by asking respondents if there were ways that they believed race affected any aspect of their work. I then asked respondents what impact, if any, major changes in the health care industry (e.g., increasing gender and racial diversity, cuts to the public sector, the Affordable Care Act, and predicted practitioner shortages) had had on the work they did. Finally, I asked respondents to conclude by evaluating their careers in health care and reflecting on what changes they would recommend to improve the issues they raised.

All interviews were recorded and transcribed. I also took detailed notes at the conclusion of each interview. I read transcriptions carefully and coded data deductively according to themes that emerged from the transcripts. This allowed me to highlight common themes and variables—respondents who felt that race affected them through interactions versus those who saw it as a structural process; those that believed they benefited from a labor shortage versus those who identified hassles and problems from this; black women's reactions to working in the public sector versus black men's.

I conducted the majority of interviews but assigned about twenty-five of them to two research assistants. I tasked a white woman research assistant with conducting all interviews with white respondents. I believed that these respondents might speak more openly about racial issues with a white interviewer than with me. I also tasked another research assistant, a biracial man, with conducting some of the interviews with black men technicians, physician assistants, and nurses. Both research assistants followed the established interview protocol.

As a black professional woman, I expect that racial and, in some cases, gender solidarity likely made it relatively easy to establish a quick and easy rapport with respondents. I did not observe any clear ways that gender affected my interviews with men respondents, though it is of course possible that this shaped the ways they responded to interview questions. However, given the similarities between interviews I conducted and those conducted by my male research assistant, it did not appear that the interviewer's gender demonstrably changed the scope or content of interviews with respondents who were men.

I recruited respondents through a snowball sample. This method runs the risk of creating some redundancy in the sample pool. However, given the extremely small number of black professionals in these fields, this approach actually worked out to be a valuable method of locating potential respondents. I began by reaching out to professional associations that represented doctors, nurses, physician assistants, and technicians. Once I contacted members of these associations, I described my study and research goals and invited members to follow up with me if they were interested in being interviewed. I then asked each respondent if they could refer me to others who might be interested in participating.

At the same time, I also relied on personal contacts in these professions who could point me toward potential respondents. I knew several doctors and nurses as well who referred me to colleagues willing to be interviewed. Once I made these contacts, I built on them to connect to other workers in the industry who could be potential interviewees.

One limitation of this methodological approach is that I do not have data from diversity officers in the various health care settings where respondents were employed. As a result, I am unable to gauge whether organizational efforts toward this end received administrative support. It may be that in some health care facilities, administrators took the issues of diversity, equity, and inclusion very seriously but managers implemented policies that are not shown to meet with success. In other cases, diversity managers may work without a great deal of administrative support or resources and could potentially struggle to change their organizations in ways that would be beneficial

for workers of color. My focus on how black health care workers navigate structural changes in the new economy does not provide data that allows me to offer an informed conclusion as to the inner workings of the organizations where they are employed and why some health care facilities put forth certain strategies while others do not.

main argument ‼

What does emerge from this interview data, however, is a consistent picture showing that black health care workers are, at best, underwhelmed by their assessments of the mismatch between organizational diversity efforts and their own racial experiences. While I cannot say with certainty whether organizations are unable to execute diversity initiatives successfully for black workers as a result of indifference, lack of competence, or an intentional effort to avoid change, it is clear that whatever the reason, their initiatives do not adequately resolve the racial issues black workers encounter in professional settings.

All respondents' names and identifying details have been altered to protect their privacy. In some cases, this required changing the specialty area of practitioners, particularly black women doctors. This was necessary because a few of my black women respondents informed me that there were so few black women physicians in their specific subfields that even general details about their race, gender, practice, and/or region might be enough to identify them. Thus, in the case of black doctors working in fields where they were especially underrepresented, I have changed their specialty area to one that is somewhat similar to their field of study or omitted it altogether.

shadowed doctors

FIELD OBSERVATIONS

Doc #1

The second source of data collection came from field observations. During a six-month period, I spent a few weeks shadowing three black doctors during their daily routines at work. One doctor, identified in this book as Dr. Randy Goodwin, worked in the emergency department of a large public facility that I call City Hospital. City is located in a sprawling metropolitan area. This hospital primarily served black and Latino patients from the surrounding area, many of whom were

uninsured. The city itself had a majority-minority population, with a median income well above the national average. The ER had a fairly multiracial staff, with a handful of black doctors and several women doctors who hailed from a variety of racial backgrounds. Hospital leadership was predominantly white.

The second doctor I shadowed was a black woman obstetrician/ gynecologist, identified here as Dr. Ella Chapman. She worked at a location I refer to as University Hospital, which served predominantly black patients from the city in which it was located. This city itself is also predominantly black, though long-term residential racial segregation has situated the white population in the surrounding areas. Households in the city have a lower median income than elsewhere in the United States, though households in the county boast a higher median income. However, while Randy Goodwin's hospital is one of a few completely publicly managed hospitals in the US, Ella's hospital is managed by a nonprofit group (similar to the one managing Grady Memorial Hospital). In her case, the vast majority of her coworkers were white. The nursing staff in her department included a higher percentage of black women, and the technician staff, too, was more racially diverse than the medical staff.

DOC #2

The third and final doctor I shadowed for my field observations is identified here as Dr. Jayla Flood. Unlike Ella and Randy, Jayla worked in private practice as a pediatrician. She had a partnership stake in her company and was one of four partners, the rest of whom were white men. The staff at Jayla's office was much less diverse than staffs at the hospitals I visited, with mostly white women working as nurses and technicians (though there was a lone black woman receptionist at one of the branches). Jayla also treated a more economically secure patient population than Randy or Ella. While the median income in her city was slightly below the national average, most of her patients had private insurance, and she had very few Medicaid patients who frequented her practice. This city is predominantly white, though it has a sizable black minority and a quickly growing Latinx population.

DOC #3

Gaining access to these sites was relatively simple. All three doctors were willing to let me shadow them and were very generous

with their time. That doctors were more accommodating than professionals in other fields might be due to the fact that requests to shadow and observe their work are fairly common. Each of the doctors with whom I spoke had allowed interested students to follow them during the course of their workdays, and doctors are accustomed to leading medical students through rounds. Thus, my request to join doctors in their daily routines was not particularly unusual.

In order to capture the details of doctors' work, I relied on meticulous notes that I took before, during, and after my time with them at work. I did not audio record any conversations or interactions that took place during field observations. In accordance with Institutional Review Board requirements and the parameters of this project, I did not gather any data on the patients who saw the doctors I shadowed. I have also been careful here to avoid any references to patients that could potentially compromise their privacy or anonymity. Field notes focus specifically on the details of doctors' work settings; interactions with nurses, technicians, patients, and each other; and daily routines.

SURVEY DATA

The final source of data I used in this project was the American Panel Survey, a monthly online survey of a national probability sample. The survey is distributed by the Weidenbaum Center at Washington University in St. Louis and includes about 2,000 US adults recruited in fall 2011. Most questions on the survey address economic and political topics.

Survey administrators allowed me to add questions to the survey that ran from September to December 2016. The September 2016 wave of the survey, which included the questions used for this research, went to 1,810 people. Of those, 1,585 people completed it, for a completion rate of 87.6 percent. The response rate for the survey was 4.8 percent when not estimating for unknown eligibility of those initially recruited. When we factor in the estimate for those being recruited who were not eligible to take the survey, the response rate was 10.8 percent.

The control question was: "You are troubled with recurrent headaches and want to see a doctor to determine why. Your regular practitioner is unavailable. Instead, your doctor's office sets up an appointment for you with a new doctor. How likely are you to trust your practitioner?" Variable questions specified the doctor as female, black, or black and female.

A research assistant analyzed this data by running a multivariate linear regression analysis of reported trust in the doctor. The independent variables include the experimental condition and the respondent's gender, race, income, education, and age. I interacted the respondent characteristics with the experimental condition so that gender, race, income, education, and age effects varied by condition. An abbreviated equation and variables are below, including only the experimental condition, candidate gender, and their interaction.

$$Trust = \beta_0 + \beta_1 Condition + \beta_2 Gender + \beta_{12} Condition \times Gender \ldots$$

Variables:

1. Experimental conditions: (1) female doctor, (2) black doctor, (3) black female doctor, (4) control.

2. Respondent gender: (1) male, (2) female.

3. Respondent race: (1) white, (2) black, (3) Hispanic, (4) multi/other.

4. Respondent income: (1) under $10,000, (2) $10,000–$29,999, (3) $30,000–$49,999, (4) $50,000–$79,999, (5) $80,000–$99,999, (6) $100,000 or more.

5. Respondent education: (1) college degree or more, (2) some college, (3) high school diploma or less.

6. Respondent age: 18–29 years old, 30–44 years old, 45–59 years old, 60+.

References

Acker, Joan. 1990. "Hierarchies, Jobs, Bodies." *Gender & Society* 4 (2): 139–58.
————. 2006. *Class Questions, Feminist Answers*. Thousand Oaks, CA: Sage.
The African-American Labor Force in the Recovery. 2012. Washington, DC: US Department of Labor.
Anderson, Carol. 2015. *White Rage*. New York: Bloomsbury.
Auerbach, David, Peggy G. Chen, Mark W. Friedberg, Rachel Reid, Christopher Lau, Peter I. Buerhaus, and Ateev Mehrotra. 2013. "Nurse-Managed Health Centers and Patient-Centered Medical Homes Could Mitigate Expected Primary Care Physician Shortage." *Health Affairs* 32 (11): 1933–41.
Berrey, Ellen. 2013. *The Enigma of Diversity*. Chicago: University of Chicago Press.
Bhatt, Wasudha. 2013. "The Little Brown Woman." *Gender & Society* 27 (5): 659–80.
Bivens, Josh, and Lawrence Mishel. 2015. "Understanding the Historic Divergence between Productivity and a Typical Worker's Pay." Briefing paper no. 406. Washington, DC: Economic Policy Institute.
Bobo, Lawrence, and Ryan Smith. 1998. "From Jim Crow Racism to Laissez Faire Racism: The Transformation of Racial Attitudes." In *Beyond Pluralism: The Conception of Groups and Group Identities in America*, edited by Wendy F. Katkin, Ned Landsman, and Andrea Tyree, 182–220. Urbana: University of Illinois Press.

Bonilla-Silva, Eduardo. 2001. *White Supremacy and Racism in a Post–Civil Rights Era.* Boulder, CO: Lynne Rienner.

Boulis, Ann, and Jerry Jacobs. 2008. *The Changing Face of Medicine.* Ithaca, NY: Cornell University Press.

Bourdieu, Pierre. 1986. "The Forms of Capital." In *Handbook of Theory and Research for the Sociology of Education,* edited by J. Richardson, 241–58. Westport, CT: Greenwood Press.

Branch, Anna. 2011. *Opportunity Denied.* New Brunswick, NJ: Rutgers University Press.

Browne, Irene, and Joya Misra. 2003. "The Intersection of Gender and Race in the Labor Market." *Annual Review of Sociology.* 29: 487–513.

Carnes, Molly, Claudia Morrissey, and Stacie Geller. 2008. "Women's Health and Women's Leadership in Academic Medicine: Hitting the Same Glass Ceiling?" *Journal of Women's Health* 17 (9): 1453–62.

Cassel, Joan. 2014. *Woman in the Surgeon's Body.* Cambridge, MA: Harvard University Press.

Castillo, Emilio, and Stephen Benard. 2010. "The Paradox of Meritocracy in Organizations." *Administrative Science Quarterly* 55: 543–76.

Chen, Victor. 2015. *Cut Loose: Jobless and Hopeless in an Unfair Economy.* Oakland: University of California Press.

Clawson, Dan, and Naomi Gerstel. 2014. *Unequal Time.* New York: Russell Sage.

Cohen, R., M. Martinez, and E. Zammitti. 2017. *Health Insurance Coverage: Early Release Estimates from the National Health Interview Survey, January–March 2017.* Hyattsville, MD: National Center for Health Statistics. www.cdc.gov/nchs/data/nhis/earlyrelease/insur201708.pdf.

Collins, Patricia Hill. 2000. *Black Feminist Thought.* New York: Routledge.

———. 2004. *Black Sexual Politics.* New York: Routledge.

Collins, Sharon. 1988. *Black Corporate Executives.* Philadelphia: Temple University Press.

———. 2011. "Diversity in the Post–Affirmative Action Labor Market: A Proxy for Racial Progress?" *Critical Sociology* 37 (5): 521–40.

Cooper, Marianne. 2013. *Cut Adrift.* Berkeley: University of California Press.

———. 2000. "Being the 'Go-To Guy': Fatherhood, Masculinity, and the Organization of Work in Silicon Valley." *Qualitative Sociology* 23 (4): 379–405.

Cose, Ellis. 1993. *Rage of a Privileged Class*. New York: Harper Perennial.

Cottom, Tressie McMillan. 2017. *Lower Ed: The Troubling Rise of For-Profit Colleges in the New Economy*. New York: New Press.

Denice, Patrick. 2017. "Back to School: Racial and Gender Differences in Adults' Participation in Formal Schooling, 1978–2013." *Demography* 54 (3): 1147–73.

Dill, Jeannette, Rebecca Erickson, and James Diefendorff. 2016. "Motivation and Care Dimensions in Caring Labor: Implications for Nurses' Well-Being and Employment Outcomes." *Social Science and Medicine* 167: 99–106.

Diversity in the Physician Workforce: Facts and Figures. 2014. Association of American Medical Colleges. Washington, DC.

Duffy, Mignon. 1997. "Doing the Dirty Work: Gender, Race, and Reproductive Labor in Historical Perspective." *Gender & Society* 21 (3): 313–36.

Edelman, Lauren B., Sally R. Fuller, and Iona Mara-Drita. 2001. "Diversity Rhetoric and the Managerialization of Law." *American Journal of Sociology* 106: 1589–641.

Ely, Robin, and David Thomas. 2001. "Cultural Diversity at Work: The Effects of Diversity Perspectives on Work Group Processes and Outcomes." *Administrative Science Quarterly* 46 (2): 229–73.

Embrick, David. 2011. "The Diversity Ideology in the Business World: A New Oppression for a New Age." *Critical Sociology* 37 (5): 541–56.

Evans, Louwanda. 2014. *Cabin Pressure*. Lanham, MD: Rowman and Littlefield.

Feagin, Joe, and Melvin Sikes. 1995. *Living with Racism*. Boston: Beacon Press.

Ferguson, Ann Arnett. 2000. *Bad Boys: Public Schools and the Making of Black Masculinity*. Ann Arbor: University of Michigan Press.

Govere, Linda, and Ephraim Govere. 2016. Motivation and Care Dimensions in Caring Labor: Implications for Nurses' Well-Being and Employment Outcomes. *Worldviews on Evidence-Based Nursing* 13 (6): 402–10.

Greenstone, Michael, and Adam Looney. 2012. *A Record Decline in Government Jobs: Implications for the Economy and America's Workforce*. Washington, DC: The Hamilton Project/Brookings Institute.

Harlow, Roxana. 1997. "Race Doesn't Matter, But ..." *Social Psychology Quarterly* 66 (4): 348–63.

Hoberman, John. 2012. *Black and Blue*. Berkeley: University of California Press.

Hochschild, Arlie Russell. 1988. *The Managed Heart*. Berkeley: University of California Press.

———. 2016. *Strangers in Their Own Land*. New York: New Press.

Hoffman, Kelly, Sophie Trawalter, Jordan Axt, and Norman Oliver. 2016. "Racial Bias in Pain Assessment and Treatment Recommendations, and False Beliefs about Biological Differences between Blacks and Whites." *Proceedings of the National Academy of Science* 113 (16): 4296–5301.

Houts Picca, Leslie, and Joe Feagin. 2013. *Two-Faced Racism*. New York: Routledge.

Humes, Karen R., Nicholas Jones, and Roberto Ramirez. 2011. *Overview of Race and Hispanic Origin: 2010*. Washington, DC: United States Census Bureau. www.census.gov/prod/cen2010/briefs/c2010br-02.pdf.

Hunter, Margaret. 2005. *Race, Gender, and the Politics of Skin Tone*. New York: Routledge.

Ibarra, Herminia, Nancy Carter, and Christine Silva. 2010. "Why Men Still Get More Promotions Than Women." *Harvard Business Review*, September 10.

Jackson, Pamela Braboy, Peggy Thoits, and Howard Taylor. 1995. "Composition of the Workplace and Psychological Well-Being: The Effects of Tokenism on America's Black Elite." *Social Forces* 74 (2): 53–57.

Jones, Charisse, and Kumea Shorter-Gooden. 2003. *Shifting*. New York: HarperCollins.

Kalev, Alexandra, Frank Dobbin, and Erin Kelly. 2006. "Best Practices or Best Guesses? Assessing the Efficacy of Corporate Affirmative Action and Diversity Policies." *American Sociological Review* 71: 589–617.

Kalleberg, Arne. 2013. *Good Jobs, Bad Jobs*. New York: Sage.

Kanter, Rosabeth Moss. 1977. *Men and Women of the Corporation*. New York: Basic Books.

Kass, Rena, Wiley Souba, and Luanne Thorndyke. 2006. "Challenges Confronting Female Surgical Leaders: Overcoming the Barriers." *Journal of Surgical Research* 132: 179–87.

Kelly, Erin, and Frank Dobbin. 1998. "How Affirmative Action Became Diversity Management: Employer Response to Antidiscrimination Law." *American Behavioral Scientist* 41: 960–84.

Kennelly, Ivy. 1999. "That Single-Mother Element." *Gender & Society* 13 (2): 168–92.

Kirschenman, Joleen, and Katherine Neckerman. 1991. "'We'd Love to Hire Them, But …': The Meaning of Race for Employers." *Urban Underclass* 203: 203–32.

Kitzerow, Phyllis. 2014. *Women Attorneys and the Changing Workplace*. Boulder, CO: First Forum Press.

Kulik, Carol T., and Loriann Roberson. 2008. "Common Goals and Golden Opportunities: Evaluations of Diversity Education in Academic and Organizational Settings." *Academy of Management Learning and Education* 7 (3): 309–31.

Lacy, Karyn. 2007. *Blue Chip Black*. Berkeley: University of California Press.

Laird, Jennifer. 2017. "Public Sector Unemployment Inequality in the United States and the Great Recession." *Demography* 54: 391–411.

Lamont, Michèle, Stefan Beljean, and Matthew Clair. 2014. "What Is Missing? Cultural Processes and Causal Pathways to Inequality." *Socio-Economic Review*, 1–36.

Lewis-McCoy, L'Hereux. 2010. *Inequality in the Promised Land*. Palo Alto, CA: Stanford University Press.

Monk, Ellis. 2015. "The Cost of Color: Skin Color, Discrimination, and Health among African Americans." *American Journal of Sociology* 121 (2): 396–444.

Moore, Wendy L. 2007. *Reproducing Racism*. Lanham, MD: Rowman and Littlefield.

Moore, Wendy L., and Joyce Bell. 2011. "Maneuvers of Whiteness: Diversity as a Mechanism of Retrenchment in the Affirmative Action Discourse." *Critical Sociology* 37 (5): 597–613.

Murti, Lata. 2012. "Who Benefits from the White Coat? Gender Differences in Occupational Citizenship among Asian-Indian Doctors." *Ethnic and Racial Studies* 35: 2035–53.

National Nursing Workforce Study. 2015. Chicago: National Council of State Boards of Nursing.

Newfield, Christopher. 2008. *Unmaking the Public University*. Cambridge, MA: Harvard University Press.

Newman, Katherine. 1999. *No Shame in My Game*. New York: Knopf.

Phillips, Janice, and Beverly Malone. 2014. "Increasing Racial and Ethnic Diversity in Nursing to Reduce Health Disparities." *Public Health Reports* 129 (1): 45–50.

Pierce, Jennifer. 1995. *Gender Trials.* Berkeley: University of California Press.

———. 2012. *Racing for Innocence.* Palo Alto, CA: Stanford University Press.

Piketty, Thomas, Emmanuel Saez, and Gabriel Zucman. 2016. "Distributional National Accounts: Methods and Estimates for the United States." Working paper no. 22945. Cambridge, MA: National Bureau of Economic Research.

Pitts, Steven. 2011. *Research Brief: Black Workers and the Public Sector.* Berkeley: University of California Center for Labor Research and Education. http://laborcenter.berkeley.edu/pdf/2011/blacks_public_sector11.pdf.

Pololi, Linda, Peter Conrad, Sharon Knight, and Phyllis Carr. 2009. "A Study of the Relational Aspects of the Culture of Academic Medicine." *Academic Medicine* 84 (1): 106–14.

Quadagno, Jill. 1995. *The Color of Welfare.* New York: Oxford University Press.

Ray, Victor. 2019. "A Theory of Racialized Organizations." *American Sociological Review* 84, no. 1: forthcoming.

Reskin, Barbara, and Patricia Roos. 1990. *Job Queues, Gender Queues.* Philadelphia: Temple University Press.

Ridgeway, Cecilia, and Tamar Kricheli-Katz. 2013. "Intersecting Cultural Beliefs in Social Relations: Gender, Race, and Class Binds and Freedoms." *Gender and Society* 27: 294–318.

Rivera, Lauren. 2014. *Pedigree.* Princeton, NJ: Princeton University Press.

Robnett, Belinda. 1993. *How Long? How Long?* New York: Oxford University Press.

Roscigno, Vincent. 2007. *The Face of Discrimination.* Lanham, MD: Rowman and Littlefield.

Roscigno, Vincent, George Wilson, and Reginald Byron. 2012. "Workplace Racial Discrimination and Middle Class Vulnerability." *American Behavioral Scientist* 56 (5): 696–710.

Rosenfeld, Jake. 2013. *What Unions No Longer Do.* Cambridge, MA: Harvard University Press.

Royster, Deirdre. 2003. *Race and the Invisible Hand.* Berkeley: University of California Press.

Sewell, Abigail. 2015. "Desegregating Ethnoracial Disparities in Physician Trust." *Social Science Research* 54: 1–20.

Shambaugh, Rebecca. 2008. *It's Not a Glass Ceiling, It's a Sticky Floor.* New York: McGraw-Hill.

Shapiro, Thomas. 2004. *The Hidden Cost of Being African American.* New York: Oxford.

Sharone, Ofer. 2013. *Flawed System / Flawed Self.* Chicago: University of Chicago Press.

Silva, Jennifer. 2013. *Coming Up Short: Working Class Adulthood in an Age of Uncertainty.* New York: Oxford University Press.

Sinsky, Christine, et al. 2016. "Allocation of Physician Time in Ambulatory Practice: A Time and Motion Study in Four Specialties." *Annals of Internal Medicine* 165 (11): 753–60.

Skrentny, John. 2014. *After Civil Rights.* Princeton, NJ: Princeton University Press.

Stainback, Kevin, and Donald Tomaskovic-Devey. 2012. *Documenting Desegregation.* New York: Russell Sage Foundation.

Stone, Pamela. 2007. *Opting Out.* Berkeley: University of California Press.

Tesler, Michael. 2015. "Priming Predispositions and Changing Policy Positions: An Account of When Mass Opinion Is Primed or Changed." *American Journal of Political Science* 59 (4): 806–24.

Thistle, Susan. 2006. *From Marriage to the Market.* Berkeley: University of California Press.

Tsugawa, Yusuke, et al. 2017. "Comparison of Hospital Mortality and Readmission Rates for Medicare Patients Treated by Male vs. Female Physicians." *Journal of the American Medical Association, Internal Medicine* 177 (2): 206–13.

Turco, Catherine. 2010. "The Cultural Foundations of Tokenism: Evidence from the Leveraged Buyout Industry." *American Sociological Review* 75 (6): 894–913.

Tyson, Karolyn. 2013. *Integration Interrupted.* New York: Oxford University Press.

Viglione, Jill, Lance Hannon, and Robert DeFina. 2011. "The Impact of Light Skin on Prison Time for Black Female Offenders." *Social Science Journal* 48 (1): 250–58.

Westbrook, Johanna, Christine Duffield, Ling Li, and Nerida Creswick. 2011. "How Much Time Do Nurses Have for Patients? A Longitudinal Study Quantifying Hospital Nurses' Patterns of Task Time Distribution and Interactions with Health Professionals." *BMC Health Services Research* 11, 319. doi:10.1186/1472-6963-11-319.

Western, Bruce, and Jake Rosenfeld. 2011. "Unions, Norms, and the Rise in U.S. Wage Inequality." *American Sociological Review* 76 (4): 513–37.

Williams, Christine. 1995. *Still a Man's World*. Berkeley: University of California Press.

Williams, Christine, Chandra Mueller, and Kristine Kilanski. 2012. "Gendered Organizations in the New Economy." *Gender & Society* 26 (4): 549–73.

Williams, Joan. 2015. "The Five Biases Pushing Women Out of STEM." *Harvard Business Review*. https://hbr.org/2015/03/the-5-biases-pushing-women-out-of-stem.

Wilson, George, and Vincent Roscigno. 2016. "Neo-liberal Reform, the Public Sector and Black-White Inequality." *Sociology Compass* 10: 1141–49.

Wilson, George, Vincent Roscigno, and Matt Huffman. 2013. "Public Sector Transformation, Racial Inequality and Downward Occupational Mobility." *Social Forces* 91 (3): 975–1006.

Wilson, Valerie, and William Rodgers III. 2016. "Black-White Wage Gaps Expand with Rising Wage Inequality." *Economic Policy Institute* (September 20): 1–65.

Wingfield, Adia Harvey. 2007. "The Modern Mammy and the Angry Black Man: African American Professionals' Experiences with Gendered Racism in the Workplace." *Race, Gender, and Class* 14 (1–2): 196–212.

———. 2008. *Doing Business with Beauty*. Lanham, MD: Rowman and Littlefield.

———. 2009. "Racializing the Glass Escalator: Reconsidering Minority Men's Experiences with Women's Work." *Gender & Society* 23 (1): 5–26.

———. 2010. "Are Some Emotions Marked 'Whites Only?' Racialized Feeling Rules in Professional Workplaces." *Social Problems* 57 (2): 251–68.

———. 2012. *No More Invisible Man*. Philadelphia: Temple University Press.

Wingfield, Adia Harvey, and Renee Skeete. 2014. "Maintaining Hierarchies in Predominantly White Organizations: A Theory of Racial Tasks." *American Behavioral Scientist* 58 (2): 274–87.

Zippel, Kathrin. 2006. *The Politics of Sexual Harassment*. New York: Cambridge University Press.

Index

Acker, Joan, 167–68
affirmative action policies, 31, 55–56
Affordable Care Act (ACA, 2010),
    18–20, 144–46, 163. *See also* health
    care industry
Ainsley, 142–43
Akinyele, 53, 55–56, 139–40
Alexandria, 57, 133
Aliya, 60, 153–54
Amber, 106–7, 108, 113, 116–17
American Academy of Nursing, 28
American Association of Colleges
    of Nursing, 30
American Community Survey, 135
American Health Care Act
    (AHCA, proposed), 18–19, 20
American Medical Association, 13,
    26, 177
American Nursing Association, 28
American Panel Survey, 62, 63, 64
    fig., 155, 156 *fig.*, 184
Apple, 32, 32n7
Asian American population, 19,
    20, 178

Association of American Medical
    Colleges, 165
autonomy of workers, 11–12

"backstage" racism, 54
Bart, 61
Better Care Reconciliation Act
    (proposed), 19
black doctors, 35, 71–73; cultural
    barriers facing, 49–54; experi-
    ences of interpersonal racism,
    41–45, 104–5; hierarchy of health
    care and racism toward, 46–48;
    recommendations for addressing
    inequality and racial outsourcing,
    172–73; sexism and solidarity
    among, 57–64; structural barriers
    facing, 55–57. *See also* black health
    care professionals
black health care professionals,
    2–5; and cultural competence or
    diversity trainings, 31–33, 65–67,
    92–94, 99–100, 107–10, 122;
    implications of this study for,